IMPACT

THE ARMY AIR FORCES' CONFIDENTIAL PICTURE HISTORY OF WORLD WAR II

*In eight books, declassified and now published
for the general public for the first time
with fourteen new retrospective essays
by World War II leaders and journalists*

BOOK 5

Sponsored by
THE AIR FORCE HISTORICAL FOUNDATION

Published by
HISTORICAL TIMES, INC., HARRISBURG, PA 17105

Cover: 20th Air Force B-29s line up on Saipan to attack Japan (*Impact,* January 1945)

Published by Historical Times, Inc.
2245 Kohn Road - Box 8200
Harrisburg, PA 17105-8200

Library of Congress Catalog Card Number: 79-91997

IMPACT: The Army Air Forces' Confidential Picture History
of World War II, published in eight books.

Book 5

Second Printing

Printed in the United States of America

Published simultaneously in Canada

Strategic Air Power: Destroying The Enemy's War Resources

Essays by

Colonel Beirne Lay, Jr., USAFR (Ret.)
and
General Curtis E. LeMay, USAF (Ret.)

THE BACKGROUND

by Colonel Beirne Lay, Jr., USAFR (Ret.)

About the author: *Beirne Lay won national attention with the publication of his first book,* I Wanted Wings, *in 1936. Above he is spreading his wings in an A-17 trainer at Langley Field in 1937. The next five years were spent as a bombardment, pursuit and staff pilot for the GHQ Air Force until Ira Eaker chose him as one of the six officers to accompany him to England in February 1942 to start the Eighth Air Force.*

After a year of staff work, which Lay interrupted to go on a number of B-17 combat missions, including Regensburg, "Eaker sprung me from a desk" to return home in 1943 for transitional training to the B-24 and command of the 487th Bomb Group. It arrived in England in March

1944. On April 11, while leading a combat wing, Colonel Lay's plane was shot down over France. He was hidden by the Maquis for months, until the invading Americans rescued him. This harrowing adventure was chronicled in Lay's I've Had It.

Since the war, Beirne Lay has been a full-time writer, turning out many books, articles, films and television programs. Probably the best known is Twelve O'Clock High, *which appeared first as a book (written with Major Sy Bartlett, wartime ADC to General Spaatz), then as a major motion picture for which Lay wrote the screenplay, and later as a high-rated TV series.*

Lay adds: "After my retirement from the AF Reserve

in 1963, I found wings again and a fresh exhiliration when I took up soaring. It's not only for the birds but for humans too. Logged about 700 hours before the doctors told me to quit."

—J.P.

Historically, the only acceptable vindication of a profoundly novel theory has been scientific proof. Acceptance of strategic bombing in World War II was no exception.

The theories espoused in the 1920's by Giulio Douhet, Hugh Trenchard, Billy Mitchell and their apostles were beautifully and deceptively simple: you simply leapfrogged by air over battlefields, mountains, deserts and ocean barriers to strike mortal blows at the enemy's vitals in order to gain a comparatively quick and inevitable decision.

Douhet and Trenchard stressed "frustrating" the enemy's war-making capacity by demoralizing attacks on civilian populations. As we now know, such attacks against the British and German working forces tended to make them fighting mad and stiffened their resistance. Mitchell stressed purely "strategic" bombing—destruction of the enemy's war production capability (as distinguished from tactical air power—air superiority over a battlefield to further the aims of the ground forces). The first strategic bombing plan was actually drawn up in 1918 by a Mitchell subordinate to wipe out German bomber production, too late to be put into effect.

There was a stumbling block. You could not, in the absence of a major war between 1918 and 1939, *prove* the theory in the acid test. The airmen were "visionaries." True, evidence in abundance accumulated during that controversial period to encourage the airmen of vision, but the skeptics of the traditional services scorned the evidence.

Brigadier General William "Billy" Mitchell, fresh from the lessons of World War I, believed passionately that air power represented a new dimension in warfare, transcending its use as a tool which armies and navies could apply to the increase of their overall effectiveness.

Any historical review must recognize the magnitude of the ferocity with which any revolutionary idea is bound to be opposed by those who perceive a challenge to their most cherished beliefs and a dangerous threat to their dominance. To this day there are people who believe that the Earth is flat, despite photos from space. (Lancaster, California is the headquarters of the "International Earth is Flat Research Society of America," claiming about 1,500 members.)

This essay does not seek for one moment to impugn the patriotism of the generals and admirals who defended their spheres of influence against the air power "usurper" for twenty-one years between the wars. Being flesh and blood, they reacted predictably in the absence of incontrovertible proof.

And there was another factor, viewed better in hindsight, namely the gross underestimate on the part of the theorists as to the sheer complexity and over-all industrial investment that would be required, in men and machines, to deliver the necessary tonnage of accurately placed bombs on strategic targets to be decisive. If asked today whether or not the country would be willing to live over again the near-miraculous conversion from peacetime to wartime production, the answer of America might well be: "Hell no. I couldn't stand the excitement."

The near-miracle was indeed achieved, in a madhouse atmosphere attendant on the constant headaches as combat lessons were fed into the modification centers, endlessly complicating the chances for an orderly production program. And throughout there was tombstone competition between the services for the lion's share of aircraft production, and between us and our allies and between the embattled commanders in the Pacific and their counterparts in Europe. President Roosevelt wisely regarded Hitler as the first priority target of our over-all strategy.

As of September 1, 1939, when Adolf Hitler invaded Poland, the United States had on hand only nineteen heavy bombers (not really combat-ready). Only three months previously further production of the Boeing B-17, then the world's most advanced strategic bomber, had been halted by the War Department (the B-24 was barely off the drawing boards).

Major General Frank M. Andrews, Commander of the General Headquarters Air Force (a first, though feeble, attempt toward an autonomous Air Force), described America's as a "fifth rate air force" with its roughly 20,000 men and 800 combat aircraft (mostly obsolete) by comparison with the Luftwaffe at more than half a million manpower and 4,000 planes and the RAF with more than

100,000 personnel and 1,900 planes.

Four years were to pass—learning, training and building while we fought—before this country was able to overcome the deficit with an adequate fighting force—approximately the same time period needed to this day to bring a new SAC combat wing (the "wing" was referred to as a "group" in wartime) from scratch to professional combat readiness.

Volumes have been written to explain the events which culminated in so ominous a predicament, and they do not make for light reading. But for the purposes of this essay fingerpointing would be argumentative, serving only to rekindle the dying embers of old animosities. In fairness to the skeptics, there *had* been no definitive test of the theory that strategic bombing would become the indispensable element in future wars.

Hence the United States entered upon its first truly global conflict still believing that the infantry was queen of battles and that battleships could not be sunk. Parenthetically, the battleship *Ostfriesland* had been sunk in 1921, in tests off the Virginia Capes, by vintage Army aircraft, and the battleship *Utah,* cruising at sea off California, had been successfully located in adverse weather and hit by practice water-bombs dropped by the GHQ Air Force's B-17s in 1937.

No occupant of the White House, from Harding through Roosevelt, had believed otherwise; though FDR professed to be "air-minded," he was, in fact, always Navy-minded. The country through the twenties and thirties, thanks to Billy Mitchell and Charles Lindbergh, had become largely air-minded, but its Congressional representatives lagged behind, withholding the encouragement (and dollars) so urgently needed by the struggling Army Air Corps until the brink of hostilities.

Throughout the war the President's senior service adviser, Admiral William D. Leahy, supported by Admiral Ernest J. King, was never to join the camp of the protagonists for strategic bombing, as exemplified by Gen. Henry H. ("Hap") Arnold, even after air power loomed as the indispensable factor in victory over Germany and Japan. Army Chief of Staff General George C. Marshall was a firm believer in air power, while supporting the air and ground forces about equally.

Although a base for mass production of aircraft was yet to be built in 1940, we did not have to invent the new technology. We *had* the airplane, the B-17 (and shortly the B-24). We *had* the bombsight—the Norden. Most important, we *had* a sound doctrine: bombing from high altitudes by closely flown formations in daylight to insure greater precision than could be attained at night.

But these plusses were of little avail to the seriously underfunded prewar Air Corps, exposed dramatically in early 1934 when the Air Corps was ordered to carry the U. S. mail with makeshift equipment. Carry it they did, often in open cockpits, but at a price in frostbite and lives. Air Corps planners perforce fell back on preserving the first priority essential—procuring the right bomber, even though they realized that they could not expect the funding for refinements such as self-sealing fuel tanks and mechanically operated gun turrets. (General Curtis E. LeMay tells me that *one* set of new propellers for the B-29 cost more than the entire annual appropriation for propeller R&D at Wright Field, prewar.) These could come later.

Fortunately there *was* a plan, surprisingly accurate. On Hap Arnold's orders in response to a White House directive, four gifted staff officers set to work at top speed in 1940. They were seniors Colonel Harold L. George and Lieutenant Colonel Kenneth N. Walker and juniors Major Laurence S. Kuter and Major Haywood S. Hansell. The team came up with an Air War Plan setting up the following requirements.

Manpower	(planned)	2,200,000
	(actual)	2,400,000
Combat Groups	(planned)	239
	(actual)	243, plus 108 separate squadrons
Aircraft	(planned)	63,647
	(actual)	80,000, not all needed at war's end

Note that the planning figure of 2,200,000 men represented a *one hundred to one* expansion of the peacetime force of approximately 22,000 officers and men. Little wonder then that the handful of bomber specialists in the 2nd Bomb Group at Langley Field had to be "expanded" beyond recognition into slots in the new bomb groups being activated.

But, as a tiny nucleus, they ignited and reignited *ad infinitum* the torch of time-tested Air Corps doctrine for trainees to follow, much as a single vine cutting can propagate a whole vineyard. They truly "kept the faith," albeit the venerable Morning Report gave way to the systematic Stat Control, championed by Colonel Charles B. Thornton, as the bible for up to date information.

The earthy realities of translating the theory of strategic bombing into practice can well be illustrated by the record of one individual, Colonel Curtis E. LeMay, who led the 305th Bomb Group overseas in November 1942. To this day LeMay recoils in disbelief from the recollection of his baptism under fire and his lack of experience for a Group Commander's role.

"By contrast with a combat-ready outfit," LeMay admitted recently, "the 305th was a rabble. Minimally trained gunners who could not shoot. Pilots fresh from training in BT-8s but with no experience at all in multi-engine aircraft. Only three pilots, including me, who had ever checked out on a B-17. And to top it off we started with only three flyable B-17s assigned, which ruled out the practice in formation flying that was so absolutely essential for placing a pattern of bombs on the target, and for survival.

"We lived in tents, had no hangars and did maintenance at night during the summer months, when the metal on the aircraft was too hot to touch in the daytime. When we arrived on the East Coast from our desert training base at Muroc Dry Lake, California (now Edwards Air Force Base), we had no clothing for cold weather, although we were headed for the frigid climate of England.

"Here we were with bombardiers who had never dropped a live bomb. Finally we did get thirty-six new B-17s, checked out the pilots and off we went, bound for *combat*, flying our B-17s through the clouded cold fronts of the North Atlantic route.

"I had never exercised command of anything, unless you count ten days spent as a squadron commander of a squadron with no aircraft assigned, before I took over the 305th. Everything useful

about command I acquired from Colonel Robert Olds when I served as his Group Operations Officer in the 2nd Bomb Group, Langley Field, Virginia, spearhead of Frank Andrews's GHQ Air Force. My specialty had been navigation, and my earlier background was as a pursuit (for 'fighter') pilot at Selfridge Field, Michigan."

No one, with the possible exception of his immediate superiors, could have foretold, when the green commander of the 305th landed with thirty-four of his thirty-six B-17s (two were delayed en route) at Prestwick, Scotland, in November, 1942, with greener combat crews, that the name of Curt LeMay would go down in history as the embodiment of the strategic bombing theory—"Get the bombs on the target at all costs." An ingrained pragmatist, his "show me" philosophy was tailor-made for a demonstration of the validity of the theory.

He believed that the most immoral course one could follow in war was to *waste* human lives, as in the grisly stalemate enacted in the trenches of World War I, where millions of men became cannon fodder for the sake of a few hundred yards gained or lost, for four hellish years.

He believed that the worst evil is to see an evil and do nothing about it. There was no doubt in his mind about the evil nature of Nazi Germany, obvious particularly to those nations already under Hitler's yoke and, before the fight was over, to six million Jews.

He believed that the most moral choice was to win as *quickly* as possible—that it is more humane to sacrifice a relatively few lives early in the struggle than to incur enormous casualties, civilian and military indiscriminately, while fighting a protracted "conventional" war (as we did later in Korea and Vietnam, attacking "the flies instead of the manure pile"). He also realized, in 1942, that without an adequate force in being, no quick victory was possible, although he was convinced that strategic bombing might render costly ground invasions unnecessary.

He acted on the belief that you could not hold young pilots, navigators, bombardiers or gunners responsible for professional results unless they had first received professional training, and he set out to give them just that from his earliest days in the U. K., acquiring the soubriquet "Iron Pants." Yet he was fair: "I can forgive a mistake—once anyway. But God help you if you ever lie to me." As a result, his popularity with the crews after a few missions zoomed from zero to straight up.

He never lost sight of the truth that a bomb group justified its tidy investment only in terms of bombs delivered on target. And he was possessed of an absolutely implacable determination to get them there—weather, defensive fighters or flak to the contrary.

In meetings with his peers and superiors he never hesitated to voice and defend his convictions. Green though he necessarily was at the outset, he could look back for sustenance on several peacetime achievements. He had been lead navigator on record-breaking long distance flights, in the first B-17s, to South America. Again, he was Bob Olds's navigator in the successful exercises against the battleship *Utah,* and Major Vincent Meloy's navigator when the Italian liner *Rex* was intercepted more than 700 miles at sea in Army-Navy maneuvers, giving the Navy another jolt and resulting in a ban of GHQ Air Force flights beyond a 300-mile limit (at one time this was reduced to 100 miles). It goes without saying that navigators in the 305th Group were in for a hard time.

If one had to invent the prototype for translating the classical theory of strategic bombing into actuality through personal example in combat, history must record that, against Germany and Japan and in the postwar Strategic Air Command (at last a combat-ready force in being for instant retaliation), the embodiment of the requirements was invested in the scowling person of that green commander of the 305th Bomb Group.

On those wide shoulders of his rested a heavy burden of destiny.

Brigadier General Ira C. Eaker had landed in England on February 20, 1942, only nine months previously, carrying orders from Hap Arnold to build a strategic bombing force, to be incorporated in due course into General Carl Spaatz's Eighth Air Force (still forming up at Bolling Field, Maryland). Eaker, a fighter pilot by trade, enjoyed no previous bomber experience. Arnold had shrugged off this deficiency by telling Eaker, "I want the fighter spirit in this bomber command."

Eaker had no airplanes, no bases, no office, nor even a paper clip, let alone a headquarters, when he arrived in the U. K. He succeeded at once in stalling on the offer of Major General James E. Chaney, Theater Commander, that he set up shop under the aegis of Chaney's own headquarters at 20 Grosvenor Square, London, a trap which would have "swallowed him up" at the start, contrary to the intent of the orders he had been given by Arnold.

Further, like Pershing before him, he adroitly sidestepped other snares set before him by his ally. British Bomber Command eagerly offered to feed American troops with British rations, house them in British tents and provide them with British Intelligence, and invited Eaker to funnel his incoming bomber units into the stream of the RAF's night-flying fleet.

Eaker, politely but firmly, declined. If he had taken the responsibility for no other decisions in the ensuing two years, he should be remembered for setting these early precedents, which were to breed results of incalculable significance.

I was one of the original six of the cadre which accompanied Eaker to England. Major Peter Beasley and Captain Fred Castle came from business backgrounds. Castle was also a West Point graduate and a rated Air Corps pilot. Lieutenant Colonel Frank A. Armstrong had an attack pilot's background. (The role of "attack" was taken over by medium bombardment and fighter-bombers during the war.) First Lieutenant Harris B. Hull, with a newspaper and public relations background, was Eaker's Intelligence Officer, expected to deal on an equal basis with his opposite number, a Group Captain (Colonel) in the RAF. Second Lieutenant William Cowart, Eaker's first aide, was a fighter pilot. I was a captain in the Air Reserve with peacetime active duty as a pilot in the 2nd Bomb Group, Eighth Pursuit Group and Headquarters Squadron, GHQ Air Force, along with experience was a writer; I was the original VIII Bomber Command historian and filled a variety of roles on Eaker's staff.

Arnold had advised Eaker, in choosing his staff: "You can make an officer out of a smart civilian faster than you can make an officer out of a dumb soldier."

Eaker had had little choice, in any event. With the single exception of Frank Armstrong, there were no "smart professional soldiers" available, thanks to the 100-1 explosion of the Army Air Forces (wartime designation) then in full swing.

I was privileged to witness these "amateurs," followed by many more of the same, dig in their cleats and germinate the original seedling into an oak—the greatest Air Force, the Eighth, that ever attempted daylight strategic bombing. Eaker directed, and virtually completed, his Herculean task by the end of 1943, when he was transferred (inwardly hurt) to command of the Mediterranean Allied Air Forces headquartered in Italy. Eaker considered it a demotion, but Arnold justified the transfer on "global" considerations and Churchill assuaged the wound by pointing out that MAAF was a larger command than the Eighth, with prestigious RAF officers (Air Marshal Arthur Tedder, for one) reporting to him. The fact was that General Dwight E. Eisenhower had carte blanche in choosing his key personnel when he left Africa to become Supreme Commander in the European Theater of Operations (ETO), and he wanted Spaatz and Lieutenant General James H. Doolittle to stay with him—Doolittle to command the Eighth, Spaatz as his top dog airman.

Eaker had reared the Eighth from infancy to full manhood through a combination of diplomacy, patience, courage and that enormous capacity for organization more commonly associated with the chairman of a giant corporation. A professional bomber expert, at the beginning, he was not. But he more than made up for lost time in on-the-job training. Further, he had been steeped throughout his long Air Corps career in the precepts of Mitchell, Spaatz, Arnold, Harold George, Hugh Knerr, Frank Andrews, and many more. He and Sir Hugh Trenchard, the father of the independent RAF, enjoyed a meeting of the minds on bombardment matters when they met again in London. Fortunately, he and Air Chief Marshal Sir Arthur Harris of British Bomber Command operated on the same frequency in spite of their differences over the merits of night versus day strategic bombing.

History will record that Hap Arnold won handsomely when he bet on Ira Eaker to represent the AFF in the U. K. in its assignment of sprouting from a fallow field the first strategic bombing force capable at long last of destroying an enemy's war production capability.

A postscript on the later fortunes of four of Eaker's original cadre may be in order.

Frank Armstrong interrupted his staff duties in Operations to serve two combat tours, in command of the 97th Bomb Group and later of the 306th, having led the first mission of twelve B-17s from Polebrook on August 17, 1942. The war's end found him in command of the 315th Combat Wing of B-29s under LeMay.

I, after extricating myself from a desk job (Chief, Eighth Air Force Film Unit, which produced William Wyler's classic documentary, "The Memphis Belle"), returned to the U. S. for training with the 490th Bomb Group, and returned to the U. K. in command of the 487th Bomb Group. For my pains, I was shot down leading an early mission and escaped through the French Underground.

Harris Hull was promoted swiftly to one-star rank and became an authority in his field—intelligence. Postwar, he served in NASA during the Apollo program as Assistant NASA Administrator.

Freddy Castle, Eaker's A-4 (Materiel), after surviving the backbreaking chore of the buildup of VIII Bombers Command's logistics (and along the way a severe case of yellow jaundice), was given command of the 94th Bomb Group, rising to Brigadier General in command of the 4th Combat Wing. On Christmas Eve, 1944, he was shot down under heroic circumstances while leading a mighty stream of 3,000 bombers and fighters. Coincidentally, he had chosen to fly with my 487th Bomb Group to lead the mission. Castle was awarded the Medal of Honor, posthumously.

★2★
THE COMMAND REALITIES

by General Curtis E. LeMay, USAF (Ret.)

About the author: *"Old Iron Pants," as his men affectionately called Curt LeMay because he personally led so many combat missions, was the greatest fighting leader of the American Air Forces in World War II.*

Arriving in England in 1942 as a Colonel commanding the 305th Bomb Group, LeMay quickly developed formation procedures and bombing techniques which were adopted throughout the Eighth Air Force. As the Eighth slowly grew in size, LeMay, now a Brigadier in command of the Third Air Division, led the famed Regensburg raid, a B-17 shuttle mission had originated in England, heavily damaged the Messerschmitt factory deep in Germany, and flew on to Africa.

In July 1944, LeMay went to the Pacific to direct B-29 missions of the 20th Bomber Command in the China-Burma-India Theater, then moved to command of the 21st Bomber Command based on Guam. Here he made one of the war's boldest gambles by stripping his B-29s of defensive guns and gunners to save weight on the long flight to Japan and sending the planes in at night, at 5,000 feet instead of the usual 30,000, loaded with incendiary bombs to burn out sixteen and a half square miles of largely wood and paper Tokyo. Chief of Staff of the Strategic Air Forces in the Pacific at war's end, he piloted a B-29 non-stop in a record flight from Hokkaido to Chicago.

In 1947, after two years in the Pentagon, LeMay was appointed commander of the U. S. Air Forces in Europe and organized air operations for the Berlin Airlift. Back again in 1948, he took command of the new Strategic Air Command, whose headquarters at Offutt Air Base, Nebraska, became the nerve center of a world-wide bomber-missile force, combining all-jet bombers and intercontinental ballistic missiles.

After ten years as SAC Commander, General LeMay in 1957 became Vice Chief of Staff of the U. S. Air Force, and in 1961 Chief, retiring four years later.

—*J.P.*

In the previous essay, Colonel Beirne Lay has pointed out that while we had a sound theory of strategic warfare, we lacked the equipment to carry out the theory and the trained people to do the job.

Let me now cover some of the operational problems we faced—proving in combat the equipment we had, learning how to fight this new kind of war, trying to inflict what damage was possible on the enemy while conserving your forces so that the survivors could teach the new crews coming into combat—so that the day would come when your forces would be adequate to do the job and you could really go to war and finish it. Living through the frustrations of building something, only to see it "shot down"—transfers back home to form new units or to other tasks in other theaters—became a difficult way of life.

Lay has also alluded to my inexperience in command when I landed at Prestwick, Scotland, in November 1942 with the 305th Bomb Group. My awareness of this fact went deep.

Command is a soul-searching experience that, as I was to discover, never ends. You keep asking yourself: "Have I thought of *everything*? Can I do more? And do it better? Can I avoid repeating a mistake? Am I really qualified to lead these men into combat? If not, can I learn in time?"

With misgivings like these foremost in my consciousness, I leaped at the chance to hear the low-down from a veteran of many combat missions who said that he could spare a few minutes to talk to us while he was waiting for his airplane to take off for Washington, D. C.

I hastily summoned all of my crews to listen to the "oracle." We hung on every word. And the word was grim.

"The flak is murder. If you fly straight and level through it for more than ten seconds, you're a dead duck."

Hell's bells, I said to myself, if you cannot fly straight and level for more than ten seconds, how are you going to get bombs on the target?

It was an utter impossibility, under even the best of circumstances in peacetime against a practice circle in the desert—not enough time to stabilize the gyro of the Norden bombsight and feed in your rate (ground speed) and drift (cross-wind). Yet this was what the veterans of four months of combat had been trying to do when flak was heavy, in their overriding concern for survival, by taking evasive action—changing direction and altitude systematically while on the bomb run between the Initial Point and the target.

From that moment the veteran's words haunted me, breaking through my preoccupation with all of the incessant demands on my attention that were an inevitable part of getting the 305th organized (if that is the right word) in the mud and confusion of our temporary base at Grafton Underwood, before moving to Chelveston, our permanent station.

I lay awake nights, wrestling with the problem. Something was wrong—terribly wrong. Finally I had a brainstorm just before our first mission against the sub pens at St. Nazaire, got out of bed, went to my foot locker and pulled out a copy of an old ROTC artillery manual and started scribbling figures.

I based my calculations on probability of hits from a French 75-millimeter cannon on a target the size of a B-17 at a range of 25,000 feet (four to five miles straight up) for the Jerry flak gunners with their roughly comparable 88-millimeter flak batteries. The answer came out to 273 rounds fired per hit on a B-17.

By golly, I told myself, those are pretty good odds. I am going to try flying straight and level on the bomb run even if it takes *minutes* instead of seconds. Otherwise we might as well all stay at home.

Group Commanders were, at that stage, free to advise their own tactics. So the 305th's first bomb run was from the time the target was identified until the bombs dropped. The bombs landed on target. No losses to flak. It worked. And it became S.O.P. (Standard Operating Procedure), for all groups, with the endorsement of Brigadier General Laurence S. "Larry" Kuter, Wing Commander, after statistics submitted to him and other Group C.O.'s showed that we had fewer losses to flak (but more battle damage) and far better bombing.

Having slain my first dragon, I took on others of varying sizes, and with varying degrees of success, with fresh confidence.

1. *The Field Order.* This was the blueprint for a mission, teletyped to all Groups from VIII Bomber Command (through Wing), and prepared by earnest but inexperienced non-bomber pilots, overwhelmed by new problems. It was a hodgepodge. I visited Wing headquarters and furnished the Operations section with a sample copy of the Field Order

which had been S.O.P. in the 2nd Bomb Group at Langley Field, grouping all pertinent operational information under sub-headings of five paragraphs, always the same. You could find what you needed to know without hunting through the whole field order. It made sense and was adopted.

2. *Standardization of group formations.* When I arrived, each group commander was going his own way with formations flown, and Wing tactics consisted of little more than groups "getting together" en route to and over the target.

Since we had never had enough airplanes in our training period of three months to fly a formation, the first day the weather permitted I scheduled a practice mission using a type of formation I considered best at that time. It was a complete debacle. The pilots simply did not have the training to fly it.

The next day I got on the radio in the top turret and started with my ship placed with two aircraft on my wings—one about fifty feet above and behind me and the other fifty feet below and behind me. Then I placed another three-ship element above and behind the first. This formed the first (lead) squadron. The second squadron was placed above and behind the first squadron and the third squadron below and behind the first. Either the right or the left wing man could fly in the high position.

Most fighter attacks came out of the sun, so you could echelon away from the sun, thus uncovering all guns in the formation to meet the fighter attacks.

This formation was easy to fly with untrained crews, was effective—our loss rate was lower than the other Groups—and was finally adopted as standard in the Eighth Air Force.

3. *Group and Wing Integrity.* The Wing comprised always two, and normally three Groups. (Postwar, in SAC, the Group became known as the Wing.) My policy was that a following Group never under any circumstances abandoned its Lead Group, even if it became obvious that its commander was off course or heading into other trouble. It was permissible to break radio silence in an attempt to correct him, but, regardless, you stuck with him. It was part of the rigid discipline of "the larger good."

By the same token, for example, Group integrity forbade a pilot's breaking formation to "cover" a crippled buddy. The reasoning behind the rule was amply borne out, before it was adopted, by bitter experience; when a crew left formation, for whatever laudable motive, something worse invariably happened than if it had remained in formation doing its part to defend the group. For instance, you would lose *two* crews to fighters instead of one, or the weakened group formation would suffer extra losses because your defensive fire power was reduced by ten more guns.

A classical example of Wing Integrity was underlined on his first mission by Captain James M. Stewart (he of movie fame), while leading a Group of B-24s. Jimmy Stewart received a commendation from his Wing Commander for sticking with him after Stewart repeatedly warned him (correctly) that he was wandering off course. Under a subsequent heavy fighter attack, and without the support of Stewart's defensive fire power, the errant Group would have been faced with annihilation. In fact both Groups could have been lost if Stewart had tried to lead his Group back to the main bomber stream alone.

4. *Lead Crews.* I soon became convinced that it was totally unrealistic to expect bombardiers and navigators and pilots to become instant experts on unfamiliar targets *after* the target was disclosed at the briefing. Therefore I set up schools wherein the best qualified pilots, navigators and bombardiers were able to study all available target information, so that when a target was announced it was already an old friend. You had already studied the landmarks surrounding it until it was as familiar as your back yard—the bend in the river at the Initial Point and the racetrack adjacent to the factory to be bombed.

These specially trained personnel soon became known as "Lead" crews and bore the brunt of tough missions, with every bombardier in the Group "toggling" his bombs when the lead bombardier released his on the bomb run. At one stroke you raised the accuracy of the whole Group from the common denominator to the level of your best man, and navigation improved accordingly. Pilots became skilled as human "automatic pilots" in case of failure of the real auto pilot from malfunction or battle damage, able to maintain heading, airspeed, altitude or rate of climb (during assembly) to very close tolerances.

5. *Bad weather.* Two kinds of weather plagued us in the ETO, both over England and the Continent— lousy and worse—from fogged-in air bases to cloud cover over the targets to winds aloft sometimes reaching one hundred miles per hour, harassing navigators and bombardiers on the bomb run, and sometimes jeopardizing the safe return of the entire force, faced with a mass ditching in the North Sea, out of fuel. Fortunately, it never happened.

Mark Twain notwithstanding, I tried to do two

things about the weather. First, we experimented with crude radar bombing devices through the overcast, with indifferent results. Too much accuracy was compromised, resulting in "area" bombing of a "precision" target, and we were critically short of trained radar maintenance men.

Secondly, and this was crucial to the timing of the Regensburg-Schweinfurt mission of August 17, 1943, which I led, I had for some time required all takeoffs to be simulated blind takeoffs. The biggest bugaboo was the lack of ILS (Instrument Landing System) or GCA (Ground Controlled Approach) equipment, but we did have in the cockpit two reliable instruments—the DG (Directional Gyro) and the Artificial Horizon. The pilot lowered his seat at the head of the runway, concentrated on that faithful DG to hold him on a straight line down the runway, while his copilot acted as a safety measure to take over visually if the pilot got into trouble. Once airborne, the pilot ascended still relying on instruments as he circled around an assigned "splasher beacon" for a reference point, and for safe separation from other aircraft, until he broke out on top. Then different colored flares were fired to identify each Group leader.

The realistic practice program paid off on the Regensburg mission, when the fog forced you to follow a jeep to find the runway, yet all of my Groups were able to assemble roughly on time above the overcast. The Schweinfurt force, however, waited out the fog for about three hours before getting off to follow most of my route over Germany. The delay completely nullified the planned timing (fifteen minutes behind me) and allowed the Luftwaffe to land, rearm and refuel in time to meet the Schweinfurt force, after subjecting my force to the fiercest attack of the war. Nonetheless, we clobbered the ME-109 factory at Regensburg and the 1st Air Division severely damaged the ball-bearing complex at Schweinfurt, but our lack of resources with which to follow up swiftly softened the blows. (Albert Speer, in his memoirs, expresses amazement at our apparent underestimation of the damage done.)

On the whole, we never came close to an all-weather capability, for lack of sophisticated ground equipment, and the impact on crew morale of a mission scrubbed because of the weather at the last moment continued to represent a dreadful let-down for taut nerves.

6. *Major Repair.* I fought a running, and losing, battle with the Air Service Command to speed up the repair of our battle-damaged aircraft. They *owned* the bird while it was in their hands and until they were good and ready to return it. I was fortunate, however, in having a master scrounger and do-it-yourself genius of a line chief turned Engineering Officer named Ben Fulkrod and a crackerjack Armament Officer, Ralph Cohen. Bulkrod had managed to smuggle into England some priceless machine tools and other metal-working equipment and could replace a whole wing that would have been "contracted" to the manufacturer in peacetime. Through judicious bartering (helping out another Group in return for a couple of spare generators), he kept me in better shape than my envious neighbors.

The gist of it was that we were faced with a wholesale problem of repair, in combat, compared to a retail problem in peacetime, when if an aircraft was out of commission it did not fly until it was repaired—no deadline. Here in the U. K. we were snowed under by the demand for "maximum efforts," and the problem was not eased until the flow of replacement aircraft from home finally caught up with us in 1944. (I will say one good thing for bad weather: it helped us to catch up on maintenance and repair).

7. *Training of New Groups.* When I rose to Wing and then Air Division Commander, I followed the practice of putting new Group commanders under the aegis of an experienced Group for Indoctrination, easing the transition into combat. New lead crew members flew on actual missions, as individuals, with the parent group, and fairly realistic practice missions were flown over England at combat altitudes and distances. There was practice in group and wing assemblies and training in the latest wrinkles in radar bombing and gunnery. We still had to compensate for the time lag in the acceptance of combat lessons back home and perform some of the very latest modifications on arriving aircraft ourselves.

Beirne Lay has described to me the vivid contrast between my arrival in 1942 and his return in March 1944 as C. O., 487th Bomb Group, one of the last to reach England:

"We left our operational training base at

Alamogordo, New Mexico, with seventy-two (versus thirty-six) brand-new aircraft and seventy-two crews trained to fly group formation. Every crew member was far better trained than in 1942, thanks to lessons learned in combat, and most of the latest aircraft modifications had been performed at the factory. We flew individually to Kansas, to Florida, to South America and over the South Atlantic route surveyed just before the war by LeMay and General George Brett, with excellent briefing facilities at every stop, to Dakar, Marrakech, thence to England.

"Remarkably, to my mind, every one of my seventy-two pilots arrived safely, new though they were to intercontinental navigation and the responsibility for a crew of ten and a four-engine aircraft.

"We received every assistance from LeMay's staff at Elvedon Hall. By no stretch of the imagination were we combat-ready upon arrival, but we were incomparably better off than the early groups. One example: if one of my aircraft was seriously battle-damaged, a brand new replacement came in from the depot the next day. Another: I was unhappy with my Flight Surgeon, an important cog in the Group machinery. After a considerable hassle, LeMay's A-1 (personnel) section sent me down a real winner as a replacement."

8. *Mission Reports.* Early on, I started sending up detailed mission reports to give Bomber Command a comprehensive accounting of where each bomb had landed, whether on target or a gross error, and other useful information. I also initiated critiques after every mission so that we could hash over our mistakes and profit by them next time out.

9. *Gunnery.* I was never satisfied with either our proficiency or equipment in gunnery results obtained in the ETO. Prewar, we simply had not devoted enough time or attention to the problem. With a battery of ten lethal fifty-caliber machine guns on each bomber (sometimes twelve), we should have been able to defend ourselves more efficiently than we did, granted that we still needed escort fighters, also an area of neglect in peacetime. We even had to teach our gunners to lay off all of the traditional oiling of their pieces; the excess oil froze at high altitude and caused malfunctions.

I sent many a letter, both in and out of channels, to the Training Command back home in an effort to introduce more realistic training for the gunners. There was some improvement, but never enough.

Postwar, we learned that our claims of enemy fighters destroyed were grossly exaggerated— understandably enough when duplicate or even quadruplicate claims were reported from the heat of combat.

I hope that the foregoing practical considerations of a Group, Combat Wing and Air Division Commander's job will provide some understanding of what it actually took to translate the "visionary" doctrine of strategic bombing into day-to-day practice. Carrying out the theory so neatly projected by the theorists came to me, to quote our British cousins, as a "sticky wicket."

I doubt that any more complicated way to fight a war has ever been devised. The ramifications were endless. Just converting a country's peacetime industry to the production of aircraft, building huge new plants, greatly enlarging existing plants, and resorting to converted auto plants was a mighty challenge to begin with. Then, training a bomb Group in the first place, assembling hundreds of overloaded B-17s and B-24s in the congested air space over England for a mission and getting them to the target against desperate defenses and back home to fight another day would have curled the hair of a General Douhet, with his optimistic pen. I would say that it represented a practical achievement of major proportions, logistically, even had there been *no enemy opposition whatever.* We would have taken our losses if we had sent a thousand-bomber stream on a mission to Greenland and back, unopposed.

Let it be said that command of the 305th left an indelible mark on my heart and mind. The triumphs, and the scars too, will live with me always. But for the purposes of this essay I must move on to the area of higher command, beginning with my promotion to Brigadier and later Major General in command of the 3rd Air Division at Elvedon Hall, there being eventually two other Air Divisions—the 1st and the 2nd (B-24s)—as the Eighth Air Force expanded to maturity, all three Air Divisions comprising about sixteen bomb groups each.

Even at that level I was not always privy to the background of the fierce struggle behind the scenes engulfing Eaker in his efforts to keep the concept of daylight strategic bombing alive. Churchill, Sir Archibald Sinclair of the Air Ministry and Air Chief Marshal Sir Charles Portal of the RAF were all critical of our seemingly slow progress; at home, the Army and Navy were keeping Hap Arnold constantly on the defensive, anxious to divert part (or all) of our resources to their own ends. In a nutshell, strategic bombing was not proving itself, yet.

I did not see the confidential memoranda that were being circulated between the powers-that-were (nor, indeed, was Eaker always apprised). But I heaved a sigh of relief when Eaker won the "Battle of Casablanca" in early 1943. Roosevelt had already announced to Churchill that he would go along with the latter's desire to merge the American bombing effort with the RAF's night bombing strategy. Hap Arnold sent posthaste for Eaker to fly down to the Conference from London to defend the daylight concept. Eaker, with his aide Major James Parton as fact-finder and proofreader, worked day and night at Casablanca preparing a twenty-three page summary (based on Intelligence material provided by Colonel Harris B. Hull, A-2). Aware of Churchill's impatience with long-winded documents, Eaker boiled it down and presented it orally. Surprisingly, Churchill changed his mind, taking a particular fancy to the phrase, "by bombing the German devils around the clock, we can prevent them from getting any rest."

In a pivotal decision, the "Casablanca Directive" was officially adopted, becoming the basis for the "Combined Bomber Offensive."

From then on, we had a firm foundation for our daylight policy, although there continued to be shifting emphases on target priorities. Production of Luftwaffe fighter aircraft (and their destruction in the air and on the ground) continued to be given top priority, followed by transportation (primarily rail) and oil. In retrospect it appears that oil should have received a higher priority, since petroleum shortages finally sounded the death knell of the Third Reich, immobilizing both Hitler's tanks and grounding his aircraft.

Shortages of ball bearings, though acute, did not prove to be as crippling as hoped; Germany continued to receive the full output of ball bearings from neutral Sweden and Switzerland, plus the reduced output of Schweinfurt. In any case, the price had been too high, for the time being. From the end of 1943 to the Big Week in February, 1944, strategic daylight bombing perforce ground to an abrupt halt, while the Eighth Air Force waited on delivery of satisfactory long-range fuel tanks to give our fighter escorts full range to the target and back. It was a vindication of Major General Claire Chen-

nault's foresight back in the thirties, at the old Air Corps Tactical School at Montgomery, Alabama, when he championed the fighter cause in debates with Hal George. The Eighth simply could not risk repeating the unacceptable losses incurred on deep penetrations, naked over German skies for want of fighter protection.

And then there was the surprising German recuperative power from bombing attacks. You might say that we gave them a thorough course in repairing battle damage, primarily because Eaker had no choice but to violate a pertinent principle of war—mass. For too long, playing catch-up, he lacked the resources to follow up initial attacks soon enough, and with sufficient mass, as after the Regensburg and Schweinfurt missions.

Throughout my tour in the ETO, there were drains on the strategic bombing mission from many quarters: the diversion of our Bomb Groups to other theaters, i.e. to North Africa in support of Ike's ground war, the campaign against submarine pens and the use of bombers on anti-submarine patrols. And again, after I left and General James H. Doolittle took command of the Eighth, there was the diversion of bombing to support the invasion and the ground offensive. All of these diversions, though important to the Army and Navy, were at the expense of our main objective—strategic bombardment of the German war production capability. Spaatz and Doolittle were opposed but had to go along.

Summing up, we paid the price of unpreparedness, when forced by a variety of considerations to fight before we were ready to wage war by true air power, until the arrival of Jim Doolittle in early 1944. The Eighth could now attack in thousand-bomber (plus) streams and apply the principal of mass. Jim was there for the "kill," and he grasped the opportunity with that high caliber of leadership which has characterized all of his endeavors in war and peace.

In the summer of 1944, on the eve of the payoff of strategic bombing in Europe, I was ordered to India to get into the B-29 program.

Why the B-29? Our planners, while there was still a chance of losing England in 1940 as an "unsinkable aircraft carrier," during the Battle of Britain, had busied themselves with drawing-board schemes for the contingency of falling back on heavy bombers of intercontinental range—the experimental Boeing B-15 and the Douglas B-19 (underpowered and lacking in performance), the Consolidated B-32 and the Consolidated B-36. The B-32, though unpressurized, was put into limited production, while the B-36 was too far in the future for a "worst case" situation (postwar it became the early mainstay of SAC, before the B-47 and the B-52). So we put our chips on the pressurized B-29, the best bet. Curiously, even at this late stage of the war, Britain was the only other participant engaged in strategic bombing; Hitler, after losing the Battle of Britain for lack of a strategic bomber, never corrected his error; the Soviet Union, France, Italy and Japan never really attempted strategic bombing.

When I checked out on the B-29 in an effort to determine the best way to fly it (if there was one), the aircraft was in the throes of horrendous difficulties stemming from all-out efforts to come up with modifications for its defects. Engines overheated, swallowed valves, cracked their casings and caught fire with disturbing regularity. Blisters (bulging "glass windows") blew out under pressurization—sometimes catapulting crew members out into the atmosphere to boot—and they fogged over. There were bugs in the central fire-control system for gunnery, and there seemed to be no end to lesser problems.

But the B-29 could potentially haul a very big load of bombs a very long way at very high altitudes, and I believed that it represented a tool with which we could get results against Japan.

Within the confines of a short essay, I can hope only to touch on the high spots of my B-29 experience, which began in India near Calcutta, with a jump-off forward base at Chengtu, were we fueled up—a logistical nightmare that entailed *seven* B-29 flights to deliver sufficient fuel for *one* B-29 sortie. China was mostly in Japanese hands. The over-all logistical facts of life were insurmountable, topped by the fact that the B-29 just was not ready. (We never did get all of the bugs out of it right up to the Japanese surrender.) Yet history must record that it sufficed, after I was transferred to the XXI Bomber Command in the Marianas, within range for the strategic bombing of the home islands of Japan, with Guam, Tinian, Saipan and Iwo Jima at last in our hands.

When I took command on Guam on January 19, 1945, I knew without being told what was expected of me. We had not been getting results. It was going to be up to me to *get* results or let Hap Arnold down.

Arnold had achieved a miracle in getting personnel allocated for the B-29, getting it built and, above all, getting a strategic force out from under the theater commanders and directly under the Joint Chiefs (although still Dependent on General Douglas MacArthur and Admiral Chester Nimitz for logistical support). At long last the dream of autonomy fostered by General Frank Andrews with his GHQ Air Force, prewar, had come true: central direction of air power by airmen. For me, in many ways, it was the European experience all over again but with a difference. This time I had the "muscle" to carry out my basic ideas. I got aircraft-in-commission on a maximum scale through PLM (Production Line Maintenance), introduced radar operator schools and installed GCA (Ground Controlled Approach) radio installations on Iwo Jima. The first reaction of pilots was predictable: "I'm not about to put myself in the hands of some meathead on the ground," but skepticism changed overnight to amazement after B-29 pilots, struggling home from Tokyo through bad weather, battle-damaged, were "talked" into safe landings at Iwo. (After the war, in SAC, I made it S.O.P. for pilots to execute instrument takeoffs and GCA landings on every flight, routinely.)

I demanded, and supervised, the creation of an instrument for the destruction of every worthwhile target in the Japanese islands. The deed was done in seven months, with an average force of four hundred aircraft, exploiting every human and mechanical resource to its capacity. Japanese targets being largely inflammable, we hit vulnerable areas with fire bombs. Let me emphasize that this was not a deliberate deviation from precision to area bombing. We only hit areas when enemy war-making capacity was spread over large areas, as in the "cottage industries" surrounding factories or when weather forced us into radar bombing, visual precision being impossible. Helpfully, Frank Armstrong's 315th Combat Wing arrived with much improved radar equipment toward the end.

To save weight for additional bombs, we inaugurated low altitude bombing without ammunition for defensive fire power on our devastating incendiary missions, and we got our operational rate per bomber up to 120 hours per month versus 30 hours normally flown in the ETO. In fact, we ran temporarily fresh out of the munitions with which Admiral Nimitz was supposed to supply us—he did not believe I could use them up at the optimistic rate I predicted. We took our losses, but the chances of completing a combat tour proved to be actually better than surviving training accidents at home with the B-29.

"Tooey" Spaatz, triumphant in Europe, arrived in August 1945, under orders from Arnold to take over the latter's command of the Twentieth Air Force; after a thorough briefing and inspection he was satisfied that we were "getting results," sending the following telegram to Larry Norstad, his Chief of Staff:

HAVE HAD AN OPPORTUNITY TO CHECK UP ON BAKER-29 OPERATIONS AND BELIEVE THIS IS THE BEST ORGANIZED AND MOST TECHNICALLY AND TACTICALLY PROFICIENT MILITARY ORGANIZATION THAT THE WORLD HAS EVER SEEN TO DATE.

Arnold sent me back to Washington to brief the Joint Chiefs of Staff on the unpopular theme (with the Chiefs) that no invasion of Japan was now necessary. There was really nothing left to bomb, and Japan was at our mercy. I met with a cool reception. Marshall's plans for an invasion had already been made and would be carried out.

Events overtook that decision when one of my B-29s, Paul W. Tibbetts's *Enola Gay,* dropped the first atomic bomb on Hiroshima on August 6, 1945 (Arnold alone voted against it as unnecessary.) The Japanese were already suing for peace through channels in neutral Switzerland, via the Soviets, on the strength of the damage wrought by our conventional bombing, but our ally never mentioned it to us. Stalin had other fish to fry, a share of the victor's spoils, and presumably wished to place the moral onus of dropping "The Bomb" squarely on the United States.

I do not regret President Truman's decision—it speeded up the denouement—but I considered dropping the bomb no more necessary than the planned invasion of Japan. The jig was already up. Neither, for that matter, did I agree with the decision to invade Europe. I believed that once we had the complete upper hand in the air we could have waited for an inevitable German capitulation. And if we had made it clear that no invasion was planned Hitler could have transferred his West Wall divisions to the Eastern Front to stem the advance of the Soviets, far from Berlin, until a German collapse resulted in surrender to Allied policing forces. I think that the findings of The Strategic Bombing Survey, published after the war, tend to bear me out.

So there you have it. We proved, certainly the hard way, that strategic warfare by air in World War II was the indispensable element in victory. However, to be effective you must have a strategic force in being to carry out its mission in defense of this country.

We almost lost World War II by being so unprepared for it, in disregard of the advice of our first Commander in Chief that "the best road to peace is to be prepared for war." The basic lesson of World War II, hence, is that our nation must always be ready to fight, when forced to, and win.

GREAT CAPTAINS OF AIR WAR
Picture Portfolio II

The U. S. top command at the invasion front in Normandy: the AAF's
General Arnold, Chief of Naval Operations Admiral Ernest J. King,
General Eisenhower, and Army Chief of Staff General George C. Marshall.

General Arnold gets a B-29 maintenance report on Guam from Sgt. Leo F. Fliess of the 314th Bomb Wing, while General Curtis LeMay stands by.

Two years before Normandy, in England, newly arrived General Dwight D. Eisenhower confers with 8th Air Force Bomber Commander Ira C. Eaker. Behind: William Bullitt, former American Ambassador to France.

General Douglas MacArthur awards the DSM to General George C. Kenney, his brilliant commander of Allied Air Forces in the Southwest Pacific, February 1944.

The RAF's tough Bomber Commander, Sir Arthur Harris, whose nighttime heavies long carried the war alone to German vitals until the U. S. daylight forces joined them for "bombing 'round the clock," in a picture taken July 10, 1943, a fortnight before the combined attack which destroyed Hamburg.

Above, General Doolittle receives an Oak Leaf Cluster to
his DSC from General Eisenhower, with General Frederick Anderson,
8th Bomber Commander, behind. Below, Doolittle discusses
results of bombing an oil refinery at Halle, Germany, with airmen
just back from the mission. General Spaatz listens in.

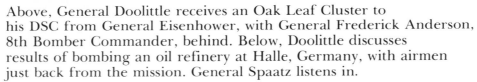

The Mediterranean High Command, Caserta, Italy, after General John K. Cannon, Chief of the 12th AF, was awarded the Order of Knight Commander of the British Empire. Left to right: Admiral H. Kent Hewitt, U. S. Navy Commander; General Ira C. Eaker, C-in-C, Mediterranean Allied Air Forces; Air Marshal Sir John Slessor, his Deputy; General Sir Harold Alexander, Commander of Allied Armies in Italy; General Cannon; General Sir Henry Maitland Wilson, Supreme Allied Commander in the Mediterranean, who made the presentation; and Admiral Sir John Cunningham, C-in-C, Mediterranean Allied Naval Forces.

General George C. Kenney, who directed the air forces under General MacArthur in the Pacific, testifying in a post-war hearing before the Senate Military Affairs Committee in Washington.

◄ Generals Spaatz and Arnold visiting a 9th AF landing strip constructed under fire in Normandy less than three days after the invasion.

Home from Tokyo, three weeks after the surrender, General Curtis E. LeMay, whose planes destroyed it and ended the war without invasion, with two of his top officers, Generals Emmet O'Donnell and Barney Giles, are greeted by General Arnold.

President Truman designates August 1, 1946, as Air Force Day, with General Spaatz, Commander of the Army Air Forces (to become independent in 1947), and his Deputy, General Eaker. The date marked the 39th anniversary of the inception of the aeronautical division of the Signal Corps with three men and no airplanes.
▼

Neil Armstrong, first man to walk on the moon, and General Carl Spaatz, first chief of the U. S. Air Force, both retired, chat at the annual Wright Brothers Memorial Banquet in 1969.

MOMENTS FROM HISTORY

America is in touch with its past as never before. And the mounting interest in our history is causing great things to happen. Historic buildings are being preserved and restored. Travel to historic sites is at an all time high. Lessons from history are helping solve today's problems and forge a new American lifestyle based on traditional values.

The four magazines of Historical Times Inc. are in the forefront of this movement. You may delve into our British roots, explore the troubled times of the Civil War, absorb the narrative of American political and social history or find out how to use antiques in your own home. There's a Historical Times magazine for you!

HOW TO FIND OUT MORE

Please write to: Circulation Director, P.O. Box 8200, Dept. IM, Harrisburg, PA 17105 and name the magazine(s) of your choice. Full, current information and subscription rates will be sent promptly.

CIVIL WAR TIMES ILLUSTRATED

Enjoy an extraordinary collection of Civil War pictures, paintings and maps as well as the best writing available today to reconstruct those troubled times through accounts of battles and stories of the common soldier. Political and social background of the times too. Published ten times per year.

BRITISH HERITAGE

Here's a magazine for every Anglophile! There are tales of empire, conquest and invasion - from Roman times to the present. But there is also much on traditions, travel, culture, food, entertainment, and the lifestyles, arts and antiques of Britain in this colorful, high quality magazine. Enjoy Britain as never before! Published six times per year.

AMERICAN HISTORY ILLUSTRATED

You'll be informed, entertained, even amused at times by this stylish magazine that's taken the lead in telling America's story in popular style. Especially for those who may never have enjoyed history before but want insight into today's problems and opportunities, this great magazine ties the news of the past to our world today. Published ten times per year.

EARLY AMERICAN LIFE

Find out what life in early America was like and how to create the warmth and beauty of colonial days in your home today! Houses, large and small, decorating, furnishing, collecting, cooking, gardening, travel and home crafts - all with an early American flavor. The first and still the best magazine on these subjects. Published six times per year.

IMPACT

PLOESTI—18 AUGUST
Scene from the Final Act

DISTRIBUTION:
SQUADRONS

OFFICE OF THE
ASSISTANT CHIEF OF AIR STAFF, INTELLIGENCE
WASHINGTON, D. C.

Vol. 2   No. 9
SEPTEMBER, 1944

**Forts en route to
Merkwiller on 3 August**

IMPACT
Contents
September, 1944

CLASSIFICATION: A combination of text and pictures or a revealing sequence of pictures is sometimes classified higher than are individual photos. For units which may use the pictures alone for instructional purposes, the following page by page list is published (unless otherwise noted, all text is CONFIDENTIAL):

FRONT COVER, CONFIDENTIAL
1-3: UNCLASSIFIED
4-5: CONFIDENTIAL
6-14: UNCLASSIFIED
15: CONFIDENTIAL
16-22: UNCLASSIFIED
23: PHOTOS UNCLASSIFIED, CHART
    CONFIDENTIAL
24-31: CONFIDENTIAL
32-33: UNCLASSIFIED
34-37: CONFIDENTIAL
38-39: UNCLASSIFIED
40: TOP TWO UNCLASSIFIED,
    BOTTOM TWO, CONFIDENTIAL
41: UNCLASSIFIED
42-THROUGH INSIDE BACK COVER:
    CONFIDENTIAL
BACK COVER: UNCLASSIFIED

CORRECTIONS: Major Generals Howard C. Davidson and St. Clair Streett were incorrectly listed as brigadier generals on Page 3, IMPACT Vol. II, No. 8. Photo on back cover IMPACT Vol. II, No. 7, was taken at Oahu, not Ponape.

CONFIDENTIAL

Remains of a railroad car
blown by MAAF bombs into
ceiling of Building at Siena

GROWTH OF AAF POWER IN EUROPE

On 16 August the Eighth Air Force celebrated two years of operations by flying mission No. 452 against targets in Europe. Three synthetic oil plants were attacked, also an oil refinery, three aircraft engine plants, two bomber assembly plants, the largest air equipment depot in Germany, and a GAF station. All together, 1,935 tons of bombs were dropped on these widely scattered objectives by 1,087 heavy bombers escorted by 708 fighters. This mission was just one in the series of air attacks which have been thundering over Europe for months. It was smaller than some of the gigantic missions flown recently as part of the all-out air-ground attack in France. Accordingly, it was buried on page eight of the New York *Times*, its news value apparently unable to compete with that of the ground situation, which saw Allied troops racing towards Paris and pouring ashore in new landings near Toulon, while Russian troops pushed into East Prussia and hammered at the gates of Warsaw to the south. It was obvious, on 17 August 1944, to the idlest amateur strategist, that Germany's military affairs had reached the critical stage.

What brought this about? There was little in the New York *Times* of two years ago, the day the Eighth AF was baptized, to explain it. The headlines then were ominous. In the East, Nazi armies were roaring through the wastes of Russia, about to encircle Stalingrad after administering a "crushing defeat" to Soviet forces at Krasnodar. The Mediterranean was an Axis lake.

The clue, however, was in the paper that morning in an account of the Eighth's first mission over the continent. This was a puny affair. Its significance is much clearer now, two years later, than it was then. But airmen here and in Germany realized what it meant: A long-range plan to knock Germany out of the war by bombing her from bases in England was at last under way.

Simplification of a war as complex as this one is always dangerous. However, a rough breakdown of the European conflict into three phases can be made. The first, running to about the middle of 1942, during which our air power was inferior to the enemy's, was one of adversity for the Allies. The second, from mid-1942 to mid-1943, with the air forces opposing each other about equal in strength, was generally a stalemate. The third, now approaching a climax, has seen the full growth of Allied air power and the tide of defeat begin to run with increasing swiftness for Germany.

A turn in the tide came first in Africa—where the Northwest African Air Force, formed in February, 1943, gave us air superiority. The Tactical Air Force, operating with General Montgomery, battled the Luftwaffe in that theater to a standstill, and ranged ahead of the Eighth Army on the desert in what has come to be regarded as a classic example of air-ground cooperation. Meanwhile, the German collapse was hastened by unceasing long-range blows by the Strategic Air Force, which dried up the German flow of personnel and equipment with strikes at ports, supplies and airdromes in Sicily and Italy, and made convoy duty a nightmare for German sailors.

Pantelleria next. The defenders hung out the white flag to escape further bombardment, and the island was formally handed over to the first Allied soldier to set foot on it. Then came Sicily, Salerno, Anzio, all of whose landings were facilitated by heavy preliminary bombardment, convoy and beach cover. Subsequent ground operations in Italy were expedited by the neutralization of the Luftwaffe there by constant blasts at its airfields and constant attrition of its planes. A few air shows put on by the enemy, like the Bari raid, make it easy to imagine what the campaign in Italy would have been like had the GAF been around in force all the time.

This brings us back to the Strategic Air Forces, now grown lusty and dangerous, and becoming more and more responsible for the absence of enemy planes on all fronts. Not only was it beginning to affect German aircraft production by attacks on the Messerschmitt and Focke-Wulf complexes, but the threat of greater blows had become so alarming to German strategists that the bulk of their defensive fighters was concentrated in Germany in an effort to smother bomber penetrations to critical targets.

The ensuing battle for the mastery of the air in Europe has so occupied public attention that one is prone to forget that it was in a sense incidental to the original purpose of building up a strategic bomber force in England, which was to destroy Germany's industry, and make it impossible for her to supply her troops at the front, effecting a collapse on the ground at a minimum cost to our own ground troops. Against a highly industrialized and determined opponent the force required to do this is huge. Despite much comment pro and con, the Eighth Air Force was not large enough to start this on a conclusive scale until the closing days of 1943.

Meanwhile, bad weather and impossible terrain had stalled the Allied ground armies in Italy in a sea of mud before Cassino. Two historically important efforts were made by air power to break this deadlock. The first was a sort of super-artillery barrage by our bombers against defensive positions in and around Cassino itself. It was a new experiment, and an inconclusive one. However, the lessons learned were applied with signal success later on in Normandy. The second attempt was the now famous Strangle Operation, which cut enemy supply lines in Italy.

By this time the German Air Force on all fronts appeared to be following in the footsteps of the Passenger Pigeon and the Dodo. Allied bombers flew to every corner of Hitler's Fortress. In three months the German oil industry was crippled.

A repetition of the Strangle Operation on an infinitely larger scale now began to take shape in preparation for the invasion of Normandy. Communications and airfields in a huge area in Northern France, Belgium, and Holland were hit day and night by the USAAF and RAF. The landings were preceded by an unprecedented bombardment of beach defenses, and implemented by parachute and glider operations on a scale never before attempted. During the critical days on the beachhead, continuous bombardment and fighter activity effectively checked enemy efforts to concentrate troops and supplies for a successful counter-attack. The beachhead grew, but exhibited a tendency to stall along a line running roughly between St. Lo and Caen. The Cassino barrage experiment was tried again, with improvements. This time it blasted a hole in the German defenses, through which our ground forces poured, folding up the Breton peninsula and rolling down the road to Paris. Smashing of all the bridges on the Seine, which originally interrupted the westward movements of German troops to reinforce units in Normandy, now prevents the orderly eastward escape of armies penned in a trap between Paris and the sea. And as the density and disorganization of Nazi troops in this pocket increases, the low-flying Allied fighter becomes a more and more devastating weapon.

This is air power's record in Europe, and it is an impressive one. On the next page will be found a graphic presentation of the growth of USAAF bomb tonnages, followed by brief statistical studies of the eight major types of targets.

Continued on next page

3

THE BOMBING RECORD

Shown are monthly tonnages dropped on European targets by the U. S. Eighth, Ninth, 15th and 12th Bomber commands and their predecessors. By June, 1943, the rate had already exceeded Germany's greatest month against England. Not included are fighter or RAF tonnages. For monthly totals by type of target, see the following 14 pages.

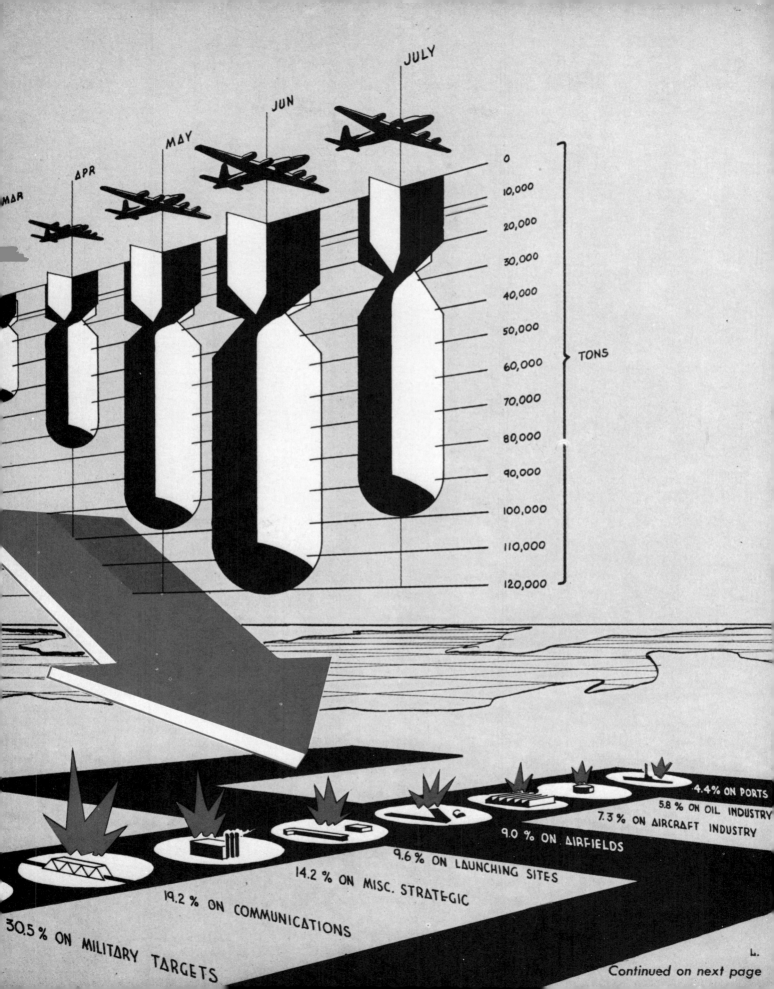

MAR   APR   MAY   JUN   JULY

TONS

0
10,000
20,000
30,000
40,000
50,000
60,000
70,000
80,000
90,000
100,000
110,000
120,000

4.4% ON PORTS

5.8% ON OIL INDUSTRY

7.3% ON AIRCRAFT INDUSTRY

9.0% ON AIRFIELDS

9.6% ON LAUNCHING SITES

14.2% ON MISC. STRATEGIC

19.2% ON COMMUNICATIONS

30.5% ON MILITARY TARGETS

L.

Continued on next page

AIRCRAFT INDUSTRY

8th AF B-17s Leaving Regensburg on 25 February

Bloody Sky Battles Fought in Campaign to Wreck GAF

By far the bloodiest air campaign in history has been the seesaw struggle to destroy Germany's production of aircraft. The comparatively small tonnage involved by no means reflects the importance or the bitterness of the battles waged. They went on for nearly a year without apparent advantage to either side, and losses of 50 or 60 heavies by us and 150 to 200 fighters by the enemy became accepted as the price to be paid many times over for control of the air over Europe. But a cancer was gnawing steadily at the GAF. The flow of replacements began to run thinner and thinner as one after another the great fighter complexes were shattered.

In July, a year ago, Warnemunde was hit, followed by Regensburg in August, Marienburg, the classic of precision bombardment, in October, Wiener Neustadt in November and Oschersleben in January. These attacks prevented a build-up of GAF strength to match the buildup of our own. By 20 February, we had a sufficient number of both bombers and long-range fighters for a decisive stroke. Taking advantage of

a break in the winter weather, we pressed home a week of uninterrupted attacks from which the enemy aircraft industry never recovered. Weather forced a lull in March. In April activity soared to new heights, and the GAF began the long skid into oblivion, climaxed by its failure to show up for either the Normandy or the Riviera invasions.

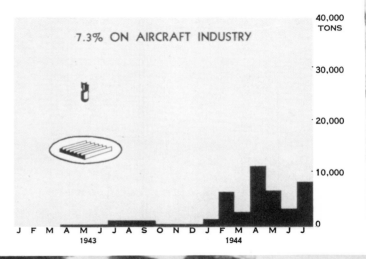

7.3% ON AIRCRAFT INDUSTRY

40,000 TONS
30,000
20,000
10,000
0

J F M A M J J A S O N D J F M A M J J
1943   1944

Continued on next page

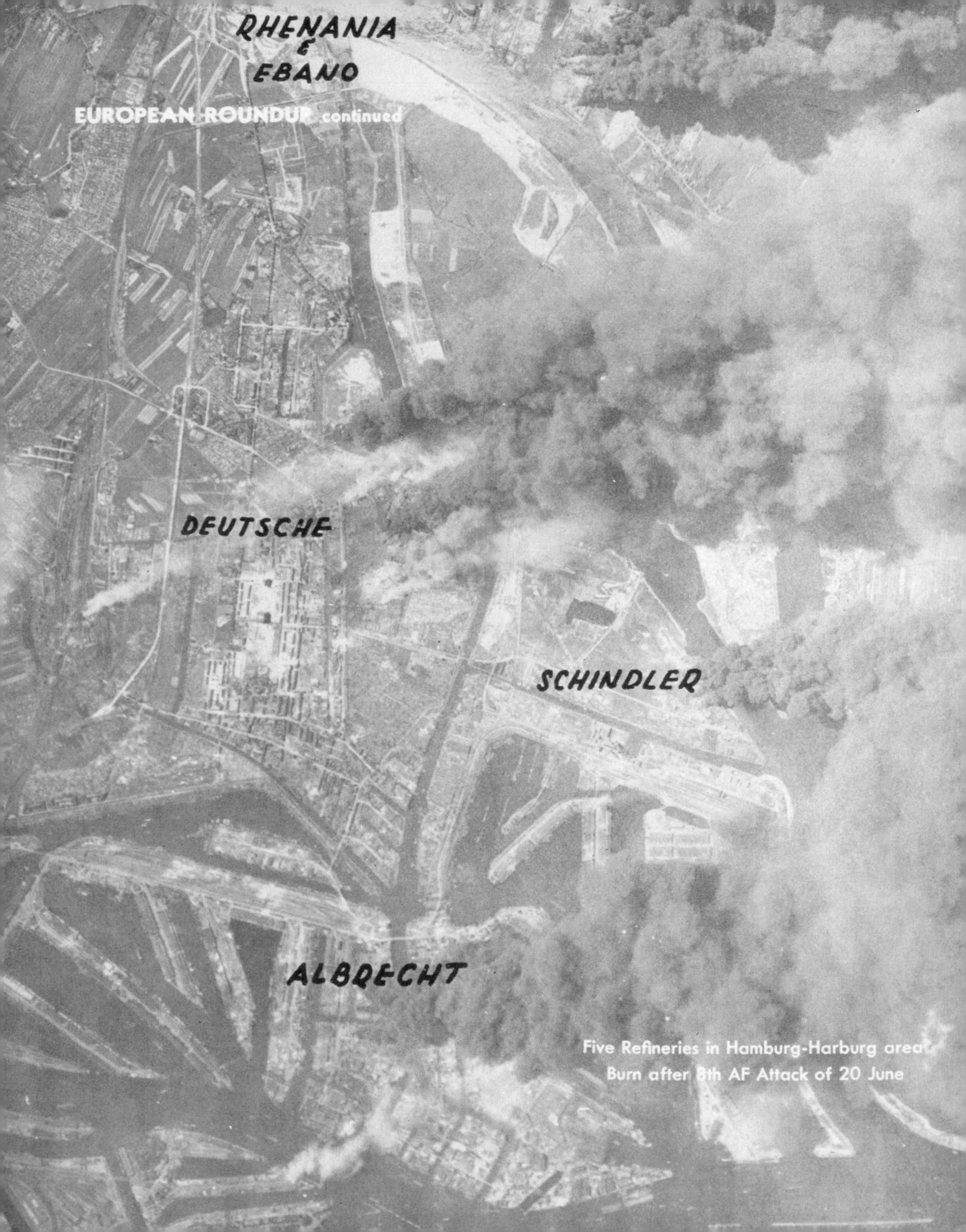
RHENANIA
&
EBANO
DEUTSCHE
SCHINDLER
ALBRECHT

Five Refineries in Hamburg-Harburg area Burn after 8th AF Attack of 20 June

OIL

Oil Campaign Begins To Immobilize German Armies

Although only a very small percentage of the total of USAAF bombs has been aimed at the German oil industry, the yield per bomb is tremendous. Germany is currently demonstrating the universality of the law that a modern war machine cannot operate without oil. Despite the enormous pressure generated by Allied armies, enemy oil consumption, instead of rising sharply to meet these threats, has decreased as follows:

Thousands of metric tons	Jan.	Feb.	March	Apr.	May	June	July
	1,306	1,300	1,280	1,115	1,054	1,129	1,050

The significant figures here are the June and July totals. While they show Germany's ability to reverse a declining trend for a few weeks to meet the initial assault in Normandy, they reveal her complete inability to keep it up in the face of relentless expansion of the Allied effort. This can mean only one thing: Germany no longer has the oil to maintain her armies in the field. This is borne out by prisoner of war reports which tellingly describe stalled tank regiments, anti-tank companies forced to fight wherever their fuel gave out, armored vehicles of all kinds abandoned in parks whence they could not be withdrawn. The situation can only grow worse as dwindling reserves vanish, and continued bombardment knocks production ever lower. It is now (in percentages of the monthly pre-attack level) down to 52% for all oil, 42% for gasoline, and 32% for lubricants.

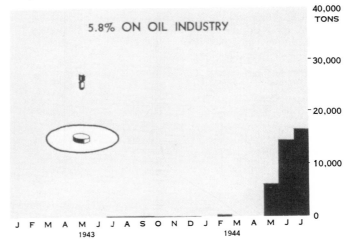

5.8% ON OIL INDUSTRY

40,000 TONS · 30,000 · 20,000 · 10,000 · 0

J F M A M J J J A S O N D J F M A M J J
1943   1944

Continued on next page

Other German War Economy "Bottlenecks" Are Blasted

Between 1 January and 31 July 1944, the U. S. Strategic Air Forces in Europe dropped a total of 350,000 tons of bombs, or enough to fill 310 average U. S. freight trains. By way of contrast, the RAF Bomber Command dropped 256,000 tons. About 43 percent of this total tonnage was aimed at industrial areas and strategic targets deep in the Axis war economy. The remainder hit targets closely related to military ground operations, such as railroads, defenses and troop concentrations, thereby supplementing the bombing activity of the various tactical air forces.

Of the 43 percent, roughly half was aimed at oil refineries and aircraft plants, discussed on other pages. The rest was dropped on targets grouped here under the heading "Miscellaneous Strategic." They include factories for making ball bearings, military vehicles, rubber, radio parts, precision tools, steel, and such small but important items as kitchen utensils. The largest part of the miscellaneous category is accounted for by area bombing and attacks on targets of opportunity.

Such attacks on industrial areas are necessitated by overcast conditions, as were found over Munich in July. The accuracy of bombing through overcast, even using Pathfinder technique, leaves something to be desired. But it does succeed in damaging industry and housing, thus causing absenteeism and lowering enemy morale.

A classic example of strategic bombing on a key industry is, of course, the long-term campaign on anti-friction bearing plants, which reached its height in the first quarter of 1944. Damage inflicted at this time, coupled with damage from previous attacks, reduced the output of bearings to about 65 percent of the level prevailing before the bombing started in August 1943. It is estimated that beginning in June 1944, the output of military equipment was significantly curtailed as a direct result of bearing shortages.

It is further estimated that the bombing of industrial areas by the RAF and U. S. Air Forces has reduced over-all industrial output from 15 to 20 percent below the level that would have prevailed in the absence of attack. Over-all shortages thus created in conjunction with the specific damage to aircraft and other industries are believed to be hastening materially the collapse of the German war machine.

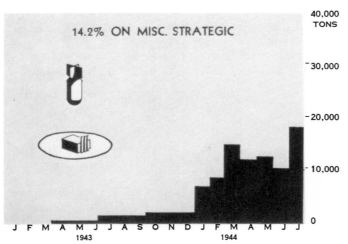

14.2% ON MISC. STRATEGIC

40,000 TONS

30,000

20,000

10,000

0

J F M A M J J A S O N D J F M A M J J
1943   1944

The MAAF gutted this war plant at Gaeta, Italy

Continued on page 12

COMMUNICATIONS

U. S. Air Attacks make Spaghetti of
Enemy Locomotive at Canisy, France

EUROPEAN ROUNDUP continued

Big Tonnages Clog Movement of Enemy Troops, Supplies

The use of grand scale air attacks to slash the enemy's arteries of communication is one of the newest and most impressive developments of the war. Before March, 1944, air power had substantially no over-all effect on continental transportation. But in March the holocaust began. Attacks were launched on three areas: (1) Italy, (2) Northern France, Belgium, Western Germany, (3) the Balkans. In March, April, and May forty-two percent of the total tonnage expended by all Allied Air Forces based in Britain and the Mediterranean was directed against transportation—the highest concentration of tonnage achieved against any single type of target.

While the Balkan attacks did not hold up enemy supplies to any material extent, the Strangle Operation in Italy (IMPACT, Vol. 2, No. 7) and the bombing of Western Europe paid off with big dividends.

In May, 906 locomotives and 16,000 cars were destroyed in Western Europe alone. In France the number of employees working on repair of bomb damage increased from 10,000 in April to 40,000 on 1 June. Prior to D-Day, rail centers in Belgium and Northern France were heavily hit, which had the advantage of diverting attention from the intended invasion zone, while still attacking the lines which would feed this zone with supplies and troops.

Increasingly, the enemy was caught with his bridges down. Prior to D-Day, bridge attacks centered on the Seine and Oise rivers, and on the main routes from Germany to Belgium.

For two weeks after D-Day, the attacks shifted to the tactical area. By 12 June, for example, all rail and highway bridges over the Seine were rendered impassable.

In July, as shown on the chart at right, the weight of attacks against transportation declined, at the same time that many planes were diverted to attacks on pilotless aircraft installations. More and more emphasis in the transportation attacks, however, was given to bridge targets. Typical July reports indicate that German troops were forced to detrain at stations in the Paris area and march on foot as much as 100 miles to the battle area. One prisoner alleged that our air superiority over communication lines in Normandy was so complete that even runners or dispatch riders could not be depended upon to get through. They delivered their messages, if at all, only after detours of miles and repeated spells of crouching in ditches while the roads were swept by machine-gun fire from aircraft.

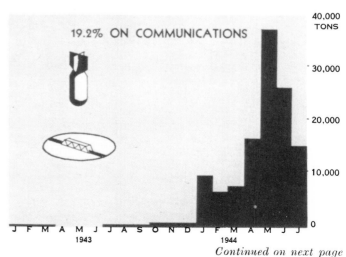

19.2% ON COMMUNICATIONS

40,000 TONS

30,000

20,000

10,000

0

J F M A M J J A S O N D J F M A M J J
1943 — 1944

Continued on next page

PORTS, SUBS

Port of Leghorn,
Smashed by MAAF

Kiel, Toulon Were No. 1 Targets

As shown on graph at right, the heaviest concentration of bombs against enemy ports, sub installations and shipping was dropped in the last quarter of 1943 when the 8th AF sent out 300 to 400 heavy bombers—huge formations for that period—to blast Bremen, Kiel, Emden, and Wilhelmshafen. These missions enabled the 8th AF to experiment with its new technique of bombing through overcast at a time when bad weather and enemy fighters curtailed unescorted precision bombing over inland targets.

While attacks against operational bases, such as Toulon, have been made from time to time, the bombing of sub yards has been much reduced. This is because it takes too long for the strength of a sub fleet to be affected by such bombing, and because naval and air attacks at sea have largely eliminated the sub menace. Since 1 January 1944 most of the tonnage in this category was dropped against the No. 1 German naval base at Kiel, and at Toulon, where enemy subs were based for their attacks on Mediterranean convoys.

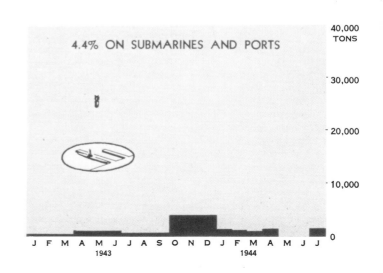

4.4% ON SUBMARINES AND PORTS

40,000 TONS

30,000

20,000

10,000

0

J F M A M J J A S O N D J F M A M J J
1943 · 1944

LAUNCHING SITES

Rocket Site (arrow)
and Blasted Area,
Siracourt, France

Robots Slowed, Not Stopped

Bombing of launching sites in the Pas de Calais area started on an appreciable scale in January 1944, increasing gradually until June, when the release of the first V-1 robots precipitated strenuous countermeasures. It has since dwindled as the development of defenses has been pushed, and as it has become more and more plain that the modified and portable sites now used by the Germans are exceptionally unprofitable targets. They contain even less damageable structure per unit of area than the ski site (see IMPACT, Vol. 2, No. 8) whose own damageable structure is only about five per cent of the site area. However, bombardment can be said to have accomplished two main objectives. The ski site program was wrecked during the first six months of 1944. So was the enemy's attempt to complete a single one of his seven large V-2 rocket sites (for detailed discussion, see pages 40-45 of this issue). Bombing of supply sites somewhat reduces flow of robots for a couple of days after attacks.

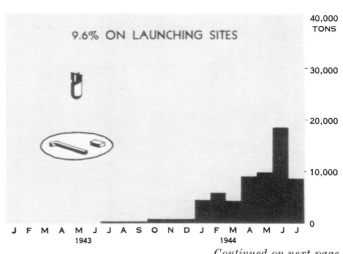

9.6% ON LAUNCHING SITES

| | 40,000 TONS |
| 30,000 |
| 20,000 |
| 10,000 |
| 0 |

J F M A M J J A S O N D J F M A M J J
1943   1944

Continued on next page

GAF Smashed on Ground, Too

At the Casablanca conference it was decided that one of the chief objectives of U. S. air power was to liquidate the Luftwaffe. The over-all strategic plan called for hitting German planes on the ground, as well as knocking them down in the air, and destroying aircraft factories. When the Luftwaffe began to decline consistent combat at the end of 1943, airfields assumed more and more importance as targets. U. S. fighters adopted the practice, after breaking off from their escort duties, of attacking enemy airfields on the way home, and also flying their own missions to specific targets.

The sudden increase of tonnage dropped on airfields early in 1944, shown on the chart at right, can be accounted for in part by the repeated B-26 attacks on German air bases in Northern France and the Low Countries, thus clearing the area for the invasion, and securing the beachheads against enemy air attack. By June literally thousands of enemy planes had been destroyed on the ground, and repair facilities badly disrupted—a major factor in the invasion success.

Remnants of the Luftwaffe, having been pushed steadily back, are now operating from hastily improvised strips, often constructed alongside bombed airfields, in order to utilize such installations as escaped bombing.

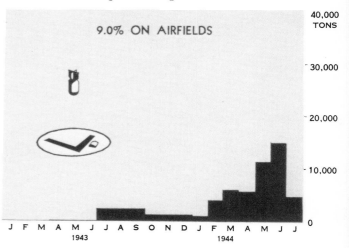

9.0% ON AIRFIELDS

B-24s from 8th AF on 24 June hit airfield at Chateaudun, France

AIRFIELDS

MILITARY

U. S. Troops Enter St. Lo after Aerial Bombing and Artillery Barrage

TARGETS

All-out AAF Effort Is Big Factor in Ground Advances

Tonnages in the chart below apply to all military (tactical) targets not covered in preceding charts.

During periods of intense ground activity the distinctions between tactical and strategic air forces disappear, as the resources of both are fused in all-out cooperation with the ground troops. This is illustrated in the graph below by the heavy tonnages of July, August and September 1943 which reflect the landings in Sicily and Italy. Between 13 and 16 September all the energies of the MAAF were concentrated in the battle area as the Germans counter-attacked strongly around Salerno. Along the beachhead 1,294 sorties were flown on 14 September alone. Tonnages continued heavy until bad midwinter weather forced a lull in both air and ground operations, but rose again in May as the drive from Cassino to Florence roared into high.

In June all records for air-ground cooperation were smashed with the opening of the western front in Normandy. A key to the part air was to play in the second Battle of France was supplied in the dawn hours of D-Day itself, when a force of 1,350 USAAF heavies dropped 3,096 tons on German beach defenses. From then on the AEAF has camped over the enemy troops opposing the Allies, walloping everything in sight with both medium bombers and the ubiquitous fighter.

When a decision was taken to force a major break through the German lines, the Strategic Air Forces were called in to supplement the work of the Tactical Air Force and a tremendous artillery barrage. On 24 June the Eighth sent 1,587 heavies and 502 fighters against German positions between Periers and St. Lo. Bad weather permitted the dropping of only 744 tons, but the attack was renewed the following day by 1,508 heavies and 591 fighters, dropping 3,370 tons. American armor rolled through the gap thus torn, in a move destined to be fatal to enemy hopes in Northwestern France. Further air smashes aided ground troops in their efforts to enclose the German Seventh Army in a pocket at Falaise.

Since July, tonnages have again increased. On 13 August, for example, the AEAF flew 3,307 sorties against the Falaise pocket, followed that night by the RAF with 3,944 tons. At the same time, preparation for landings in Southern France was begun with four days of softening up, climaxed on 15 August (D-Day) when 542 heavies, 371 mediums and hundreds of fighters struck seven landing beaches and inland communications with carrier-based Navy planes joining the attack.

30.5% ON MILITARY TARGETS

40,000 TONS

30,000

20,000

10,000

0

J F M A M J J A S O N D J F M A M J J
1943   1944

1

A truck, loaded with ammunition or gasoline, is under attack by two fighters, second of which took this picture.

2

The truck is at the start of its explosion from hits inflicted by the first plane, which is now about to fly over target.

3

Picture above was taken by the first plane; below, rear plane's camera records blast, first plane got through safely.

Matching the expanding U. S. bombardment effort in Europe as chronicled in the preceding 19 pages, our fighters have been coming along at a terrific clip. Never before have they been used in such mass and with such withering effect as since their weight has been thrown into offensive warfare. Released by the favorable fortunes of war from a

1

This typical attack on a locomotive by low-flying fighter attains primary objective by concentrating hits on the boiler.

2

Steam belches from stricken engine. During week of 13 Aug., Allied fighters destroyed more than 600 locomotives.

GREAT OFFENSIVE WEAPON

purely defensive role, they have been turned loose as low-level power punchers that smash enemy supplies and communications and provide swift and effective cooperation with ground forces. Examples of this work are illustrated by the explosive Eighth and Ninth Air Force gun camera sequences on these two pages and the one following.

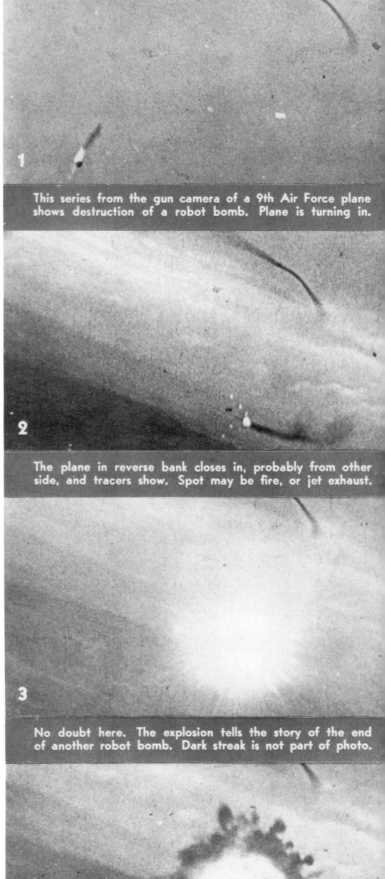

1 This series from the gun camera of a 9th Air Force plane shows destruction of a robot bomb. Plane is turning in.

2 The plane in reverse bank closes in, probably from other side, and tracers show. Spot may be fire, or jet exhaust.

3 No doubt here. The explosion tells the story of the end of another robot bomb. Dark streak is not part of photo.

4 Continued on next page

This German halftrack troop carrier in France is target for 8th Air Force fighter's .50 cal. guns as pilot starts firing.

The fighter pilot's aim is accurate as he dead-centers the troop carrier, and it explodes when bullets get the gas tank.

END OF TRAINS, PLANES

The bombers go after the rail yards and the plane concentrations. The Germans counter by dispersing planes, holding trains on jerkwater sidings. The next move (shown in these pictures) is up to the fighters. Swarming over the countryside, they terrorize the German soldier by the very personal nature of their attacks on him as he squats in a ditch, or sprints from a parked airplane.

In this strafing of train, the pilot comes in over the dust kicked up by preliminary burst, and tracers reach out ahead.

Three German planes, one crudely painted to imitate our invasion markings, are targets for strafing pilots here.

Cutting across the curve he scores an accurate concentration on several cars of the train, which is on a siding.

They got the far one the first time, came back over and got the one in the foreground, then got the middle one.

The 9th AF pilot flashes over another train on a siding. Cars in forground have had it; white spots are tracers.

TROOP TRAIN and bridge near Arezzo wrecked in one blow by MAAF fighters. Tactics are to dive-bomb rails in front of and behind train, if possible catching train on a bridge, then finish off the train at leisure with a strafing attack.

UNLEASHED FIGHTERS BREAKING ALL SORTIE RECORDS

To old time fighter men, the photos on this and the preceding three pages are especially gratifying. They have seen the fighter fulfill its primary function of conquering the enemy in the air. Now, with Allied air superiority over Europe, they see it helping conquer the enemy on the ground. Swarms of fighters are now congregating over enemy concentrations like hawks over a lemming migration. Pre-invasion fighter

sortie increases shown below first reflect the stepped-up campaign of the Strategic Air Forces and attack missions in Italy. The anti-airfield, anti-communications campaign heralding and later accompanying the invasion meant a huge increase in fighter activity, particularly in rounds of ammunition expended, because ground attack almost always provides a target, while escort duty often is accomplished without even seeing the enemy.

P-47 PILOTS examine Nazi tank they knocked out in Normandy. Allied fighters are the scourge of enemy tank forces.

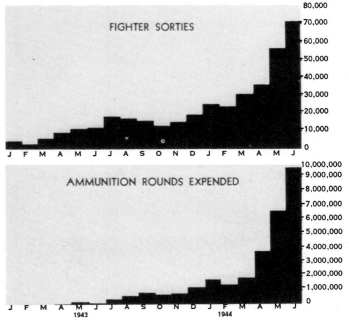

23

THE DAZZLING P-80

The future is warming up on the sidelines in the bullety shape of the AAF's jet-driven P-80, now preparing for use against enemy aircraft. The P-80 is the outcome of General Arnold's years of active leadership in the development of jet propulsion and has been carefully brought to a peak of efficiency which enables it to score brilliantly in combat-simulated tests. Details of performance cannot now be revealed, and in any case would be hard to believe, for the plane's speed in level flight and its rate of climb have outstripped all expecta-

tions. As the article following this one will show, the P-80 has a different appearance from the jet-type planes which the Germans have recently unleashed in their desperation. The result of long calculation and experiment, the P-80 is a superb example of functionalism in design, with structure smoothly adapted to purpose: its engine is a technological dream, encased in sleek and menacing contours. Airmen who have seen the P-80 test-flown say its performance leaves no doubt jet propulsion will revolutionize fighter combat.

THIS JET PLANE needs no snarling faces painted on it for frightfulness. Frontal view suggests that P-80 in head-on

attack—if enemy pilot even sees it—will look like one of the flying monsters that haunted steaming prehistoric swamps.

TAIL PIPE of new jet-propelled plane shows prominently in this view of latest model, the P-80A. Slight changes have been made in fuselage length and fin. Engine in this newest version of plane is considerably improved over early models.

 CHIEF PERCEPTIBLE DIFFERENCE in P-80A model is the landing light on the nose, illustrated above.

▼ PROFILE OF P-80A shows newest and slickest in streamlines and indicates how far forward the pilot sits.

GERMAN JET AIRCRAFT ARE TESTED IN BATTLE

The two strange aircraft pictured in these model sequences, and described in greater detail in IMPACT, Vol. 2, No. 7, represent the Luftwaffe's latest effort to redeem itself. Theoretical performance of jet types, confirmed by actual tests of the AAF P-80, led to some apprehension concerning the first operational use of the Me-163 and 262, both of which have been seen on the ground in increasing numbers for six months. Lately they have appeared in the air, and have made numerous inconclusive passes at our bombers and fighters. Although both have tremendous speed, any serious threat they may constitute is still a potential one. At this writing, they have yet to shoot down an Allied plane. At least two Me-163s have already been lost in combat. *Note: Distances between planes in these photos have been reduced because of space limitations.*

3. With P-38 closing to 300 yds., Me-163 does mile split-S. Rate of roll appears excellent, radius of turn very large.

P-38 vs Me-163: German rocket ship, after pass at bomber, is attacked by P-38 which scores hits as Me-163 climbs, weaving.

4. P-38 stays with rocket plane which spirals off into 80-degree dive. P-38 fires, observing strikes until enemy pulls away.

2. Me-163 emits smoke like thick white contrail, turns to left at 15,000 ft. P-38 turns inside, gets good deflection shot.

5. P-38 follows to 4,000 ft., breaks off. Me-163, going 500 mph plus, hits overcast in steep dive at 3,000 ft., disappears.

MOSQUITO vs Me-262: Flying at 29,000 ft., Mosquito is overhauled by Me-262 which comes alongside, looks it over.

4. Mosquito consistently turns inside Me-262, which cannot bring guns to bear, circles wide and attacks several times.

2. Dropping back, Me-262 attacks from behind, closing fast. Mosquito turns slightly, just enough to commit the Me-262.

5. Finally Me-262 goes into shallow dive, comes up under Mosquito, scoring hits. Mosquito breaks sharply to left . . .

3. Mosquito slowly tightens as Me-262 closes from 800 to 300 yards, opening fire. Mosquito whips into sharp turn.

6. . . . And dives into cloud, shaking its pursuer. Pilot estimated enemy plane 100 mph faster, less maneuverable.

B-32, RECENTLY CHRISTENED THE DOMINATOR, TRIES ITS WINGS AS IT PREPARES TO DARKEN ENEM

THE B-32 DOMINATOR

New Very Heavy Bomber Being Groomed to Join B-29 in Strategic Campaigns

The B-32 Dominator is the AAF's second plane in the VHB class. It was first planned as a twin of the B-29, and both types had important similarities. The aerial engineer, pressure-ized cabins, and central fire control were taken out of the B-32, which was redesigned as a more conventional plane in case the B-29's innovations did not prove practical in combat. Recent flight tests suggest that the Dominator is every bit as good a war horse as its big cousin, now hitting the Jap homeland.

FRONTAL VIEW OF NOSE AND INBOARD ENGINES.

SIDE VIEW OF LATER MODEL, SHOWING ARMAMEN

SKIES. EARLIER MODELS HAD TWIN TAIL, LOOKED EVEN MORE LIKE HIGH-WING LIBERATOR TYPE.

Comparison of the two VHBs reveals some interesting contrasts and surprising likenesses. Range and speed are about equal: estimates have each plane capable of ferrying well over 4,000 miles, of an operational reach beyond 2,500, and of a tactical radius of action approximating 1,500 miles. Speeds are above 350 mph at upper altitudes, the power in each case supplied by four Wright R-3350-23 engines. The B-29's maximum weight is greater, 135,000 lbs. to 123,500.

The Dominator is 83 feet in length, with a wing span of 135 feet, while the Superfortress is 141 feet, three inches across the wings and 99 feet from nose to tail. The new plane has more armament, fourteen .50 cal. guns and two .20 mm cannon contrasting with the B-29's ten guns and one cannon. And the big-bellied B-32 carries about the same bomb load as its predecessor, with each plane capable of a maximum load of 20,000 pounds. (See B-29 bomb bay story, p. 50.)

Continued on next page

OSE IS DIFFERENT FROM THAT ABOVE; PICTURE BELOW SHOWS DOMINATOR'S COMPACT STRUCTURE.

B-32—Plenty of Room for
Bombs in Its Giant Fuselage

ARMS AND RICE FOR CHINA'S ARMY

Then said the Lord unto Moses, I will rain bread from heaven for you.—Exodus, Chapter 16, Verse 4.

Quoted above is the first recorded instance of air supply. Under somewhat different circumstances, Troop Carrier Squadrons of the 14th Air Force operate now over China. But it is a safe bet that the rice and ammunition dropped to Chinese troops fighting the Japs is as welcome, and seems almost as miraculous, as the manna dropped to the Israelites during their exodus from Egypt.

In the CBI theater air supply operations are conducted both in Burma and China. In Burma, where troops at one time were supplied almost exclusively by air, much more tonnage by the so-called "biscuit bombers" is dropped per week than in China. But in China air supply is still vitally important. It reinforces native troops when they are in tight spots, as at Hengyang, and in some inaccessible Salween areas, where cliffs, ravines, and mountains make overland supply very tough indeed.

Due largely to a break-down of the Chinese supply system, there has often been a shortage of ammunition. Soldiers are sent into battle with a limited number of rounds, and when that is used up, it is generally a long time before they are resupplied.

The antiquated supply system, upon which Chinese troops in many sections depend, follows this course:

1. War zone to Army group by truck.
2. Army group to division by cart.
3. Division to regiment by cart and wheel barrow.
4. Regiment to battalion by coolie.
5. Battalion to company by coolie.

Thus, on a fluid and complicated front, the means of supply in lower echelons often becomes confused and cannot keep pace. How the 14th Air Force is remedying this situation, assisted by willing civilian armies of men, women, and children, is illustrated in the following sequence of pictures.

1. IN SUPPLY DEPOT in China a GI supervises packing of supplies to be dropped by the 27th Troop Carrier Squadron.

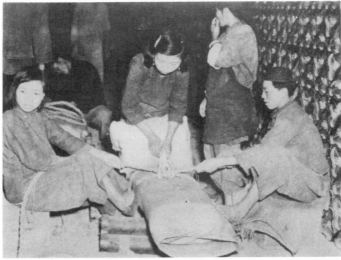

2. CHINESE WORKERS attach parachutes to ammunition bundles. Heavy 25-lb. bags of rice drop without chutes.

3. AFTER PACKING, supplies are carried to trucks. Cargo is loaded inversely in the order in which it is dropped.

4. TRUCKS LINE UP ready to have their food and ammunition supplies loaded on plane when it returns from mission.

5. ABOVE TERRACED RICE PADDIES these C-47 Troop Carrier planes, with their cargoes, fly in formation to the battle area. Here is a good example of the rough, mountainous territory that makes overland supply so difficult.

6. AT A SIGNAL from the pilot, these "Kickers" push much-needed supplies of ammunition and rice from plane.

7. WITHOUT BENEFIT OF PARACHUTE, life-sustaining rice and other supplies hurtle down to specified target.

8. AIRBORNE CARGOS, mostly of ammunition, drift accurately toward troops below. Some have already landed.

9. INTO ACTION! Chinese soldiers carry supplies, detached from chutes, through burned village to waiting comrades.

BOMBING THROUGH SMOKE

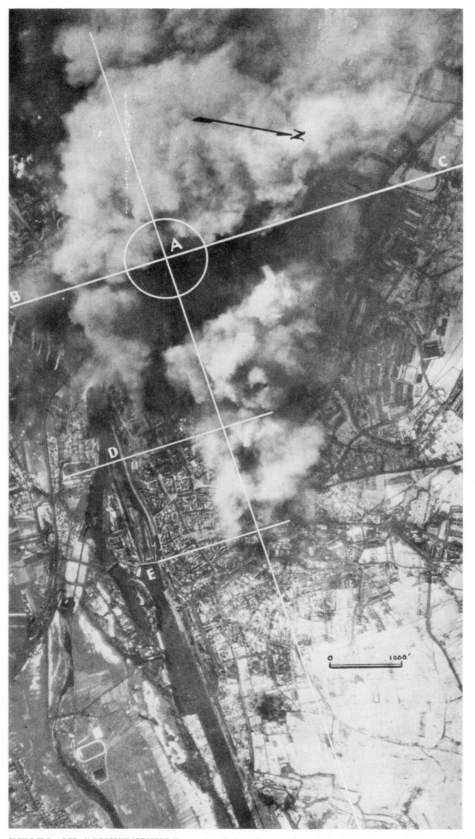

PHOTO OF SCHWEINFURT on 24 Feb. shows pinpoint (A) obscured by bomb bursts. Factory (B) and athletic fields (C) are visible. By referring to target map, bombardier could have seen that a line drawn between B and C would have passed through A. By synchronizing cross hair on this line, pinpoint would have been hit. By correcting with grid (see next page) he could have sighted on either D or E.

On 25 February 1944, the citizens of Schweinfurt were probably very busy cleaning up. The bluing factory, the jam factory, the gelatine factory, and the malt works, which next to the ball bearing factories, are the town's main sources of wealth, had shared in varying degrees the pasting handed out the day before by the Eighth Air Force. Schweinfurt was undoubtedly a mess.

It has never been the policy of the USAAF to destroy gelatine factories. So, it is logical that an analysis of the 24 February attack should have been made to see why the Deutsche Gelatine Fabricken A. G. was flattened, while the giant VKF Werke II bearing plant received no hits whatsoever. The weather was perfect, the attacking force on course, a local smoke screen highly ineffective, and enemy air attacks mild compared to what had been experienced by the more successfully attacking force of 14 October 1943. A glance at the photograph at the left will show what the trouble was. The clouds of dust and smoke raised by the explosions of the bombs themselves so obscured the entire target area that all but the first few groups over the target had to estimate where the aiming point was. This was aggravated by the fact that the first group over had dropped its bombs short.

The results of this mission were disappointing, considering the fact that 235 bombers were tied up in it, that 11 of them were lost, and that neither of the principal objectives of the attack was touched. However, they could have been hit, if a method, described here and later widely used for bombing through smoke and dust had been employed. This method, known as offset bombing, assumes that if you cannot see your pinpoint, it is still possible to synchronize your bombsight on some other point between you and the target and then make a correction by taking a reading from the grid pictured at the right. This "phony" or offset aiming point doesn't even have to be on the run-up course of the bomber, although it is better if it is not too far to the left or right. The correction obtained from the grid is then fed into the bombsight, which automatically delays release of the bombs until the proper moment.

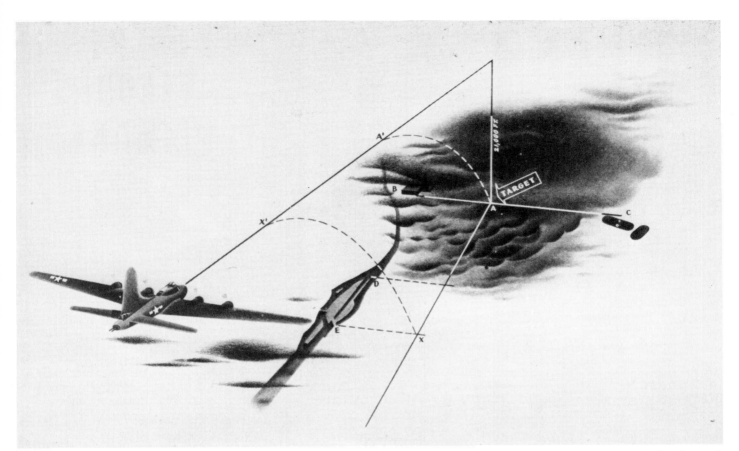

PERSPECTIVE DRAWING of photo on opposite page shows how aiming points short of target and off line of bomber approach can be used. Bombardier first gets plane flying on course to target and kills drift. He then picks out a good aiming point (ends of island at D and E are good examples) which he can locate both on the ground and on his map. He then adjusts horizontal cross hair in bombsight until its passes through this aiming point (E), and synchronizes movement

of scope so that cross hair remains on E despite forward motion of plane. Inasmuch as cross hair extends completely across optic, it will cross course of bomber at right angles to it at point X. Result is the same as if bombardier had been able to pick out a point at X, on course and short of target. If he did nothing more, bombs would be automatically released at X[1] and would fall on X. How he delays release of bombs (by using grid) until plane reaches point A[1] is explained below.

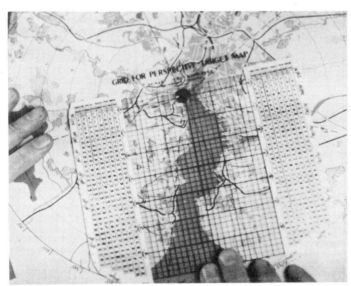

COMPUTER GRID is pinned to target chart as shown, with zero intersection at top of grid directly over true aiming point on chart. Vertical center line of grid is swung to coincide with course of bomber. The horizontal grid line (measured in 1,000-ft. intervals from true aiming point) that passes through

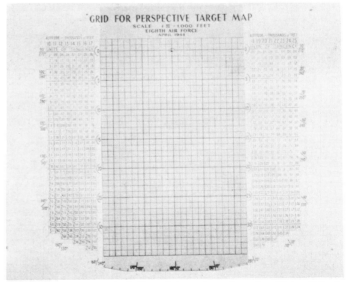

offset aiming point is followed to outer edge of grid to altitude scale. If offset aiming point is 15,000 ft. from target, and plane is 21,000 ft. up, bombardier reads to right, finding figure .71 in 21,000 ft. column. He then rolls back rate indices setting on bombsight .71 points. Bombs will then release at A[1].

Continued on next page

H2X BOMBING
IS EVEN BETTER

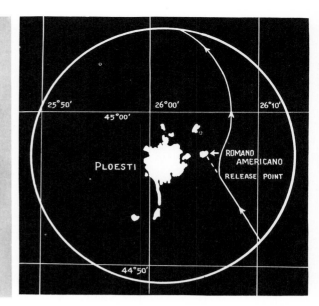

ROMANO AMERICANO: This Ploesti refinery was attacked on 15 July by 153 heavies. Photo at top left shows target completely cloud covered. No alternative aiming points were visible for offset bombing, so H2X radar methods were used. Artist's conception of radar scope (showing outline of Ploesti and relation to refinery), is shown at top right, with course of attacking planes indicated by curved line. Broken line shows path of bombs from release point to target. Damage photo (below) shows good concentration of hits despite fact that target was completely invisible, with stabilization plant (1) damaged; storage tanks (2, 3, 4) destroyed; sheds, heating tanks and process tanks (5, 6) damaged; large tank (7) damaged; distillation unit (8) damaged; blast wall (9) damaged; heating tanks (10) destroyed, tracks cut, cars derailed (11).

DISCIPLINE LAPSE DOWNS THIS B-17

The story of a tragic double error is told, unfortunately not for the first time, by the stomach-jolting sequence just below. In the first picture the bomb that is going to do the damage is shown just before the impact, with a second on the way. Next, the bomb has carried away the left horizontal stabilizer, clearing the way for those following. In the third picture the stricken ship, knocked off course by the impact, sharply has lost altitude, and in the last one the dive has begun.

The place, over Berlin. The date, 19 May 1944. The cause, as indicated by 8th AF sources: heads-up-and-locked in the ship above, the lower plane out of position.

Thus what the Germans failed to accomplish, we somehow managed to bring about. This plane had arrived at a distant target through intervening flak and safely past German fighters. It carried a crew trained individually at many places and now brought together to form, with the plane, a striking unit of fine balance and power. Then at the instant of potential impact it was betrayed by slips in air discipline—a discipline in itself the fruition of endless plans and study, as essential in the air as in any other form of attack, both to avoid enemy defenses and to make possible the massive concentrations of our planes in the missions of today.

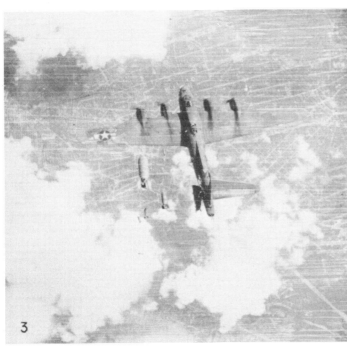

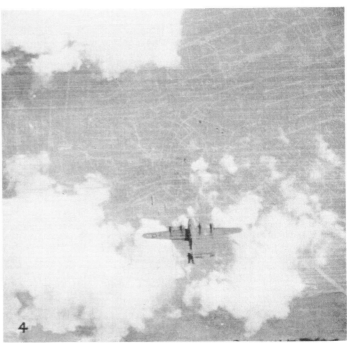

THE FLAK IS GETTING ROUGHER

A-20s ATTACK JAPS AT KOKAS, DUTCH NEW GUINEA, 22 JULY

ONE A-20 IS CAUGHT BY JAP FLAK, SWERVES OUT OF CONTROL

A-20 DIVES TO ITS DOOM, DISAPPEARS IN SMOKE AND SPRAY

The two victims of enemy flak shown on these two pages are a reminder that both German and Jap A/A fire is becoming more effective. At left, a B-24 over Germany on 30 June bursts into flame after being hit by flak. The plane was lost.

The Luftwaffe, with its back to the wall, is fighting the world's greatest concentration of air power with the world's greatest concentration of flak. The Jap, too, is reacting with all the determination of a cornered rat, and is getting results as shown at right. *The best countermeasure is Intelligence.* Any squadron or Group S-2 whose unit comes in contact with enemy A/A fire is a potential source of vital information, the kind that saves AAF men and planes if it is promptly, accurately reported to the Wing Flak Analysis Officer for evaluation and dissemination. For more information on current enemy flak tactics, see the Informational Intelligence Summary (first article, 10 July 1944).

HUN HARD AT WORK ON V-2 ROCKET

BIGGEST SINGLE PIECE of V-2 that landed in Sweden is jet unit at rear.

On 13 June the countryside north of Kalmar, Sweden, was rocked by a blast from an errant projectile launched in Germany, which broke windows nine miles away, scattered debris over a large area, and whose detonation was heard for 60 miles. Thus was the V-2 rocket accidentally and prematurely introduced to the outside world.

The V-2, or "Big Ben," together with sites for launching it, has been in process of development for at least a year. Rockets of various sizes have been observed at Peenemunde, have been reported fired into the Baltic Sea and in Poland. But there has been no operational use at this writing, delay apparently being caused by defects in the control mechanism.

The V-2 is a true rocket with an estimated maximum range of 200 miles. Its power is probably derived from a mixture of low-grade fuel and liquid oxygen, the latter being necessary to sustain combustion while the rocket is at the top of its flight curve in the rarefied air of the stratosphere, about fifty miles above the earth's surface.

Known large sites originally numbered seven. They are elaborate concrete structures built into hills and quarries. Originally regarded as the actual launching sites, their true purpose is now not clear, as present indications are that the rocket needs only a small portable base, onto which it is tipped by a dolly, to get it in the air.

V-2 has 18 separate jets. Swedish landfall indicates lack of proper control.

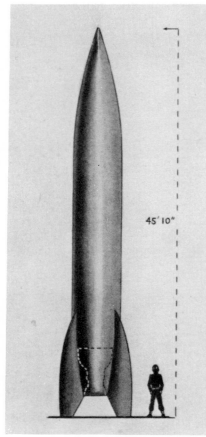

V-2 is probably 45 ft. long, six ft. across, weighs approximately 24 tons.

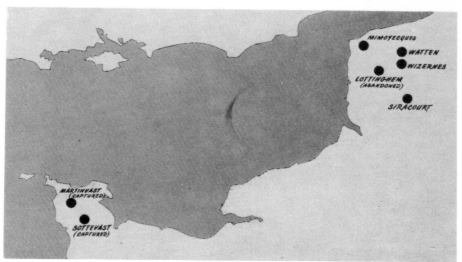

LOCATION OF "LARGE SITES" is shown on map. Two on Cherbourg peninsula have been captured, one at Lottinghem has been abandoned, other four blitzed.

SOTTEVAAST. Large site on Cherbourg peninsula was less than half finished when captured on 21 June. On completion of excavation work, whole structure would probably have been covered with concrete roof almost flush with ground.

SOTTEVAAST is inspected by General Eisenhower (next to right) and General Bradley (right). Compare picture with that of Siracourt on next page for appearance of similar structure after roofing. No two large sites are alike.

Continued on next page

2

LONDON

4

1

3

SIRACOURT: Construction started here prior to October, 1943. Site is over 700 feet long, has main central gallery, with narrow passage on each side, separated by heavy concrete walls (see elevation sketch at right). Direct hits by large bombs made five-foot crater (1), dislodged roof and revealed passage (2), scored near miss with crater 20 x 96 feet (3). Projectile may be launched from opening at (4), aimed towards London. Objects on roof are probably ventilators.

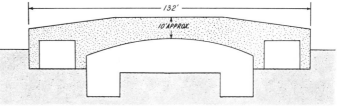

132'

10' APPROX.

SIRACOURT VERTICAL was taken on 15 May, two months before picture opposite, shows southwest end of site. Scale of activity may be measured by numerous cranes, tracks and enormous piles of lumber. Launching opening (4) is still under construction. Intense bombing has virtually isolated this site, has filled surrounding area for hundreds of yards with craters, devastated rail tracks, auxiliary buildings, equipment, tunnels, roads, halting work for long periods.

WATTEN was first large site discovered. PR of 16 May, 1943, revealed a concrete structure taking shape in a deep pit in a forest and served by two rail tracks. Heavily bombed and damaged on 27 August, further work was abandoned until November. Since then the rail lines have been repaired and a building erected on top of the previous construction. Annotations refer to results of attacks in June, 1944, show 120-ft. crater from near miss (1), blast mark from direct hit (2), obliteration of storage area (3), hit on conveyor ramp (4), damage to end of ramp (5), hits on new construction (6), railway buried for 40 yards by direct hit (7), road and rail line cut by crater (8).

MIMOYECQUES was started in September, 1943. It has elaborate underground excavations, a tunnel with standard gauge railway running from (1) to (2), and a launching struc-ture at (3). To get proper perspective of bomb craters, turn this photo sideways. Taken 6 June, 1944, photo shows huge craters from six-ton RAF bombs, one of which has hit (3).

WIZERNES, most unusual of all large sites, is located on edge of a cliff overlooking a quarry. Work began in August, 1943, with digging of circular trench above quarry. This was then covered with a concrete dome about 15 feet thick and 200 feet across, then covered with dirt as an added protection. Dome and trench have an opening, presumably for launching, aimed at London. On completion of dome enormous quantities of rubble have been removed indicating presence of large hollow space under it. In addition there are a number of tunnels in the face of the cliff at various levels, one connected with a rail line which runs through the cliff to the quarry on the other side, also used as a dump for spoil. Stereo dated 11 April, 1944, shows dome in process of construction.

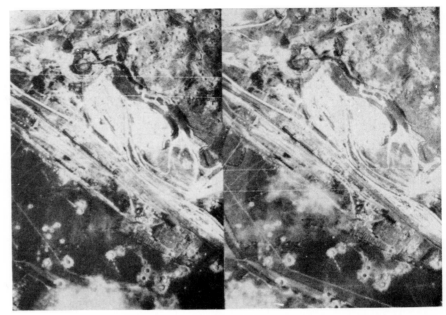

WIZERNES. Photo was taken on 21 July by a plane flying down into quarry. Bombs have caused landslide which has opened up concrete braces under dome (1), undercut and caved in concrete platform (3), completely buried tunnel (5). Main tunnel (4) and fire control tower (2) appear undamaged. Tracks on quarry floor have been obliterated.

SIX ABREAST TAKEOFFS AND LANDINGS

A FLIGHT OF B-26s IN TAKEOFF FROM DESERT STRIP DURING EXPERIMENTS WITH THE 6-PLANE SYSTEM

Time-Saving Joinup System is Adopted by 319th Group

A take-off and landing system based on operation of six ships abreast out of and into the airstrip has been adopted by the 319th Medium Bomb Group, 12th AF. For a formation of 24 B-26s the system reduces the joinup problem to assembling four intact flights instead of 24 separate planes and shaves total time in the air by as much as 25 minutes.

All four flights of a 24-ship mission line up before the first starts off, in assembly as shown in the diagram directly below. With manifold pressure pushed to about 25 inches, the pilots release locks and hold the brakes by foot. At the flag, the pilots let go the brakes and start easing up their throttles. From the start, wing men fly on element leaders to keep the line even. First pilots concentrate on throttling to keep abreast, relying on the co-pilots to handle the other gadgets. A fifth of the 6,000-foot runway is used in getting up to full throttle, and the deliberate easing of throttle makes necessary the use of about 600 feet of runway in excess of that needed for single-ship takeoff.

The system was worked out in its application to their field by the group and taken on as SOP last April. They have used the six-abreast takeoffs and landings for more than 100 missions without mishap, and now are planning a lighting arrangement to permit night use of the system. The diagrams on these pages and one following show how it works out.

DOGLEG JOINUP PATTERN is demonstrated by the diagram below. The first flight off (No. 2) flies for 5 minutes, the others, at 1-minute intervals, for 4, 3, 2. The turns are 120, 107, 93 and 80 degrees, respectively. The first flight, maintaining 175 mph, is at bomber R/V 5 minutes after the first turn, at 1,500 feet. The Group CO estimates this pattern puts the formation on course only two minutes later than one taking off on course and closing by speed differential.

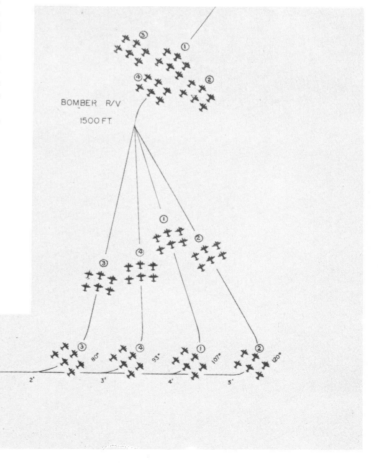

BOMBER R/V 1500 FT

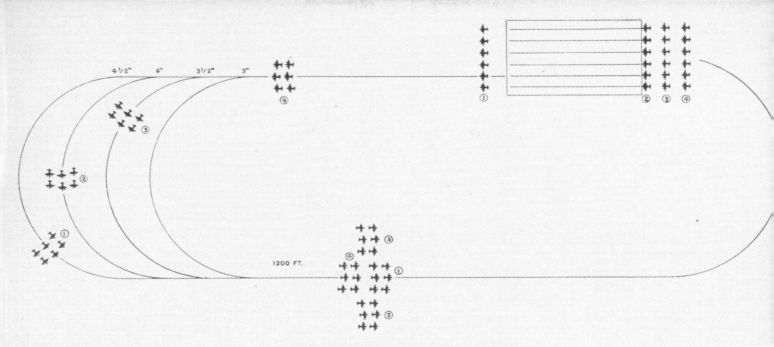

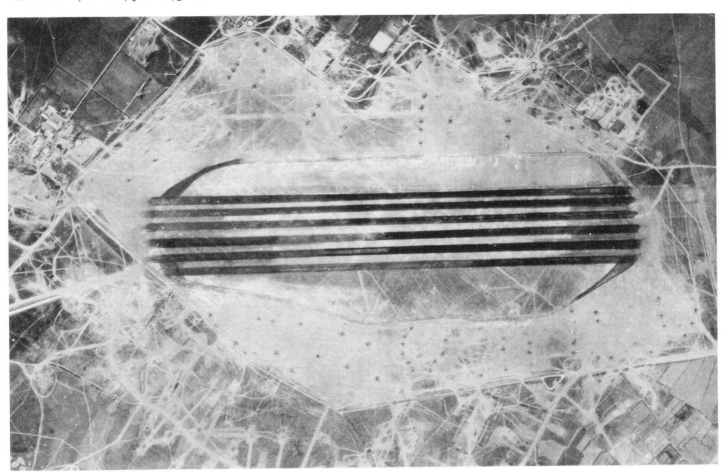

ELLIPTICAL JOINUP is shown by the pattern diagrammed above. Takeoff, unlike that for the dogleg (opposite page, below) is in order of flights. The takeoff interval is one minute, and each flight makes its first turn at 30 seconds less, from the end of the runway, than that of the preceding flight. The flights turn 360 degrees, each in a tighter ellipse than its predecessor. Bomber rendezvous is at 1,200 feet, and the on-course position is accomplished over the field at 1,800 feet, just 12½ minutes after the takeoff.

STRIPED RUNWAY used for the six-abreast takeoffs and landings is shown below. Width of runway is 1,000 feet. It is divided into the six lanes by the simple expedient of oiling the dirt and gravel surface in strips as shown here. The six planes of the first-off flight line up on yellow-painted tire scraps centered in each of the six lanes, the others lining on the plane ahead, all being in position before the first starts away. Danger of collision in takeoffs and landings has been found to be practically nil. For landing pattern, see next page.

Continued on next page

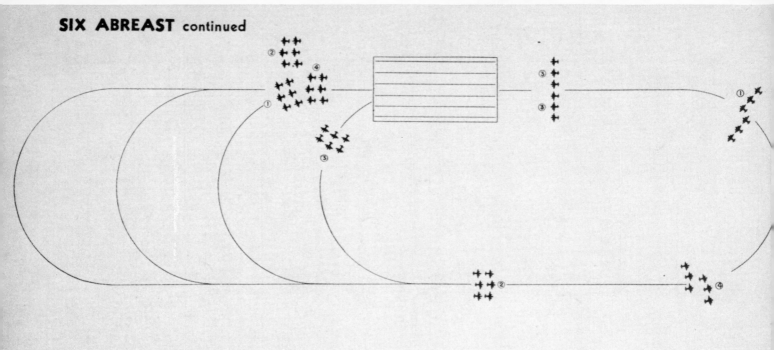

THE FORMATION LANDING is completed in 8½ minutes from the time the returning mission reaches the field, cutting 9 minutes from the time the crews of the last planes in formation spent circling the field for single-ship landings. The formation is over the field at 2,000 feet. The No. 3 (inside) flight breaks off in a half needlewidth turn. The succeeding flights, in the order 1-4-2, break at 30-second intervals, each describing a 360-degree ellipse 30 seconds longer than the one ahead. Flights turn off the downwind leg for the approach 45 seconds past the end of the runway, the second element uncovering to the inside of the turn, as shown above. Landing interval is one minute. Below, a flight of planes comes in.

COMING IN TO THE LANES (SEE PRECEDING PAGE) OF THEIR LANDING STRIP ARE SIX 319TH GP B-26s

WITH A BIG WHOOSH INITIAL "EXPLOSION" OF FIRE BOMB SEARS A JAP POSITION IN THE MARIANAS.

New Fire Bomb with Napalm Jell Is Hottest Thing This Side of Hell

The big blaze pictured above was caused by a new "fire bomb" dropped on Tinian island during its capture from the Japs. The bomb was dropped by a P-47 operating out of Aslito airfield on Saipan. In one day as much as 10,000 gallons of the liquid fire was released from altitudes as low as 50 feet by 7th AF Thunderbolts, each carrying two 165-gal. belly tanks full of it, on pillboxes, gun positions, and troop concentrations well in advance of our ground forces.

Developed at Eglin field, the new bomb is simply a belly tank loaded with standard QM gasoline thickened with napalm jell and equipped with an igniting mechanism. Since gasoline by itself explodes with too much flash and not enough burning, the jell was added for thickening, thus causing the liquid to burn on the ground with maximum effectiveness. It shoots into crannies and crevices, is highly recommended for attacks on supply dumps, ammunition, and for support of ground troops. When a sodium igniter is used the bomb is highly effective against water targets such as the small-size shipping and flimsy docks of the Pacific and Asia. When the bomb is released from minimum altitude, the conflagration usually covers an area from 200 to 300 feet long and 120 feet wide. In glide bombing attacks, the fire is more localized. Aside from its incendiary value, the "fire bomb" is a good anti-personnel weapon with a tremendous psychological effect. Used by 9th AF fighters in Normandy, it will also be used by 8th AF fighters. It is now ordered for all combat theaters.

FIRE-BOMBED JAPS who will fight no more. They were caught by napalm conflagration at mouth of Tinian dugout.

49

TWENTY 500-LB. BOMBS, TEN ON EACH SIDE, ARE READY TO BE HOISTED INTO REAR BOMB BAY OF B-29

CAVERNOUS SIZE is evident here. This picture was taken during a test of manual loading of the rear bay of the ship.

REAR BAY LOADED with twenty 500-lb. bombs. Time taken to load the bay in first test was 1 hour and 10 minutes.

TWO OF THESE 610-GALLON TANKS USED FOR FERRYING GAS FIT INTO EACH OF TWO B-29 BOMB BAYS

B-29's Bomb Bays Are Really Big—Can Tote 2440 Gallons of Gas

The pictures on the opposite page were taken during AAF Board bomb-loading tests with the B-29 at the AAF Tactical Center, Orlando, Florida. Those on this page show how the bomb bays of these ships are used for flying gasoline over the Himalayan "hump" from India, to be used later for the missions from bases in China. Gasoline burned by these planes on missions to Japan, Manchuria, and the N.E.I. has been ferried this way. Both bomb bays, with a total capacity of 2,440 gals., in four tanks, ordinarily are used.

The AAF Board tests included loading the bombs manually and by use of internal hoists, during trials to determine standard procedure.

Bomb loads that can be carried by B-29 include 80 x 100-lbs., 56 x 250-lbs., 56 x 300-lbs., 40 x 500-lbs., 12 x 1,000-lbs., 8 x 2,000-lbs., all demolition, GP; 80 x 100-lbs. incendiary, liquid filled; 12 x 1,600-lbs. demolition, and 4 x 4,000-lbs., demolition, light case. Fragmentation cluster capacity is 80 x 100-lbs. Capacities in the incendiary group range all the way up to 40 x 500-lbs.

TANKS FIT NEATLY into bomb bay, are standard auxiliary equipment for the B-29. This gas is for ferry to base, but tanks also can be connected to fuel system.

29s HIT JAP STEEL

AFTER AN EMERGENCY LANDING AT LIANGSHAM, CHINA, THIS B-29 WAS REFUELED BY CAN-AND-HAND-POWER

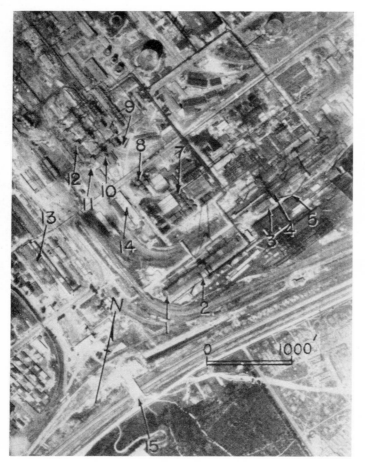

Twentieth Air Force attacks with B-29 bombers on Far Eastern targets, particularly those on the Japanese islands and in Jap-held Manchuria, continue. Following the attack of 15 June, 1944, on the Yawata steel mills (IMPACT, July) the bombers on 7 July struck at the naval docks and installations at Sasebo, Kyushu, and again at Yawata; on 29 July targets were the Showa Steel Works at Anshan, Manchuria, just south of Mukden, and Tangku, the port of Tientsin. The Pladjoe Oil Refinery at Palembang, Sumatra, N.E.I., the industrial area of Nagasaki, Kyushu, and again the Sasebo docks, were hit on 10 August. Results of the Anshan attack are indicated by the photos at the left and on opposite page.

DURING ATTACK on the Showa Steel Works at Anshan, fires from bombs dropped by earlier planes are shown burning. More bombs fell later. Only a part of these extensive works is covered by this picture. Strike was in vital area.

ANNOTATION on before-bombing photo at the left, which covers the area outlined by the white line in the large picture, indicates where the damage was done. Assessment was made from photos taken during strike, and is provisional. Numbers indicate: (1) direct hits on coke battery, (2) near miss on tower, probably damaged pusher for battery, (3) direct hit on coaling tower, (4) direct hit and near miss, or another direct hit, on coke oven battery, (5) two direct hits on building housing facilities for coke battery, (6) two very near misses on coke battery, (7) probable origin of fire and explosion, (8) burst among six tanks, (9) direct hit or near miss on stoves and stack, (10) near miss on blast furnace, (11) direct hits or near misses on shed, (12) one or two hits on blast furnace installations, (13) damage to large machine shop, (14) damage to laboratory, and (15) hit on bridge approach.

P-38s OVER ENGLAND

This plan view is of a formation developed in the U.K. for high-altitude P-38 bombardment missions

IMPACT

NIPS ON THE LAM
See p. 20

DISTRIBUTION:
SQUADRONS

OFFICE OF THE
ASSISTANT CHIEF OF AIR STAFF, INTELLIGENCE
WASHINGTON, D. C.

Vol. 2   No. 10
OCTOBER, 1944

IMPACT
Contents
October, 1944

Three-Dimensional Attack on Westwall:
C-47s over Flooded Holland, 17 Sept.
(See p. 22)

CONFIDENTIAL

Around the World with the Rocketeers

FRAMES FROM GUN CAMERA FILM ILLUSTRATE SALVO OF FOUR ROCKETS FIRED BY BRITISH TYPHOON

VERSATILE NEW WEAPON FOR FIGHTERS IS PRODUCT OF WORLD WAR II

The rise of the fighter plane as a devastating weapon of attack in the present war has been paralleled by the development of a projectile which is now being used by fighters to make them more formidable than ever. Rockets were first used effectively on the ground. The Germans developed them. So did the Russians, whose "Katusha" barrages are credited with helping to turn back Nazi ground forces before Stalingrad. American ground forces pioneered in the development of a destructive light rocket, the Bazooka. In England, large antiaircraft rockets have long done extensive damage to enemy night bombing operations.

Adaptation of the rocket as a weapon for fighter aircraft enormously increases their versatility and wallop. Through its use, fighters now have the striking power of artillery without the prohibitive weight and recoil attendant to the use of guns of a comparable caliber. (The 75 mm shell fired from a cannon-equipped B-25 is less than three inches in diameter and much lighter than the rockets now being used on British and American fighters.)

The rocket rounds out the armament of the fighter, falling between the machine gun and the bomb. The former is most suitable for strafing attacks against personnel and light and medium materiel, the latter against cities and large concentrations of buildings, leaving to the rocket the military installation, which, in accordance with general practice, is dispersed and of relatively rugged construction. The machine gun is usually too light and the bomb not sufficiently accurate to destroy such a target, unless it is fired from such short range as to make dead-center hits a virtual certainty.

Objectives against which rockets are most effective are: oil storage tanks, AA positions, small boats, hangars, warehouses, revetted fuel tanks or dumps, trains, tanks, other armored vehicles, barges, ammunition dumps, supply dumps and dispersed aircraft. In fact, almost anything which would be put under artillery fire if it were within artillery range can be considered a good rocket target. A large amount of high explosive is not needed for good results. The accuracy with which a small charge can be placed, plus the penetration of the projectile, make it unnecessary. In fact, the British have for some time been using rockets with solid heads against submarines. A hit with one of these, because of their greater weight, enormous penetration and speed, plus the usual presence, on impact, of an unconsumed portion of the propellant, results in fragmentation, incendiary effect, and sometimes a low-grade explosion.

USAAF planes are now using two types of rocket. The first

FIRST FIGHTER plane in CBI Theater with new launchers for 4.5″ M8 type rocket is this P-38J of 459th Squadron.

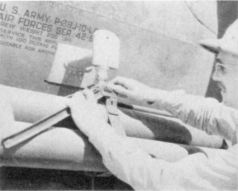

SHACKLE OF LAUNCHER is adjusted on front mount. It may be lowered in the air to jettison rockets if necessary.

PROJECTILE weighs approximately 40 lbs., is about 33 in. long. Triple plastic launchers are clustered under each wing.

NEWEST AMERICAN ROCKET IS FIVE-INCH HVAR (HIGH VELOCITY AIRCRAFT ROCKET) SHOWN ON WING OF P-51

is four and one-half inches in diameter, about three feet long and weighs 40 pounds. The forward portion or "head" carries a nose fuse and five pounds of HE. The after portion is the "motor" and contains the propellant charge, which is a solvent base, wet extruded grain with zone charges. As issued, the zone is adjusted for firing at temperatures between 20°F and 90°F. If fired at a higher temperature, the buildup of too great a pressure may result, which leads to separation. Accordingly, there are three marked grains among the 30 grains in the trap of the rocket motor. Removal of these three grains modifies the rocket so that it may be fired at temperatures between 50°F and 130°F. Later modifications (M8A1, M8A2, and M8A3) have safe operating temperature limits of —10°F to 110°F. Zone charging (marked grains) is eliminated. A further modification, now being developed, will increase these limits to —20°F to 120°F.

The propellant for the 4.5 rocket is of the rapid-burning type, lasting about one-tenth of a second. This gives it excellent acceleration characteristics and makes it a fine weapon for medium-range attack. However, its velocity is not so great, or its accurate range so long, as might be obtained with a slower-burning propellant. Maximum velocity is 865 feet per second (to which must be added the velocity of the aircraft firing the rocket), giving a maximum accurate range, under normal conditions, of 800 yards. At this range the projectile

will penetrate one inch of homogenized face-hardened armor and approximately one foot of reinforced concrete.

The rocket is carried in and fired from launcher tubes. These are three in number, mounted together as an integral cluster. A set is suspended under each wing of the aircraft in such a way as not to interfere with carrying the normal bomb load or external fuel tanks. The launcher tubes are bore-sighted so as to harmonize the rockets with the machine guns, making possible a single sight setting which can be used for both.

Each round carries a fuse in the nose which can be adjusted *on the ground only* for .015 second delay or for instantaneous setting. The round is loaded in the tube from the rear, fastened in place, and the electrical firing connections made. The round is fired electrically through the use of a control box and an intervalometer. This allows selective firing or salvo firing with one-tenth of a second interval. The use of a tube for launching suggests that the launcher can be put in the fuselage of the aircraft. This will permit automatic loading and launching of several rounds from the same tube.

As an example of the effectiveness of the 4.5 rocket, note the record in Burma of four P-51s equipped to carry six rockets each. Firing a total of 290 rounds, they destroyed the following: six large warehouses, 12 medium warehouses, one foundry, four locomotives, 10 Japanese aircraft, two river

ROUND IS PLACED in the launcher tube, while release assembly and electrical contactors are carefully adjusted.

FINS OF ROCKET are tested before insertion into launcher. Fins open as rocket leaves tube, stabilize its flight.

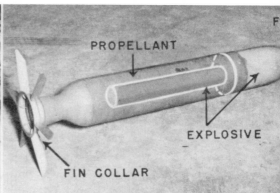

RED GLARE not yet unfurled, projectile lies quietly waiting to take up duties. Type: Rocket, 4½ inch, 3 tube, AC-M10.

Continued on next page

1. ROCKETS IN EUROPE. Attack on rail line by 2 Typhoons shows lead aircraft at moment of release of first volley.

2. LEAD AIRCRAFT continues in dive, releases second pair of rockets (flashes on wings) as first two streak for track.

ROCKETS continued

boats, four native shacks, four trucks and one medium building. Damaged were: two medium warehouses, five medium buildings, one locomotive and 13 Japanese aircraft.

The other U. S. rocket is the 5″ HVAR (five-inch high velocity aircraft rocket). It is five inches in diameter, six feet long, weighs 140 pounds, and has slightly under eight pounds of HE in the head. The propellant used is a non-solvent base, dry extruded grain. Its comparatively slow burning time (1.2 seconds) gives slower acceleration with a higher maximum velocity and a greater accurate range than is obtained with the 4.5 rocket. Maximum velocity is 1,300 feet per second (to which must be added the velocity of the aircraft firing it) and the maximum accurate range is 1,000 yards. At this range it will penetrate one and three-quarters inches of homogenized face-hardened armor and three feet of reinforced concrete. Safe operating temperature limits are from —10°F to 120°F.

The 5″ HVAR is suspended and launched from what is known as a "zero" rail launcher, consisting of two streamlined struts or studs which hold the rocket at two points about six inches below the surface of the wing. This type of launcher is easily installed on almost any type of aircraft. It has far less weight (15 pounds for a six-rocket installation) and drag than any other kind of launcher. The latter is a particularly serious problem, for the addition of any devices which will affect the smooth configuration, thus adding to the drag, of our new very-high-speed aircraft, cannot be tolerated.

The characteristics of a fin-stabilized rocket launched from the "zero" rail launcher are such that the rocket immediately assumes a "line of flight" attitude therefore its trajectory cannot be harmonized with the guns, which means that a different sight setting is required for firing guns and rockets. There is no danger of hitting the rocket with machine gun bullets when both are fired together. The bullets will be aimed at a point on the ground beyond the aiming point of the rocket.

The 5″ HVAR carries a nose fuse with instantaneous setting, which can be removed and replaced with an armor-piercing plug. Under development is a fuse which will make the rocket effective against under-water targets. The ratio of length to diameter gives the rocket an excellent under-water trajectory. For example, after traveling through the air for 1,000 yards, then striking the water and traveling for 200 feet under water, it still has the amazing velocity of 950 feet per second.

For the 5″ HVAR in combat, see page 6.

5. SECOND PAIR HITS intersection of track and road, just to right of water tower. Wingman now fires his first volley.

ROCKETS IN THE PACIFIC. Use of rockets by Navy TBFs has paid off handsomely against land installations at Mili, Palau, Woleai, Hollandia, and Truk. Attacks were in 20° glides from 4,000 feet, weather permitting. Release was at 1,200 yds. or less. Picture above shows rocket attack on radio station in background. Other TBFs strafe AA installation.

3. **A THIRD PAIR** of rockets is released by lead plane. Tiny dot on track at bottom of picture is first pair hitting.

6. **WINGMAN'S ROCKETS,** four in number, can now be seen at lower left. These are British, have bulging head.

AT PALAU, Jap naval vessel above had shot down one TBF, and killed a man in another with very accurate AA which also caused 14 bombers to miss their target. Two rocket-firing TBFs attacked, second plane firing after first had turned away as shown. Sixteen rockets were launched, 13 of which were hits. No further AA fire was observed from this crippled vessel.

4. **BURST OF FIRST PAIR** of rockets is now clearly visible in center of track. It is time for lead plane to level out.

7. **LEADER SCORES** third bull's-eye on track. As wingman pulls out, camera cannot record where his rockets went.

THE EXPERIMENT to combine rocket and glide-bombing attacks by TBFs was not successful. With glide bomb released at 2,000-yard range and 2,000-foot altitude in 25-degree dive, it was found that the TBF could not close to 1,500 yards or less (limit of effective range of rocket) without running considerable risk of becoming involved in its own glide-bomb blast.

P-47 LAUNCHES ROCKET attack near Marigny during St. Lo break-through, hitting first tank in German Mk-5 spear- head which was waiting under camouflage to blast approaching American tank column. Crippled tank crept through gate.

UNABLE TO GET FARTHER, first tank was spotted again by attacking plane and completely demolished by .50 cal. fire.

SECOND TANK, after rocket strike on tank in front of it, was backed in narrow lane to its left rear, and then abandoned.

SAME P-47, same morning, fires single rocket at leader of two Mk-5 German tanks scooting down a road away from the Americans. Pilot was Group Captain Dean, RAF, who scored direct hit on rear end of tank. For results, see photograph below.

HVAR 5-INCH IS ROUGH ON TANKS

At present the most lethal U. S. rocket is the 5″ HVAR pictured and described on page 3. Originally developed to destroy flying bomb installations on the Pas de Calais, it later proved particularly effective against armored vehicles, trains, locomotives, roundhouses, and airfield installations. To test it under rigorous battle conditions, a P-47 group was put into action in Northwest France. Results were spectacular. On 17 July 12 aircraft, carrying four rockets each, attacked the rail yard at Tiger-Quail. A direct hit was made on a flak tower on the first run, silencing it. In subsequent runs 25 locomotives were damaged, also three repair shops and a round house. On the following day 12 aircraft attacked the airfield at Coulommiers. Thirty-seven rockets were launched at 1,000-yard range from a 30° dive. One large hangar, four small hangars were hit, an Me-110 and a fuel dump destroyed. Later a rocket was fired from 800 yards at two staff cars, passing through the first and exploding in the second. A rail bridge at Montford was claimed destroyed by seven rockets. On 25 and 26 July a total of 64 rocket sorties were flown, destroying 12 tanks, damaging 13, scoring many near misses, and destroying three and damaging three other vehicles.

The drawings on these pages show attacks on tanks by Group Captain H. W. Dean, an RAF rocket pioneer, who flew with the Americans during the 5″ HVAR tests in France. His claims are substantiated by the photographs at left and right.

TANK WAS FOUND blocking road a day later, its engine burnt out. Second tank mired self trying to get around first.

Continued on next page

West China Front

Pictures on this page illustrate the bombing of Tengchung, seen smoking in the photo above. Tengchung has been a Japanese stronghold on the Burma Road Front, together with Lashio, Lungling, and Mangshih, and like them it has been subject to severe and frequent bombing by the 14th Air Force.

The photos at the right, taken during a low-level attack by seven B-25s on 29 July, show effective air cooperation with Chinese troops. The B-25s dropped 44 x 100-lb. fragmentation clusters and 6 x 1,000-lb. demolition bombs. The arrow in the lower picture points to one of the four breaches made in the city wall by the bombing. These breaches enabled Chinese troops to penetrate into Tengchung. They eventually captured the entire city on 14 September.

14th SMASHES AT JAP SUPPLY LINES ON 3 CHINA FRONTS

The 14th is a small Air Force that operates against terrific obstacles: Chinese weather, with its long rainy seasons; the uneven terrain, over which the few air bases are widely scattered; dependence upon air-flown supply; lack of U. S. ground forces; and the constant threat of an enemy almost ceaselessly on the offensive, pressing in from all sides. In the face of every handicap, the 14th has steadily carried on its blasting of Jap shipping and lines of communication. Its cooperation with the harassed Chinese armies has been a powerful factor in bolstering the morale of the Chinese people.

During the enemy advance through the great rice bowl of Hunan Province, which started from the Tung Ting Lake region in May, the 14th played a vital role in hampering the Nip armies: enemy soldiers and their pack animals were hit in and near the battle lines, while supply centers, airfields, motor convoys and river transport were bombed and strafed. The Chinese garrison was at length overwhelmed by the superior equipment of the Japanese army, which took Hengyang in August and rolled on to capture Lingling, where the 14th had an airfield. The Japs then turned towards Kweilin, capital of Kwangsi Province, aided by another force thrusting up in that direction from Canton. The 14th was compelled to evacuate its big bases at Kweilin in mid-September, and demolish all installations there.

The Yellow River Front (Honan Province) has been comparatively quiet since the Japs' spring advance to the west to protect their positions along the Pekin-Hankow railway line, but the 14th has continued to hammer important targets in that area. The third main front, West China (Burma Road), has been the scene of some recent victories by the Chinese armies which have been on the offensive against continually reinforced Japanese positions along the Salween river. Chinese forces captured Tengchung in mid-September and claimed to have taken Lungling.

Continued on next page

LASHIO, FORMER BASE of the Flying Tigers and Burma Road terminus, has lately been far behind the Japanese lines and can now be visited only by air. The picture above demonstrates how effectively the 14th AF visits this important town.

Lashio And Lungling

The attack on Lashio shown in the picture above was made on 5 June by eighteen B-24s, escorted by a dozen P-40s. The bombers dropped 720 x 100-lb. demos., inst. fused. At least 35 storage buildings and barracks were hit, and strikes were made on or near reported Jap headquarters. Widespread damage to military buildings on former visits may be seen in areas enclosed by unannotated black lines.

The 30 May attack on Lungling, shown in the picture at the right, was made by nine unescorted B-25s which peppered the target from 4,800 feet with 136 x 100-lb. HE dem. (inst. fusing) and 13 x 500-lb. incendiary bombs. Four storage buildings were destroyed, four more severely damaged, and numerous other buildings shattered. Old bomb damage is represented by white circles, camouflaged installations by dotted-line circles. Trench defenses are shown at upper left.

LUNGLING HOLOCAUST of 30 May shows how 14th AF blasts Jap-held cities on Burma battle line. ▶

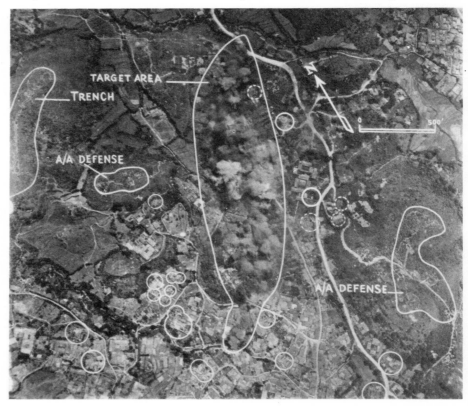

LIBERATORS over serpentine landscape of Hunan Province on 3 August mission against Yochow, big Jap supply base on Tung Ting Lake. RR yards were severely damaged; the B-24 gunners brought down two of ten intercepting Jap fighters.

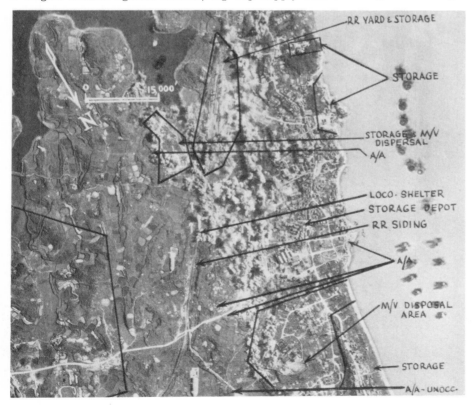

RR YARD & STORAGE

STORAGE

15,000

N

STORAGE & M/V
DISPERSAL

A/A

LOCO- SHELTER

STORAGE DEPOT

RR SIDING

A/A

M/V DISPOSAL
AREA

STORAGE

A/A-UNOCC-

The Hunan Front

Some idea of the effectiveness of the 14th's tireless slashing at the Japanese armies in the Hunan-Kwangsi campaign may be gleaned from figures released by the Chinese Army showing the results of air force activity (including the work of the Chinese Air Force). From 26 May to 15 July, the Chinese claim, there were 16,620 casualties to enemy personnel; three large gunboats and 47 large steamboats were sunk, along with thousands of junks and sampans; 778 motor cars and trucks were destroyed, as well as 32 bridges (some of them pontoon). Total Jap casualties from all causes—including ground and air action, heat, malaria, and dysentery—are put at 53,551 for the period. U. S. official estimate of Jap ground strength south of Yochow is 200,000, with 165,000 combat troops, including reinforcements since May, with 45,000 soldiers in the front lines.

◀ YOCHOW RIPPED by 216 x 250-lb. demos. dropped by two dozen B-24s during devastating 25 July attack.

Continued on next page

Yellow River Front

The 14th AF has effectively bombed the main Japanese supply centers on the Yellow River Front, such as Kaifeng, Chengsien, and Sinsiang, and has repeatedly smashed bridges spanning the wide river. Pictures at left show damage to a pair of bridges near Kaifeng. The strikes in Nos. 1 and 2 were made by B-25s on 24 June; No. 3 is a reconnaissance cover of 10 July. In each photo the circle indicates damage to the main bridge, whose 2nd, 3rd, 6th and 7th spans were knocked out (8th span also hit). The arrow in No. 3 shows destruction at north end of new bridge.

Although pictures in this article deal mainly with accomplishments of the 14th's medium and heavy bombers, a very heavy share of the burden has been carried by bombing and strafing fighters. From 4 July 1942 to 9 August 1944, the 14th AF reported that it destroyed 984 Japanese planes in the air and 333 on the ground, a total of 1,317. During the same period the 14th lost 99 aircraft in the air, and a total of 239 to the enemy in the air, on the ground, and from flak. This is an approximate ratio of 5½ to 1.

YELLOW RIVER bridges, feed-lines from North China to Japs' southern fronts, are shown hit in Nos. 1 and 2 by some of the 12 x 1,000-lb. demos. dropped on 24 June.

Strategic Missions

Cooperation with the Chinese ground troops is not the only task of the 14th AF, which also performs strategic bombing missions throughout China, over neighboring territories, and on the China seas. The 14th has made devastating attacks on important Japanese bases in Formosa and French Indo-China, and has been the scourge of enemy shipping. From the end of May through the middle of August, the 14th sunk some 70 vessels 100 feet long and over (plus probables), and 1,400 vessels of under 100 feet. Figures include river shipping.

The picture at the right shows a few of the 26 Liberators that on 29 July attacked Samah, large Hainan Island base and main Jap supply center for the South China Sea. The B-24s were escorted by 16 P-38s; seven intercepting enemy aircraft were destroyed, and eight more were reported as probables. The heavies dropped 864 x 100-lb. GP bombs with inst. fusing, destroying six revetted fuel storages and six barracks, severely damaging five more barracks and smashing a servicing hangar. Several aircraft were also destroyed on the ground. Hainan-based planes are defense for Japanese shipping along the South China coast.

FLAK HIGH AND TRAILING...

SMOKE PLUMES TESTIFY TO EFFECTIVENESS OF HAINAN ATTACK

THE LEAPING 7th LEAPS AGAIN

CAMOUFLAGED JAP CONTROL TOWER OF CONCRETE WAS CAPTURED AT SAIPAN BY U. S. INFANTRY ON 23 JUNE

NEW ARRIVALS are (above) the first C-46 to land at Aslito airfield, 24 June, carrying parts for P-61s and mail, and (below) a B-24 on 28 June bringing Maj. Gen. Willis H. Hale, Com. Gen. COMAIRFORWARD, to inspect new base.

And Keeps House at Saipan

Join the 7th and See the World.

While other Air Force Headquarters remain in one spot, at least long enough for the laundry to dry, the 7th no sooner cleans up the rubble on one newly won island, than its advance base jumps to another, still nearer Tokio. Thus it has hopped from Makin to Funafuti to Tarawa to Kwajalein, and now to Saipan, where the G.I., in the picture at left, examines a shinto temple in the town of Garapan.

With the occupation of the three main Mariana islands, Saipan, Guam and Tinian, land-based bombers of the 7th began operations against the Japs in the Bonin group (see page 15). This island chain begins 629 nautical miles north of Saipan, stretches north for 145 miles, and ends some 500 miles from the Jap mainland. On 10 August the first B-24 attack was directed against Iwo Jima in the Bonins, principal Jap air base between Saipan and the Jap empire. The next day, Chichi Jima (main Jap anchorage) was struck. There was no interception. And since then, heavies of the 7th have regularly given these two Bonin bases the business.

On 1 September the 7th reported that no enemy aircraft had been met in the Marianas since the first week of August. The Japs have steadily attempted to build up airfields at Yap. But on 20 August when 7th AF B-24s for the first time bombed Yap, no interception was met. Although teeming with aircraft a few months ago, there are today in the entire Central, South Pacific Area (excluding Philippines and the empire) only two Jap bases offering nominal air resistance: Truk and Iwo Jima.

Continued on next page

P-47 AT SAIPAN met its doom on 26 June when about 150 Japs broke into engineer area (IMPACT, Vol. 2, No. 8). In a pitched battle most Japs were killed, but one sneaked through, set fire to P-47. He was shot before he could get away.

JAP DUMMY PLANE is examined at captured Aslito airfield by two 7th AF engineers. This is one of many such planes, made of cloth, and spread out in Jap parking areas in hopes of making our bombers believe they were the real McCoy.

AT ASLITO AIRFIELD the Japs, realizing that hangars and buildings would be targets for U. S. bombing and shelling, dispersed various supply items away from buildings. Prominent in photo above are auxiliary gas tanks for Jap fighters.

From Saipan the 7th Batters the Bonins

AT CHICHI JIMA, JAP NAVAL BASE, A B-24 DROPS FIRST BOMBS (SEE UNDER WING TIP), 12 AUGUST

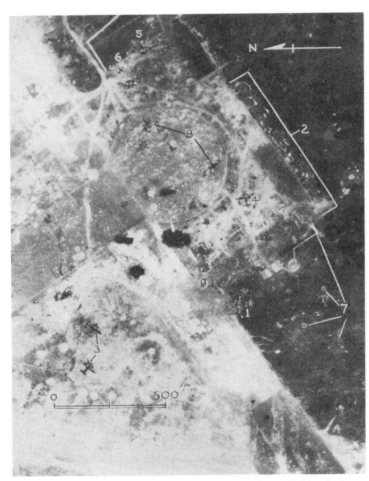

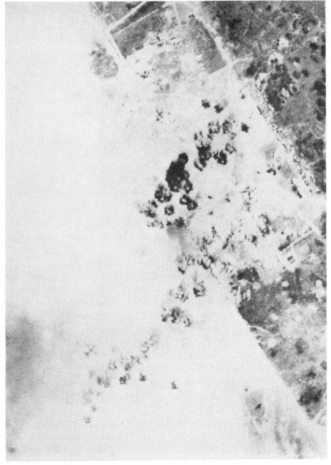

AT IWO JIMA airfield accumulated damage from B-24 missions beginning 10 August includes (1) Nell; (2) dump of damaged aircraft; (3) two Bettys; (4) Betty with damaged starboard wing; (5) Betty; (6) Zeke; (7) four L.A.A. positions; (8) two Kates; (9) Nell with damaged wing. In picture above this same field hit again by 7th AF frag. bombs.

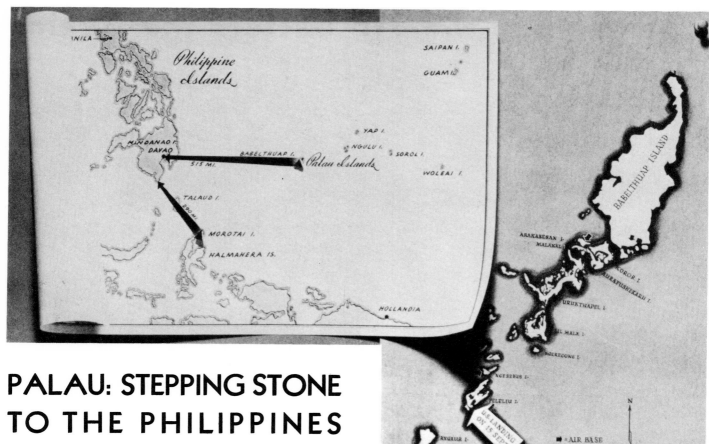

PALAU ISLANDS

PALAU: STEPPING STONE TO THE PHILIPPINES

On 15 September the dawn came up like thunder over the far Pacific, and ominous shadows fell upon the Philippines. At Jap-held Palau, the Marines were landing less than 600 miles from the Philippine islands, while only a few hours earlier General MacArthur's troops had invaded Morotai, off Halmahera, some 290 miles from the southern tip of Mindanao.

Of the two landings, the tougher was at Palau. This was partly because the Japs were unprepared at Morotai, believing the attack would be at Halmahera, and partly because the Palaus were heavily fortified on beaches and in the hills. In the actual Morotai landing there were no casualties, except for one soldier who broke a leg.

For a litter of obscure little islands (see map above), the Palaus have seen a lot of history—perhaps more than any of the small Pacific islands yet conquered by the U. S. Held by Spain for two centuries, they were purchased by Germany in 1899. In 1914 the Japs seized the Palaus, and have held them ever since, nominally as mandates of the Versailles Treaty, but actually as colonies. The small island of Koror was administrative center of all the Japanese Mandates, Malakal harbor was an important shipping center, and Arakabesan a major air base. Phosphate and copra were the chief industries. U. S. troops will no doubt be warned of the poisonous sea snakes that lurk off shore, and swat the biting midges, that are the islands' prize pest.

The softening-up of Palau was primarily a Navy job, with assistance from the 13th AF. On 30 March a Naval task force destroyed at least 100,000 tons of shipping and 200 Jap planes (IMPACT, Vol. 2, No. 6). Four days before the invasion the Navy intensified its attacks, sent in more than 250 carrier-based planes to bomb AA positions at Angaur, and other installations at Pelelieu, Ngesebus, and Babelthuap. Attacks continued at this same pitch until D-Day, with special attention to Pelelieu, where the Marines made their first landing.

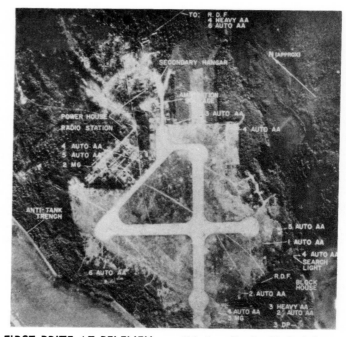

FIRST PRIZE AT PELELIEU was this heavily fortified airfield, captured by Marines during second day's fighting. Runways are 3,850 and 3,990 feet long. Marines made a second landing on 17 September on Angaur island. Other landings followed.

AT KOROR, capital of Palau islands and home office for the Japanese South Seas Government, a 13th AF B-24 takes part in one of nine daylight attacks made on the Palaus by 13th AF from 23 August to 3 September, dropping 625 tons of bombs.

PHILIPPINES BOMBED FIRST TIME SINCE 1942

A milestone in General MacArthur's inexorable advance towards the Philippines was reached on 1 September when 57 5th AF heavy bombers of the FEAF, escorted by long-range fighters, made the first heavy bombing strike on the Philippines since 1942. The targets were three enemy air bases in the Davao area, Mindanao, which were plowed up with 100 tons of fragmentation bombs. Damage at the three bases, Licanan, Sassa, and Matina, was extensive and large fires were started. A total of 38 enemy planes was destroyed, including 26 bombers and 11 fighters on the ground. One of eight enemy fighters intercepting our formations was shot down. We lost two bombers to A/A fire and six were slightly damaged.

This historic attack, heralding a new phase of air war against the Philippines, was followed up the next day when the three airfields, and Davao's port area and shipyards, were blasted with 230 tons of heavy demolition bombs, dropped from 58 B-24s covered by P-38s. Great fires and explosions in all targets followed. Our fighters, operating at the greatest distance from base in the history of this theater, swept down to tree-top level and strafed the area.

BEFORE AND AFTER pictures of barracks area at Licanan airfield near Davao show how 13th AF B-24s with frag bombs started fires on 1 September attack.

THE RICH EAST INDIES

Japan is Already Threatened with their Loss

As if Japan didn't have troubles enough with U. S. forces thrusting closer every week to her homeland, she must also face the loss of supplies from the Netherlands East Indies. This is inevitable on two scores. First, from newly won bases in the Halmaheras and Western New Guinea, the AAF can increasingly bomb the N.E.I. Second, as we move toward control of the Philippines and South China Sea area, our air and naval forces will be in a position to cut Japan's supply lines to her Indies empire.

A current report from Target Analysis Branch, AC/AS Intelligence, on the economic contribution of the Indies to Japan's war effort, states, "It is estimated that 67 percent of total 1944 Japanese oil production comes from here, and that 77 percent of the total Jap aviation gasoline and 75 percent of total fuel oil production are supplied by the area. In terms of estimated 1944 consumption, the Indies supply over 85 percent of aviation gasoline, more than 75 percent of the fuel oil, and 29 percent of the lube oils." Obtaining fuel oil has been one of the big problems in the operations of the Jap fleet. Main sources of supply for oil and petroleum products are Sumatra and Borneo.

Most of Japan's nickel comes from mines in the Pomelaa area on the Celebes, which formerly supplied about 250,000 tons of dry ore per year. A concentration plant at Pomelaa was badly damaged by Allied attacks, but may be in operation again.

Other resources, of varying importance, are itemized on the map below.

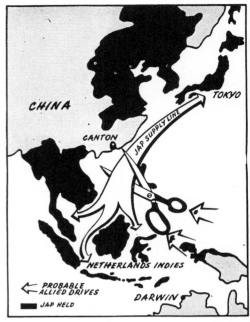

JAP SUPPLY LINE through the South China Sea to the East Indies may thus be cut by the U. S. as we move toward the mainland of China.

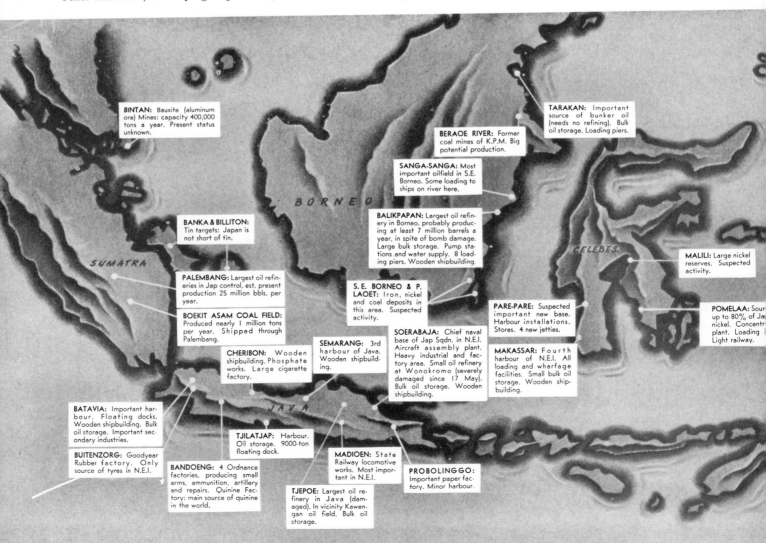

BINTAN: Bauxite (aluminum ore) Mines: capacity 400,000 tons a year. Present status unknown.

TARAKAN: Important source of bunker oil (needs no refining). Bulk oil storage. Loading piers.

BERAOE RIVER: Former coal mines of K.P.M. Big potential production.

SANGA-SANGA: Most important oilfield in S.E. Borneo. Some loading to ships on river here.

BANKA & BILLITON: Tin targets: Japan is not short of tin.

BALIKPAPAN: Largest oil refinery in Borneo, probably producing at least 7 million barrels a year, in spite of bomb damage. Large bulk storage. Pump stations and water supply. 8 loading piers. Wooden shipbuilding.

MALILI: Large nickel reserves. Suspected activity.

PALEMBANG: Largest oil refineries in Jap control, est. present production 25 million bbls. per year.

S. E. BORNEO & P. LAOET: Iron, nickel and coal deposits in this area. Suspected activity.

PARE-PARE: Suspected important new base. Harbour installations. Stores. 4 new jetties.

POMELAA: Source up to 80% of Jap nickel. Concentration plant. Loading Light railway.

BOEKIT ASAM COAL FIELD: Produced nearly 1 million tons per year. Shipped through Palembang.

SOERABAJA: Chief naval base of Jap Sqdn. in N.E.I. Aircraft assembly plant. Heavy industrial and factory area. Small oil refinery at Wonokromo (severely damaged since 17 May). Bulk oil storage. Wooden shipbuilding.

MAKASSAR: Fourth harbour of N.E.I. All loading and wharfage facilities. Small bulk oil storage. Wooden shipbuilding.

CHERIBON: Wooden shipbuilding. Phosphate works. Large cigarette factory.

SEMARANG: 3rd harbour of Java. Wooden shipbuilding.

BATAVIA: Important harbour. Floating docks. Wooden shipbuilding. Bulk oil storage. Important secondary industries.

TJILATJAP: Harbour. Oil storage. 9000-ton floating dock.

MADIOEN: State Railway locomotive works. Most important in N.E.I.

PROBOLINGGO: Important paper factory. Minor harbour.

BUITENZORG: Goodyear Rubber factory. Only source of tyres in N.E.I.

BANDOENG: 4 Ordnance factories, producing small arms, ammunition, artillery and repairs. Quinine Factory: main source of quinine in the world.

TJEPOE: Largest oil refinery in Java (damaged). In vicinity Kawengan oil field. Bulk oil storage.

IMPORTANT ECONOMIC TARGETS IN N.E.I.
AS OF 15TH AUG.

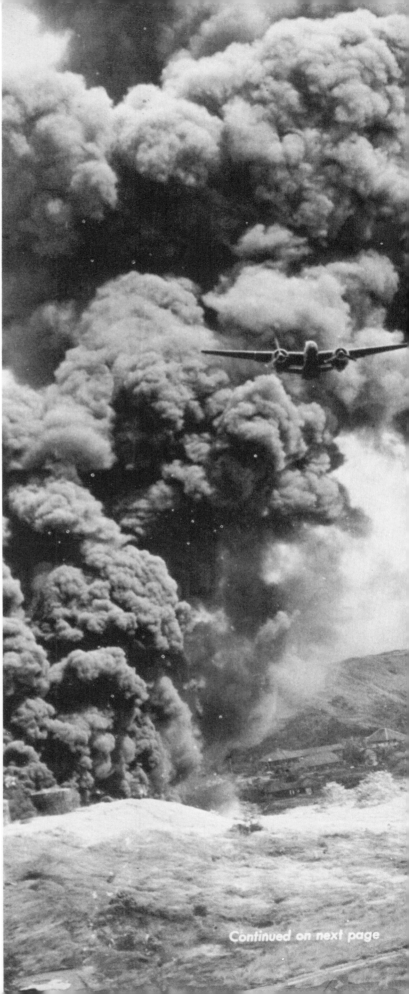

JAP OIL TANKS at Boela on Ceram were hit by A-20s on 14 July. Above: Before strike. Right: During strike an A-20 skims tanks. For more on Boela, see page 21.

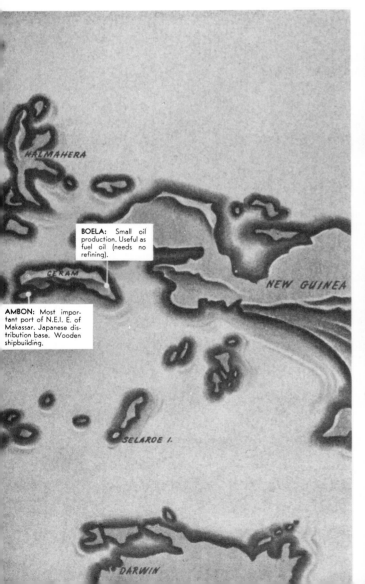

HALMAHERA

BOELA: Small oil production. Useful as fuel oil (needs no refining).

CERAM

NEW GUINEA

AMBON: Most important port of N.E.I. E. of Makassar. Japanese distribution base. Wooden shipbuilding.

SELAROE I.

DARWIN

Continued on next page

ONE OUT OF ONE. This Jap Topsy, type MC-20 transport, was the only plane on strip at Selaroe island when on 22 July three RAAF Beaufighters strafed the strip, killed six Japs (see same attack on front cover), and cremated poor Topsy.

AIR BLOWS KEEP THE JAPS GROGGY IN N. E. I.

Considering the output of other big oil targets in the Netherlands East Indies, Boela on the island of Ceram (see map on previous page) may not seem important. Of the total oil tonnage produced in the Indies annually, Boela contributes only four percent. But Boela is a handy filling station on a long road, and on 14 July was the scene of a successful mission by 72 A-20s, which took on added significance because it was the first time Ceram had been attacked from new 5th AF bases in Western New Guinea instead of from Darwin. Thus, the

Boela mission marked another milestone in the advance of the Allied air front. As for the attack itself, one 7,000-ton and two 500-ton tanks, and possibly another, were destroyed. One A-20 was downed by A/A, and one was damaged. Including a 7,000-ton tank destroyed by an Allied vessel on 13 June, the total estimated storage at Boela is now greatly reduced.

Boela has been hit subsequently, including a mission on 25 Sept. when 26 B-25s dropped 25 tons on the oil installations. Business at Boela is definitely not going on as usual.

CAUGHT IN THE ACT. Japs construct revetments for four-gun A/A battery, barracks, storage, and other installations along coast of Dutch New Guinea near Sorong. B-25s did this reconnaissance while attacking Jap shipping on 20 July.

OFF SHORE OIL WELLS at Boela, numbering about 20, looked like this as the attack begins on 14 July. Of a total of 60 well sites, an estimated 35 are capable of production. The total annual production is estimated at 15 million gallons.

DURING THE ATTACK, the off shore wells were shrouded in geysers of smoke and spray. Two out of the three wells smoking at left were damaged. Other damage in shore area included 20 houses, but not the tennis court or the swimming pool.

DOUBLE COLUMN OF CG-4s LINES UP NOSE TO TAIL WITH OVERLAPPING WINGS, WAITING FOR HOOK-UP

PARATROOPERS LUG THEIR EQUIPMENT TO A LONG LINE OF C-47s VANISHING IN THE MIST AT LEFT

AIRBORNE BLITZ LAUNCHED IN HOLLAND

Lt. Gen. Brereton's airborne army launched on 17 September the most ambitious parachute and glider operation yet undertaken by the Allies, first pictures of which are shown here and on page 1. As an indication of its size, over 7,000 transport sorties were flown between 17-23 September. Its purpose: to sieze strategic points in the region of the lower Rhine and Maas rivers to facilitate flanking of the Westwall at its northern end. At this writing the U. S. 82nd and 101st Airborne Divisions, dropping at Nijmegen and Eindhoven respectively, have been joined in force by advancing ground troops. The 1st British Parachute Division, dropping at Arnhem north of the others and farther from the front lines, was withdrawn after 10 days' heavy fighting. A detailed discussion of the airborne invasion of Southern France will be found on page 32.

ALREADY looking like a Christmas tree, laden paratrooper picks up his rations.

ARMED JEEPS mounting .50 cal. machine guns await loading into CG-4s on steel mat runway in England prior to takeoff. Gliders carried all heavy equipment used.

FLATNESS OF FORMATION FLOWN IS SHOWN BY PHOTO OF C-47s ON WAY TO DROPPING ZONE ON 17 SEPT.

DUTCH CASTLE IS DRENCHED WITH PARACHUTES FROM ONE FLEET OF C-47s AS ANOTHER PASSES ABOVE

APPROXIMATE NORTH

IN UKRAINE THE GAF SHOWED IT STILL CAN TOSS A WICKED PUNCH

Proof, if any was needed, that the GAF still was able to muster some bombardment strength of its own and to direct it at the most unsuspecting targets was given on the night of 21 June 1944 at the Poltava airfield, in the Ukraine, when 47

Eighth AF B-17s, having just completed their first shuttle-bombing mission from England, were destroyed on the ground in a perfectly timed and well executed attack.

What happened is graphically shown in the photo above, taken the next day.

On the Poltava airfield that night were 73 B-17s, six transports, three photo planes, a P-38. Bombs were stored in perimeter revetments, gasoline drums were in dispersed piles outside the field. The dispersed planes, even in dispersal somewhat crowded for room because of the size of the field, were under guard; slit trenches had been dug, two oxygen service crews were at work around the planes, other servicing work was in progress up to 2200. More than 1,000 American personnel were in the camp area.

The first warning was at 2335, when Russian authorities notified American headquarters that enemy aircraft had crossed

APPROXIMATE SCALE

1000' 0 1000'

the Russian front lines, headed toward the Poltava area. Air raid alarms were sounded; the men took to the slit trenches and other cover. The Germans arrived at 0015, were met by Russian antiaircraft fire, and dropped flares. The bombing started about ten minutes later. The first assault lasted until 0145, during which, from medium to high altitudes, a small quantity of demolition and short-delay demolition bombs, and large quantities of small incendiaries and anti-personnel bombs were dropped. After a 15-minute pause, the attack was renewed, for 20 minutes when planes flew in low, dropping anti-personnel bombs and strafing.

Photo planes took over with flash bombs at 0220, then the enemy withdrew.

Tonnage dropped was 110, of which 15 were demolition, 78 anti-personnel, and 17 incendiary. Two Americans were killed, six wounded, 50 aircraft destroyed, 29 damaged. Soviet losses were 30 killed, 95 wounded, one aircraft destroyed, 25 damaged. More than 400,000 gallons of gasoline were destroyed. Three weeks were required to put the field back into full operation.

During the attack Soviet antiaircraft fire, mostly of small caliber, was continuous, and night fighters were sent up. There was no destruction of enemy aircraft. About 80 Ju-88s and He-111s took part.

Recommendations of a U. S. Army investigating board included limitation of the number of aircraft to be on the field at any one time, complete use of dispersal areas, and that American planes should remain on the field briefly. Camouflage painting of aircraft and adequate suspended camouflage were recommended, as was camouflage of storage facilities, runways, and other features of the airfield. Further attacks by the Germans on American-used bases in the USSR following the Poltava bombing were not successful.

BOMBING RESULTS AT PLOESTI

Production Down Four-Fifths in Long Campaign

If the United States should suddenly lose one half of all the oil produced in Arkansas, Colorado, Ohio, Pennsylvania, West Virginia, New York, Indiana, Kansas, Kentucky, Louisiana, Michigan, Mississippi, Montana, Nebraska, New Mexico, Oklahoma and Wyoming (all oil-producing states), the catastrophe would make it impossible for us to make war on the scale to which we are presently committed. Yet the proportionate loss to us as the result of such a blow is no greater than that actually suffered by the Germans when they lost Ploesti, four-fifths of whose refinery capacity had been already destroyed by bombing, cutting production proportionately.

Ploesti is by far the largest oil area in Europe. It supplied the enemy war machine with a third of its total fuel requirements. It is the one target in the whole enemy economy which Germany could least afford to lose. Annual capacity before attacks by USAAF bombers was 9,300,000 metric tons a year, actual production of refined products 4,800,000 metric tons a year. The pictures shown of three of Ploesti's ten main refineries give a preview of U. S. bombing results.

◄ **CONCORDIA VEGA.** Pump house and treating plant are shown destroyed. Gasoline was pumped from small pumps at left into agitators (towers at right) then to storage tanks (rear).

CONCORDIA VEGA. Packaging unit is completely destroyed. Greases and lubes were kept in tanks (rear), piped as needed into wide-mouth cans (stacked at right) prior to distribution.

CONCORDIA VEGA. Another view of treating plant. Gasoline goes into agitators, where it is treated by chemicals to remove sulphur and other impurities. This is the last step in production.

Continued on next page

CONCORDIA VEGA. Power house interior. Old-type fire tube boilers (rows of small pipe projecting from rubble at right center) were destroyed. Germans put in water tube boiler (large square unit in background), never finished it.

CONCORDIA VEGA. This is part of low-pressure fractionating unit smashed by bomb which made crater in foreground. Fuel comes from still in vapor form, is turned into liquid in condensors (left), goes to run-off tanks (right).

CONCORDIA VEGA. Another view of power house shows useless fire tube boilers at lower right. Destruction here shuts down refinery because steam is used in fractionating towers, runs pumps. In background, damaged coking stills.

ASTRA ROMANA. Blast wall in background was erected to minimize bomb blast to large storage tank inside. Direct hit has not only destroyed tank, but has also knocked down the wall which was supposed to have insured its protection.

Continued on next page

ASTRA ROMANA. Large storage tank is completely destroyed. It was probably empty at time of attack because paint on metal has not been burned, and metal is not fused, as would have been the case if fuel in tank had been ignited by bomb burst. Total collapse here insures total loss. If top of tank is blown off, fuel in bottom can sometimes be salvaged.

ASTRA ROMANA. Burst in foreground has made such mincemeat of Trumble unit that Germans made no effort to repair it. This is an old-fashioned thermal cracking plant. Bomb blast has destroyed most pipe, has perforated much that remains, has also damaged fractionating stills (row of vertical tanks at top), and decapitated brick chimney in rear of picture.

ASTRA ROMANA. Main offices and laboratories have developed alarming sag. Astra Romana is the largest, most important, and one of the most modern refineries in Ploesti area.

CREDITUL MINIER. Pipe from which photo was taken, and section in front of it are parts of new bubble tower for primary distillation which Germans moved in, hoped to get installed.

Statistics on the Campaign

Save for two attacks in 1943 by the Eighth and Ninth Air Forces (one of these the historic low-level B-24 smash on 1 August), a small P-38 mission, and four attacks by RAF night bombers, the campaign to level Ploesti was carried on exclusively by the 15th Air Force. All together over 2,200 fliers were shot down over Ploesti. Of these, 1,166 were liberated by the Rumanians and flown out to Italy by MAAF B-17s between 27 August and 3 September. Statistics of the 15th's effort are given below. The decline in the number of enemy fighters shot down reflects the gradual elimination of the GAF in that area. Our losses were increasingly due to flak. At the end the enemy had over 240 heavy AA installations in Ploesti, one of the three densest concentrations in Europe.

15th AF ATTACKS ON PLOESTI

Date 1944	Heavy Bombers Attacking	Tons Dropped	Heavy Bomber Losses	Enemy Aircraft Destroyed in Air
5 April	230	587	13	41
15 April	137	316	3	1
24 April	290	793	8	11
5 May	485	1,257	19	18
5 May	135	329	6	14
18 May	206	493	14	23
31 May	481	1,116	16	22
6 June	310	698	14	22
23 June	139	283	6	10
24 June	135	329	14	11
9 July	222	605	6	7
15 July	607	1,526	20	2
22 July	495	1,334	24	5
28 July	349	913	20	0
31 July	154	435	2	0
10 August	414	952	16	1
17 August	248	534	15	0
18 August	377	825	7	0
19 August	65	144	0	0
Total	5,479	13,469	223	188

CREDITUL MINIER. Germans actually erected bubble towers in this fractionating unit, had begun to connect them up, had time only to put one 88 mm. shell in before Russians arrived.

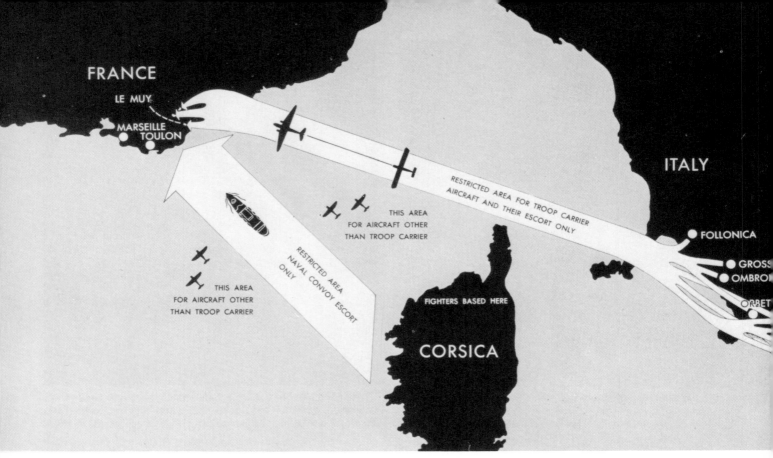

MAP shows path of air task force from bases in Italy to three dropping zones near Le Muy, France. Formations were guided on this route by Eureka signal devices, one at tip of Corsica, others in boats along course. Combat air traffic was restricted to areas shown to avoid mistakes in recognition. Convoy, escorted by a large force of naval vessels, formed

TOULON, hit many times to insure minimum submarine activity during invasion, was struck on 6 August by 146 B-24s. Bursts shown in photo damaged quays, blew stern off ship, wrecked crane (1); wrecked power station and lock gates in two sub docks (3). Four sunken destroyers (2), a tanker (4), and the Battleship Dunkerque (5) had previously been scuttled by the French Navy.

ANTHEOR VIADUCT, rail bridge west of Nice, was smashed as part of campaign to interdict landing areas. This vital communications target is on main coastal line from Marseille and Toulon

off coast of Corsica. Fighters were based on coastal fields built for this operation in northern part of Corsica.

to Genoa and central Italy. Its destruction stopped rail traffic between southern France and Italy except for what could be run on a roundabout route to the north through Lyon and Turin.

SOUTHERN FRANCE INVASION

Writers for AMAZING STORIES and similar imaginative journals have for years beguiled their readers with accounts of armies landing by parachute and glider behind enemy lines and causing indescribable confusion while a more conventional attack is launched along the ground. The fairy tale came true in May 1941 when citizens the world over opened their papers to learn that 30,000 Germans had undertaken to capture Crete from the air. This operation, in which 750 glider troops and 10,000 parachutists took and held an airfield on which 12,000 more troops and supplies were landed by air, completely subdued Crete in 10 days, aided in the final stages by 7,000 troops landed by water. It stands as a test case for students and taught an interesting lesson. It almost failed, because the defending ground forces were not sufficiently blitzed from the air in advance to be prevented from decimating the Germans as they floated in. An interesting corollary may be read in what happened to the British fleet in the Eastern Mediterranean. A force estimated at 1,200 planes attacked the ships which had gathered to protect Crete, sank three cruisers, six destroyers, and damaged *every other ship,* some so badly that they barely made it back to Alexandria. This proved to interested Allied observers that a major task of air in a three-dimensional operation over water was to assure the protection of a seaborne assault from counterattack by air.

The nature of the present war has forced America into a series of air envelopments, some pure, some part of triphibious operations, until the technique can be said to have become peculiarly our own. It has been developed in New Guinea, Sicily, Salerno, Burma, and tested (with the British) in the crucible of Normandy. It was brought to a peak of efficiency and economy in the invasion of Southern France, and is at this writing being pushed on an unprecedented scale among the fens and canals of Southern Holland. The Riviera invasion has been chosen for analysis here because it was a triphibious operation in all whose phases air played a dominant part, and because it was so extraordinarily successful. This was partly due to planning and execution, partly to the pre-occupation of the Germans with the ominous bulges appearing in the Normandy front, partly to the earlier neutralization of the GAF and partly to the effective activities of Maquis in Central and Southern France.

Operations to prepare for the Riviera invasion started as far back as D minus 110 (28 April) with a heavy bomber attack at the sub installations at Toulon. They continued to D minus 5 (10 August), during which time 6,000 sorties were flown and 12,500 tons of bombs were dropped. As D-Day grew closer, the focus of attack was continually narrowed around sub, rail, and air installations in the Marseille-Toulon area.

A second phase ran from D minus 5 to 0350 hours on D-Day. Its task was to neutralize coastal batteries and radar stations on beaches in the Frejus area midway between Toulon and Nice. In accomplishing this 5,408 sorties were flown and 6,740 tons of bombs dropped.

A third phase, from 0350 hours to H-Hour (0800) on D-Day, called for the use of all available force to destroy coastal and beach defenses on the following schedule:

0550-0610	Four-ship patrols of fighters over beaches to dive bomb any guns seen firing.
0610-0730	Small formations of mediums, heavies and fighters to attack selected gun positions.
0630-0730	Further dive-bombing of gun positions.
0700-0730	Medium and heavy bombers to beat down beach defenses and underwater obstacles with saturation attacks.
0800-on	Continuous patrols of 16 Navy and 16 Army planes on call for further dive-bombing.

The schedule was adhered to. The defenses were overwhelmed and the landing force hit the beach with low casualties. Meanwhile, any possibility of slow strangulation of this force on the beach was being averted a few miles inland. A stream of men and equipment had begun before dawn to drop into Le Muy from the air. Pathfinders came first, setting up Eureka and other homing devices, followed by paratroopers who seized a landing field for gliders carrying more troops and heavier weapons. Resupply went on throughout that and the following day. No aircraft or gliders were lost to enemy action although landing casualties were inflicted by poles stuck in open fields by the enemy.

Continued on next page

Preliminary Study of Beaches from Air Helped Determine Best Invasion Spots

Dicing missions along the entire French Riviera revealed amazing differences in the strength of shore defenses, and influenced the choice of landing points accordingly. As a graphic example, the placid little cove shown on the next page was chosen instead of the area pictured above, whose beach was studded with concrete pyramids, with barbed wire back of them, and pill boxes (not visible) in back of that. Pyramids are shown in process of installation. Those at right of picture have been transported to the beach in small flat cars, will be run down to shallow water and dumped off. To get the pyramids into deeper water, the raft shown at left was used. When it had been maneuvered by a rowboat to the correct spot, a pyramid was lowered through the hole in the center by a block and tackle. This work was done by locally impressed laborers who, judging from the relaxed attitude of the bathers above and the denizens of the raft at left, were not making the coast any more impregnable than they could help. Although everything looks peaceful in these pictures, German AA made the low-level dicing missions extremely hazardous. For his work in obtaining pre-invasion photographs, Lt. Carl Dolk, Third Photo Group, won the Distinguished Service Cross.

PHOTO PLANE SNAPS RAFT USED TO DROP PYRAMIDS

ST. RAPHAEL IN FREJUS BEACH AREA, MID-POINT OF RIVIERA LANDINGS, LOOKED LIKE THIS ON 17 JULY

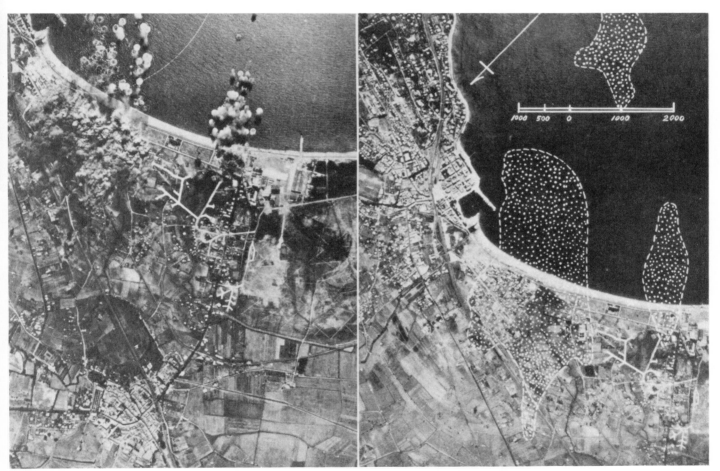

VERTICAL OF ST. RAPHAEL shows start of D-Day bombardment aimed at saturation of all beach defenses. Greatest weight of bombs is falling in area behind beach, whose sands, as photo at top shows, were free of obstacles. Attack started at 0700 after dive bombing and strafing of specific gun positions.

ST. RAPHAEL BOMB PLOT shows carpet-like pattern of bursts. Load here was 1,014 x 100-lb. bombs, altitude 15,000 feet. Also used were frags and demolition bombs of weights up to 260 lbs., all instantaneously fused for maximum blast effect. Pattern started 75 yards from shore, went 400 yards inland.

Continued on next page

H-HOUR MINUS 30 MINUTES. Landing craft of the assault force wait just off Frejus Beach. Saturation attack by medium and heavy bombers is at its height. Heavy gun positions have already been silenced by a succession of dive-bombing attacks.

H-HOUR PLUS 30 MINUTES. Consolidation of beachhead is complete and patrols are moving inland to join airborne forces at Le Muy. Column of men at left center consists of German prisoners who quit willingly after two hours of aerial attack.

PARATROOPERS of the Troop Carrier Air Division, 12th Air Force, have a smoke and listen to final words of their jump-master before boarding their plane in Italy. C-47s and 532 glider pilots were flown as inconspicuously as possible from England, and 354 gliders delivered directly from the U. S.

NEARING THE DROPPING POINT, paratroopers hook static lines. Of 9,000 paratroopers carried, only 37 plane loads missed their target. Less than two percent of those jumping suffered jump casualties. Of the 746 glider pilots dispatched, eleven were killed, 16 hospitalized, four are missing.

C-47s APPROACH DROPPING ZONE. (For details of formations flown, see page 40). By 23 August, paratroops, planes and glider pilots had begun to move back to England in a steady stream in preparation for Holland landings on 17 Sept.

Continued on next page

PARATROOPERS, SUPPLIES cascade down on area outside of Le Muy. First pathfinder drop was at 0323 on D-Day, first regular paratroop drop at 0423, followed by nine others at four to eight minute intervals.

OPEN FIELDS suitable for glider landings were filled with poles sticking from the ground at a height of about ten feet. These were arranged irregularly so that gliders would hit them, whatever their angle of approach would be.

GLIDERS CAME IN in nine waves between 0814 and 1907. CG-4 shown has just coasted to a stop as another circles to land. Holes in wings were torn by trees and posts such as one at left. Two men wearing berets are Maquis.

BAKER'S DOZEN OF CG-4s comes to earth in briefed dropping area outside Le Muy. Dust clouds at top of picture, kicked up by gliders, have not yet settled. Glider at left has lit where dust streak behind it is beginning to develop, will probably stop outside of picture in corner of field before it gets to road. All together, 408 glider sorties were flown on D-Day. Earlier-landing paratroopers had everything under control by the time gliders began to land, eliminating possibility of heavy casualties from ground fire, which had decimated German gliders in Crete.

THESE GERMAN SOLDIERS were captured at dawn by first wave of paratroopers. They are shown in an improvised prisoner-of-war pen at temporary airborne headquarters, watching with utter incredulity a sky full of vari-colored parachutes dropped by 300 C-47s on the first re-supply mission, and wondering where the Luftwaffe is. On D-Day and D plus 1, the following were landed by air: 9,000 troops, 221 jeeps, 213 artillery pieces, 1,270 gallons of gas, 4,938 lbs. of bombs, 759,112 rounds of ammo, 56,896 lbs. rations, 744,831 lbs. miscellaneous equipment. Further dropping was unnecessary. By D+2 junction had been effected with landing forces.

Continued on next page

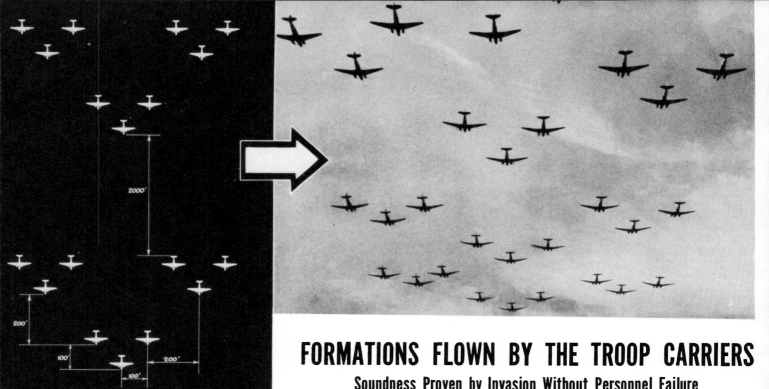

FORMATIONS FLOWN BY THE TROOP CARRIERS
Soundness Proven by Invasion Without Personnel Failure

The amazing record of no formation mixups, only two mechanical failures, and the premature release of only nine gliders and two paratroop loads out of 1,394 aircraft and glider sorties flown in the airborne invasion of Southern France is a tribute not only to the training and ability of those who took part in it but also to the operational soundness of the formations diagrammed at the left and pictured in action above and below.

PARACHUTE COLUMN: This consisted of a nine-ship V of Vs in serials of up to 45 aircraft, in trail, with five-minute interval head-to-head between serial lead aircraft. In each V, distance between planes, from nose to nose, was 100 feet to the side and 100 feet to the rear of the lead aircraft. Distance, front to rear, between each nine-ship formation was 2,000 feet. Formation was to be flown as flat as possible, at an altitude of 2,000 feet from command departure point to target.

GLIDER COLUMN: This was to be flown in pairs of pairs, echeloned to the right, serials up to 48 aircraft towing gliders, in trail, with eight-minute intervals between serial lead aircraft.

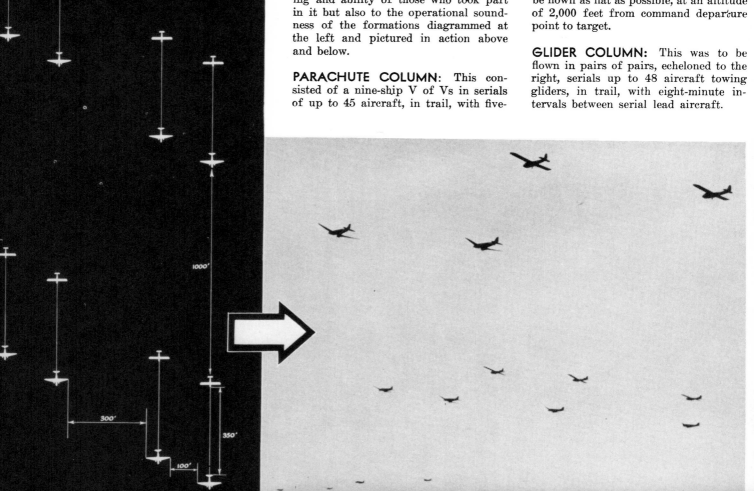

INVASION WRECKAGE

So fast did invasion columns pour north and west from the Riviera beachhead, so complete was the dominance of Allied air power in the area, and so determined the rising tide of French resistance, that the German materiel loss there was very high —out of all proportion to the heaviness of the fighting that actually took place. The photographs on this page give point to the story of the young American platoon leader who ac-cepted the surrender of 20,000 Germans and then marched them fully armed across France. The Germans were afraid to turn over their arms and throw themselves on the mercy of the Maquis. They could not fight their way to safety because of the methodical destruction of their trucks, tanks, and trains by MAAF fighters. Results of such attacks are visible (above) at Montelimar in the skeletons of war machines which dot the Marseille-Lyon road for miles. Below is shown one of seven ammunition trains dive bombed north of Montelimar.

1. ATTACK BY ME-163 on B-17 on 16 Aug. is from one o'clock low. Angle of climb is about 50° at 5,000 ft. a minute.

2. ME-163 CLIMBS at over 200 mph until 1,500 feet above B-17 at 5 o'clock, cuts power and makes slow turn into tail.

5. AS ME-163 INCREASES DIVE angle, latter's pilot and co-pilot together pull up nose and skid with full rudder.

6. TAIL, WAIST, and ball-turret gunners fire as Me-163 does partial wing-over, goes down to 1,000 feet below Fort.

JU-88 FILLED WITH EXPLOSIVE charge (total warhead weight estimated at 8,000 lbs.) to be used against capital ships, is flown by pilot in Me-109 attached to its back. Ju-88 is released below 2,000 ft. at 15°-20° angle and 325 mph speed. It is guided to target by automatic pilot (best guess from study of crashed remains).

NEWEST ATTEMPTS

Allied bombers have been meeting Me-163s with increasing frequency recently, but the latter are still apparently committed to a policy of warming-up exercises, and do not press home their attacks as resolutely as other German fighters on which the GAF has voluminous combat notes and does not hesitate to sacrifice in order to attack bombers. Also, the Me-163s are still scarce, and pilots have undoubtedly been instructed not to waste them. A typical combat sequence is illustrated in the model photographs shown above. Of this engagement the pilot reported, "The tail gunner told me later that our evasive action was perfect, that the enemy aircraft was sliding back and forth with us and

3. WITH POWER OFF, and in a shallow dive, Me-163 closes steadily on B-17 and opens up with cannon and machine gun.

4. TAIL GUNNER of Fort reports Me-163 firing. Pilot dumps stick for 3 seconds, causing Me-163 to shoot too high.

7. ME-163 LEVELS OUT and flies (still gliding) at same speed as bomber for 2 minutes. P-51 comes in from 5 o'clock.

8. AS P-51 FIRES, Me-163 goes into nearly vertical dive, both planes disappear. P-51 was observed not catching up.

OF THE LUFTWAFFE

couldn't get his guns trained on us."

At the left and right are innovations by an enemy who has dug deep into the barrel to produce the two makeshifts shown. At the left is illustrated a use for war weary Ju-88s. They are filled with explosives and then, with Me-109s on top of them, used as glide- or rather power-bombs against priority targets or concentrations of shipping. The Me-109 pilot is apparently able to control the engines of the Ju-88 and draw fuel from its tanks.

At the right, the obsolescent He-111 is pressed into service as an airborne launcher for the flying bomb. This is where the latest ones striking London are coming from.

FLYING BOMB IS CARRIED on top of fuselage of He-111 as shown. Problem of aiming is simple, could be solved by providing two or more light beacons on ground, oriented to target, and instructing He-111 pilot to fly straight and level across them. Bomb is then released by He-111, which goes into slight dive to get itself clear.

STEEL—STRATEGIC

In Japan the first industrial target to feel the weight of U. S. bombs was steel. To date, two of the enemy's greatest plants, at Yawata and Anshan, have been hit. And that is only a hint of things to come.

For these pages, the P.I. Section of AC/AS, Intelligence, has prepared a pictorial analysis of these two typical plants. Because they contain practically all of the installations to be found in any steel plant, this study will be helpful to other P.I.s in analyzing future targets. The photographs, taken by the 21st Photo Reconnaissance Squadron of the 14th AF, and the 20th Bomber Command, constitute the finest coverage yet published of any Jap industry.

The importance of steel in the enemy's war economy hardly needs to be emphasized. Ship construction, munitions,

B-29s ON 20 AUGUST BOMB YAWATA STEEL PLANT, START FIRES

TARGET IN JAPAN

railroads, maintenance, all depend on the operation of the big Jap steel plants illustrated in the following series of annotated photographs.

The key below refers to the annotated picture of Yawata steel mills at right, taken on 4 August: (1) coke oven plant, five batteries with a total of about 375 ovens; (2) by-products plant; (3, 5, 13, 14, 15, 19, 20, 24, 25, 29, 30) mills; (4) Bessemer converters; (6, 18) blast furnaces; (7) storage yard, finished products; (8) warehouse finished products; (9) nail mills; (10) electric power plant; (11) administration buildings; (12, 23, 28) open hearth furnaces; (16) coke oven plant, probably four batteries with a total of about 250 ovens; (17) by-products plant; (21) unidentified; (22) foundry; (26) electric power plant; (27) refractory brick plant; (31) ore, scrap, coal and limestone storage.

ANNOTATED PHOTO OF YAWATA MILLS SHOWS MAIN TARGET AREA

FOUR-PART STEREO of Yawata mills, at left and below, can be studied by placing stereo glasses across any two panels. To identify installations, compare with annotated photograph above, which covers same area.

Continued on next page

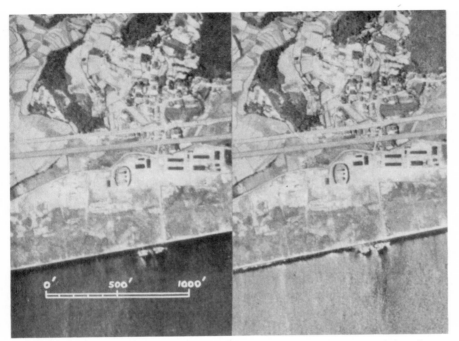

PUZZLE FOR P.I.s was this horseshoe revetment near Yawata containing three balloon-like objects, each about 60 feet long, first noted in stereo, 18 June.

PUZZLE SOLVED: 20 August photo shows revetment empty, balloon aloft (in circle).

ANSHAN STEEL PLANT IS VITAL FACTOR IN JAP MANCHURIAN ECONOMY

One of Japan's big steel plants, second in size only to Yawata, is the Showa Steel Works at Anshan, Manchuria, south of Mukden, where the 20th Bomber Command attacked on 29 July (IMPACT, Vol. 2, No. 9) and also on 8 September. The following three photos give the layout of this important Japanese target.

The Anshan works are vital to Japan because, unlike some other mills on the homeland, they do not depend on ore from overseas. Manchuria is a railroad country, in the U. S. sense, able to supply its own mills. When Anshan is knocked out, Japan loses one of its top plants, where production capacity has been 100 per cent utilized. Also Anshan's loss will hurt the Japs because it has been a major unit in the army plan for military and economic self-sufficiency in Manchuria.

GENERAL TARGET AREA FOR B-29s IS SHOWN ON PHOTO OF ANSHAN MILLS, TAKEN FROM 30,000 FEET

IT CONTAINS ALL STEPS FOR PROCESSING STEEL

To the P.I. expert, the Anshan plant is a rich field for study. It contains two concentrating plants, briquetting plant, luppe plant, brick plant, nine blast furnaces, 16 coke oven batteries with about 625 ovens, a coke oven by-products plant, an electric power plant, and two open hearth plants. Annotations at right are keyed below: (1) ore and limestone storage yard; (2, 3) blast furnaces; (4, 5) gas cleaning plants; (6) boiler house and blowers; (7) boiler house and electric power generators; (8) boiler house; (9) blowing house; (10, 11) cooling towers; (12) blast furnace gas holder; (13) chemical and metallurgical lab; (14, A, B, C) coke oven by-products plant; (15, 16, 17) coke oven installations, each with four Otto batteries with a total of approximately 150 ovens; (18) coke oven installations, four Koppers batteries with a total of approximately 175 ovens; (19) coal crusher; (20) coal bins; (21, 22) storage yard, finished products; (23) coke oven gas holder; (24) storage sheds; (25, 34) open hearth furnaces; (26 to 29) bar, sheet, rail mills; (30, 33) soaking pit, rolling mills; (31, 32) mill and plate mill.

ANNOTATED PHOTO OF ANSHAN IDENTIFIES AREAS SHOWN BELOW

STEREOS OF ANSHAN TAKEN ON 4 AUGUST SHOW COKING, BLAST FURNACE, OPEN HEARTH, MILL AREAS

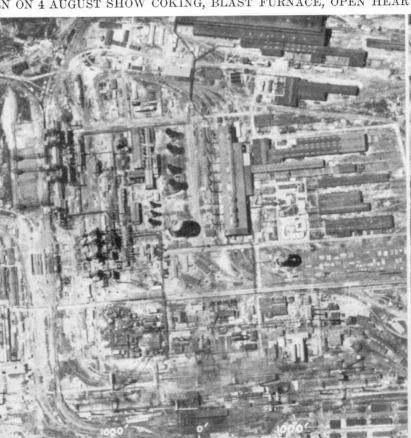

NEW TAIL RADAR REAL NECK SAVER

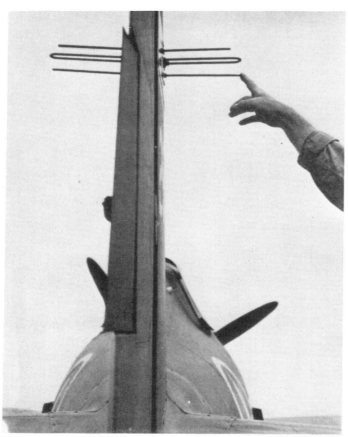

Saving pilots' necks from wear and tear, both the kind that comes from trying to keep that blind spot covered as well as the more permanent kind, is the function of the Radar Tail Warning Device, now in production and recommended by the AAF Board for installation in all day and night fighters.

The equipment consists of a tail antenna, a transmitter-receiver unit, a pilot control box and a warning light beside the gunsight. The light can be pre-set to operate when another aircraft enters, at any point up to a maximum distance of 800 yards, the zone of radar coverage. This is an elliptical cone with axes 60 degrees horizontally and 90 vertically, extending to the rear of the plane.

Tests have shown that the device not only provides adequate warning of attack but is especially valuable in telling the pilot when his tail is clear during evasive action.

TAIL ATTACK WARNING is given by the AN/APS-13 radar equipment, antenna of which is shown here on a P-47.

WARNING LIGHT mounted (right) beside reflector gunsight in a P-47 flashes on when planes enter zone of radar coverage.

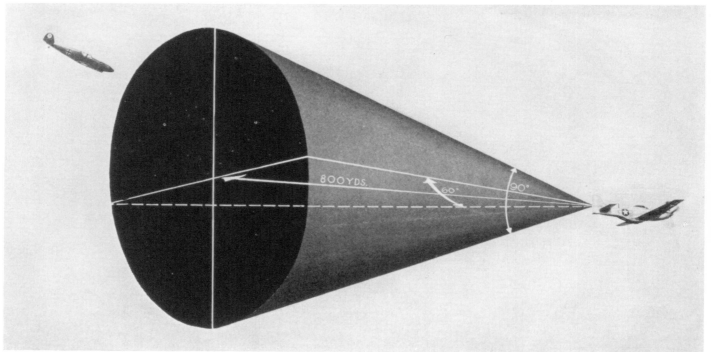

CONE OF RADAR COVERAGE is shown in this conventionalized diagram. Entrance of plane into it from any direction at any point is registered. Note that cone is higher than wide, to catch diving planes. Maximum effectiveness is 800 yards.

HUNS' HANGARS TOPPLE IN FRANCE

These two pictures are a sample of what U. S. bombardment did to German air bases in Northern France. Above is the interior of a permanent concrete hangar near Chateau- dun, taken on 18 August, where a huge pillar has buckled as if Samson were on the job again. Notice here how the Germans tried to store bombs after the building was damaged. Below is all that remains of another German hangar near St. André Leure, taken on 22 August. The heavy pounding of this area preceded the fall of the area to advancing American forces.

8th AF FIGHTERS BLAST AMMUNITION TRAINS

Ammunition trains have been special targets of strafing fighter pilots hitting the German rail lines behind the Western front. The six pictures above, taken from 8th AF gun-camera films, give a glimpse of these train attacks as seen by the pilot. The first three show **(1)** start of an explosion as a car loaded with ammunition is hit, **(2)** the explosion bursting wide open as the plane comes in, and **(3)** the roaring flare-up of flame, which in this case burned the camouflage from the bottom of the plane. The pilot who did this job wrote in his report: "Box cars were being loaded with ammunition for the front. Time and again we would dive in . . . Our concentration of incendiaries and armor-piercing shells tore into everything. At one time I had to fly through one of the explosions . . . I saw a box car wheel go up by my wing . . . It threw a large piece of timber through a window of my canopy."

Shots **4, 5** above, taken during another mission, show the first car of a train exploding. No. **6**, same mission after more passes, shows virtually the entire train in flames. Note how the cars have been spaced on the siding in an effort to isolate explosions during attack.

IMPACT

130 MPH HUMAN PICK-UP
See p. 48

DISTRIBUTION:
SQUADRONS

OFFICE OF THE
ASSISTANT CHIEF OF AIR STAFF, INTELLIGENCE
WASHINGTON, D. C.

Vol. 2   No. 11
NOVEMBER, 1944

CRISS-CROSSING THUNDERBOLTS GUARD 8th AF FORTS
See Strategic Campaign in Europe p. 2

IMPACT

CONTENTS
NOVEMBER, 1944

Confidential

ETO STRATEGIC SLUGGERS STILL SLUGGING HARD;

The tendency (noted in the June IMPACT) of our strategic air forces in Europe to concentrate an increasingly large proportion of their tonnages on tactical rather than on strategic targets, has lately begun to reverse itself. During the first half of October the Eighth Air Force dropped 12,857 strategic as against only 9,406 tactical tons. There are several reasons for this. First, the interdiction campaign in France (see pages 12-21) is over. Second, the greatly increased size of our tactical air forces, plus the fact that low-level attacks are more effective against personnel and small dispersed military targets than high-altitude bombardment, has relieved our heavies of much of their tactical work. Third, new German industries have been earmarked for concentrated attacks. Fourth, the phoenix-like quality of German industry as a whole makes constant surveillance an absolute necessity. For example, with Ploesti gone and the Hungarian fields almost within the grasp of Russian armies, the Germans have redoubled their efforts to keep both their synthetic plants and their natural refineries operating. Two of the largest refineries in Hamburg are going at this writing, despite recent heavy attacks which had completely halted operations. Accordingly, tonnage statistics have shown oil to be the top priority for the Eighth for several months,

NEW TARGETS ARE ADDED TO THE OLD FAVORITES

followed in order by tank, truck, and ordnance works, then by aircraft and aero engine plants. Rail yards, a few months ago at the top, are now fourth on the target priority list.

Ordnance, tank, and truck works are now regarded vulnerable because of the enormous wastage by German armies on three fronts, which has more than consumed whatever excess productive capacity the enemy may have had prior to this; because of the numerous stresses to which an overburdened and overbombed industrial empire is now subject; and because of the loss of huge amounts of truck-producing capacity as a result of the liberation of France. Pictures of this phase of our strategic campaign will be found on pages 6 and 7.

The well-known recuperative ability of the German aircraft industry has been responsible for a continuance of the kind of attack pictured below. Production of conventional single-engine fighters has risen sharply during the summer and fall months, as has that of two types of jet-propelled aircraft, the Me-262 and Me-163. Linked with the campaign to reduce effectiveness of the latter are the blows at Peenemunde (see pages 4 and 5), one of five main producing centers for jet and rocket fuels, and long a station for experiments with robot bombs, rockets, glide bombs, and other types of controlled missiles.

ROSTOCK. Oblique photograph at left shows the Heinkel Flugzeugwerke smoking from the 8th AF attack of 4 August, during which 148 bombers dropped 370 tons of GP and IB. Hit again with 311 tons on 25 August by 116 8th AF heavies, the northern half of the factory is shown (above) blanketed by these attacks. Large assembly shop (lower left) is severely damaged. Smaller shop next to it is slightly damaged. In center of picture two flight hangars, a large assembly shop, a paint shop and a canteen are all damaged. This plant has been making the He-111, now regarded obsolescent, and the He-219, a twin-engine long-range fighter.

Continued on next page

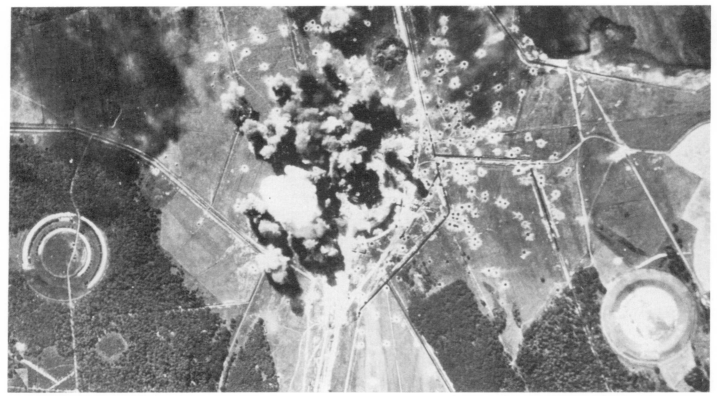

ELECTROSTATIC PLANT for manufacturing hydrogen peroxide was hit on 4 August by 221 B-17s dropping 522 tons (note craters from previous attacks). Center installation is the only one completed by the Germans. Characteristic circular embankment has been finished in unit at right, and preliminary work begun in unit at left. Both have since been abandoned.

ELECTROSTATIC PLANT (top of picture) is shown demolished in cover of 25 August during strike at electrolytic plant (bottom). Location of two main buildings is shown by dotted lines.

8th AF BLASTS PEENEMUNDE

One German target which is, in a sense, an industry in itself is Peenemunde, the huge experimental station on the shore of the Baltic. It is here that extensive tests in jet and rocket propulsion have been carried on for several years by the Germans, with projectiles being shot along the coast or out over the sea while they are tracked and tested for accuracy. Of particular interest at Peenemunde are the hydrogen peroxide plants shown here. Hydrogen peroxide (H_2O_2) in concentrated form, mixed with small quantities of alcohol, is an excellent propellant for pure rockets, which must draw on their own fuel for their supply of oxygen, as opposed to jet-driven projectiles, which depend on oxygen from the atmosphere. The mixture is forced into a combustion chamber under pressure, where it ignites in the presence of a catalyst such as potassium permanganate.

Two processes for manufacturing H_2O_2 are used at Peenemunde, the electrolytic and electrostatic. The former, and older, takes place in the rectangular buildings shown at the right, the latter (about which very little is known at present) in the round installations above and at the left. In the electrolytic process sulphuric acid is subjected to electrolysis, which turns it into persulphuric acid and hydrogen. Water is added to the persulphuric acid and this is distilled, giving off H_2O_2 with a top concentration of about 20 per cent. This is then subjected to further chemical treatment to bring it up to a strength of 85-90 per cent. Even at these high concentrations H_2O_2 is inherently stable. However, it is extremely delicate, and will disintegrate rapidly if exposed to heat, light, or dust.

In addition to Peenemunde, H_2O_2 plants at Friedrichshaven, Rheinfelden, Hollriegelskreuth, and Dusseldorf have been attacked in the campaign to reduce Germany's effectiveness in the use of rockets.

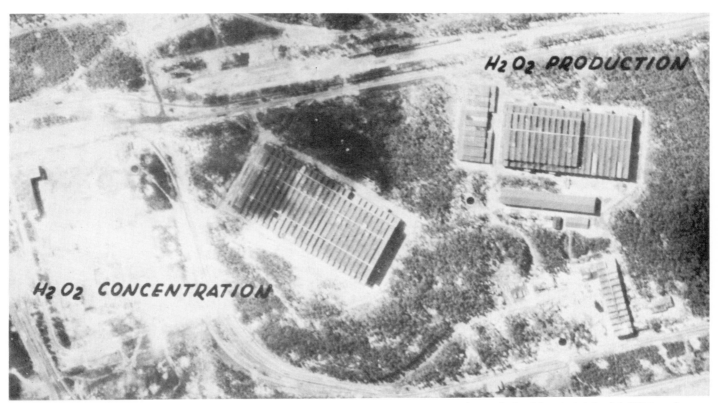

ELECTROLYTIC PLANT BEFORE. Photograph was taken on 4 August during strike attack on electrostatic plant shown at top of opposite page. This mission was only a small part of the day's operations of the 8th. A total of 1,417 heavies was dispatched, dropping 3,252 tons on three refineries, three aircraft factories, three airfields and port installations at Kiel.

ELECTROLYTIC PLANT AFTER. This photo shows installations still smoking from mission of 25 August. Two main electrolysis buildings have each sustained numerous direct hits. Three smaller buildings have been severely damaged. Attack was made by 146 B-17s which dropped 288 tons of GP, 77.5 tons of IB. The incendiaries were particularly effective.

Continued on next page

WEIMAR ARMAMENT WORKS was attacked on 24 August by 129 8th AF heavies. Load was 175 1,000-lb. GP, 583 500-lb. GP and 279 500-lb. incendiaries, a total of 303 tons.

ORDNANCE PRODUCTION IN SILESIA AND RUHR BEING WHITTLED DOWN

The bulk of German ordnance is centered in the two great iron and steel areas of the Ruhr and Silesia. The largest Ruhr plant is the Krupp works at Essen, followed by the Rheinmetall Borsig works at Dusseldorf. All the heavy instruments of war are made here, including large caliber guns and shells, aerial bombs, naval mine components, gun mounts, turrets and armor plate. Such heavy industrial areas have been pounded for several years, RAF pilots claiming that they can find their way down the Ruhr valley by following the pattern of flak bursts better than they can navigate in Piccadilly Circus on a foggy night.

Small arms manufacture is scattered among numerous firms throughout Germany, and small arms ammunition even more widely dispersed, no one firm producing more than a small percentage of total German output. One of the larger light armament plants is at Weimar/Buchenwald, shown under attack on this page. Rifles, self-propelled gun carriages, and armored military vehicles are made here. The target is made more attractive by the presence of a radio factory and a Gestapo headquarters and barracks, all of which were also hit.

WEIMAR AFTER. Reconnaissance photo shows tremendous damage. In the armament works (bottom center) seven of ten main workshops have been destroyed, the boiler house gutted, and other smaller buildings damaged. In the garage and storage area directly above 14 buildings were destroyed, nine severely damaged, and large numbers of trucks destroyed. The dotted rectangle to the right encloses a radio factory in which 13 buildings were destroyed and two gutted. This attack also destroyed seven buildings in the concentration camp next door. In the Gestapo headquarters, 11 buildings were destroyed.

TRUCK, TANK FACTORIES SMASHED

The pictures on this page illustrate the growing severity of attacks against German tank and truck plants which have contributed strongly to the M/T shortage now plaguing the Wehrmacht. **Above** is shown the huge Fallersleben works as it looked after the 5 August mission when 85 Eighth AF heavies dropped 270 tons. It is estimated that six football games could be played simultaneously in the damaged area. Fallersleben produces flying bombs, Ju-88 parts, cars, jeeps, and has one of the largest metal pressing shops in Germany. **Below** is shown

the Borgward tank and truck plant in Bremen after 1,057 tons had been dropped on it by 394 8th AF heavies on 26 September. The main machine shop, assembly plant, foundry and finishing works all have suffered direct hits. This plant is one of six main truck producers in Germany. The other five have all been attacked as follows: Daimler Benz at Stuttgart (very heavily damaged on 5, 12 and 13 September), Ford at Cologne (a target for numerous attacks, this plant is so near the front lines that further production by it is not expected), Opel at Brandenberg (very severely damaged on 6 August), Bussing at Brunswick (damaged in several RAF saturation attacks), Auto Union at Chemnitz (severely damaged on 11 September).

OIL. Standard Oil Gennevilliers plant in Paris was hit on 22 June and 10 August by a total of 190 Eighth AF heavies dropping 743 tons. Tank cars shown above were caught beneath girders of grease manufacturing shop when roof fell in. Company had extensive storage facilities and a well-equipped mixing plant for raw materials. Both were virtually demolished.

OIL. Another view of Gennevilliers shows main works wrecked. Estimated monthly production of 2,200 tons and storage capacity of 13,000 tons were destroyed during these attacks, a serious blow to German armored force operations in France, as the chief products of this plant were lubricants and tank grease. Rail attacks made this loss almost impossible to replace.

AIRPLANE ENGINES. Hispano Suiza plant was taken over by Germans on entry into Paris, used for repair of 250 Mercedes and Daimler Benz engines a month. Hit by 8th AF bombs on 15 September and 31 December 1943, and plagued by constant sabotage by French workers, activity was thereafter limited to the finishing of engine parts from factories in the Pyrenees.

MOTOR VEHICLES. Renault plant in Paris produced 2,550 trucks, 500 tanks a month when taken over by Germans in June 1940. Blasted by the RAF and 8th AF, isolated by rail bom- bardment, chilled by strikes at fuel and electrical plants, de- nuded of its best workers, production skidded to zero in four years. The pictures below show details of 8th AF bomb damage.

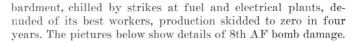

TAKING WING, the XP-47N makes one of its experimental flights in preparation for its role as escort of very heavy bombers. Additional fuel tanks in inboard wing sections give new model far greater range than other types of fighter plane.

NEW, IMPROVED P-47 HAS MUCH MORE RANGE

The P-47N is an improved Thunderbolt whose new features extend the plane's combat radius of action so that it can be used to escort Very Heavy Bombers on long-range missions. This model has the same fuselage as the older types, and the P-47's characteristic stubby nose, but the wings have been altered in span and shape and the landing gear has been widened. New internal tanks add 100 gallons' fuel capacity in the inboard panels of each wing, which had to be lengthened about 18 inches; eight inches were then taken off each wing at the tip. The total wing spread was increased from 40 feet, nine inches to 42 feet, six inches. With 600 gallons in drop tanks, the P-47N will have a gas load of 1,170 gallons, and it is estimated that this will enlarge the Thunderbolt's combat radius to more than 1,200 miles. With CH-5 turbosupercharger, critical altitude is expected to be well above 30,000 feet.

The engineer's diagram on the lower half of the following page illustrates the principal features of the P-47N with the exception of the engine, which is an R-2800-C. The R-2800-B, now installed in the P-47D series, has a War Emergency Rating of 2,550 horsepower with water injection, using Grade 100/130 fuel. With water injection and Grade 100/150 fuel, the War Emergency Rating of this engine has been stepped up to 2,800 h.p. The R-2800-C power plant in the P-47N now has a WER of 2,800 h.p. when using a 50-50 mixture of water-alcohol injection and Grade 100/130 fuel. As IMPACT goes to press, tests are getting under way with Grade 100/150 and Grade 115/145 fuels. Based on War Emergency power obtainable with improved fuel with the R-2800-B engine, an increase in horsepower to above 2,800 can be logically expected with the R-2800-C power plant.

FLIGHT-LINE VIEW OF CURRENT P-47 (LEFT) AND XP-47N GIVES COMPARISON OF OLD WING WITH NEW

XP-47N SEEN from above, over Ohio grainland, shows pilot looking up at photo plane through teardrop canopy.

DIAGRAM of P-47N shows not only new major features but also smaller changes made in new model Thunderbolt.

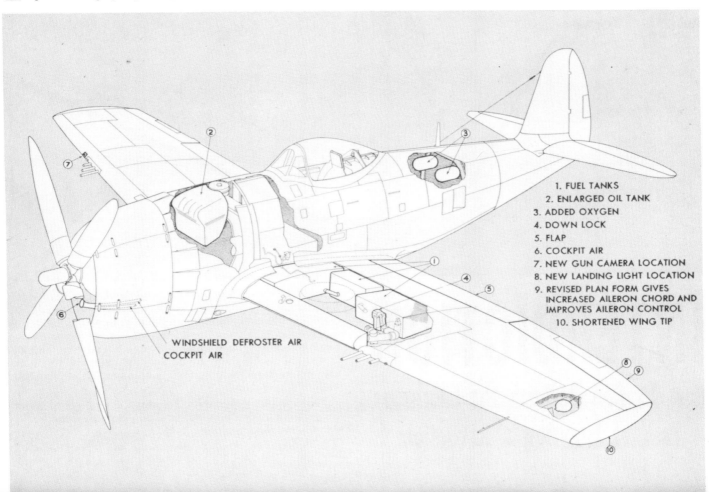

1. FUEL TANKS
2. ENLARGED OIL TANK
3. ADDED OXYGEN
4. DOWN LOCK
5. FLAP
6. COCKPIT AIR
7. NEW GUN CAMERA LOCATION
8. NEW LANDING LIGHT LOCATION
9. REVISED PLAN FORM GIVES INCREASED AILERON CHORD AND IMPROVES AILERON CONTROL
10. SHORTENED WING TIP

WINDSHIELD DEFROSTER AIR
COCKPIT AIR

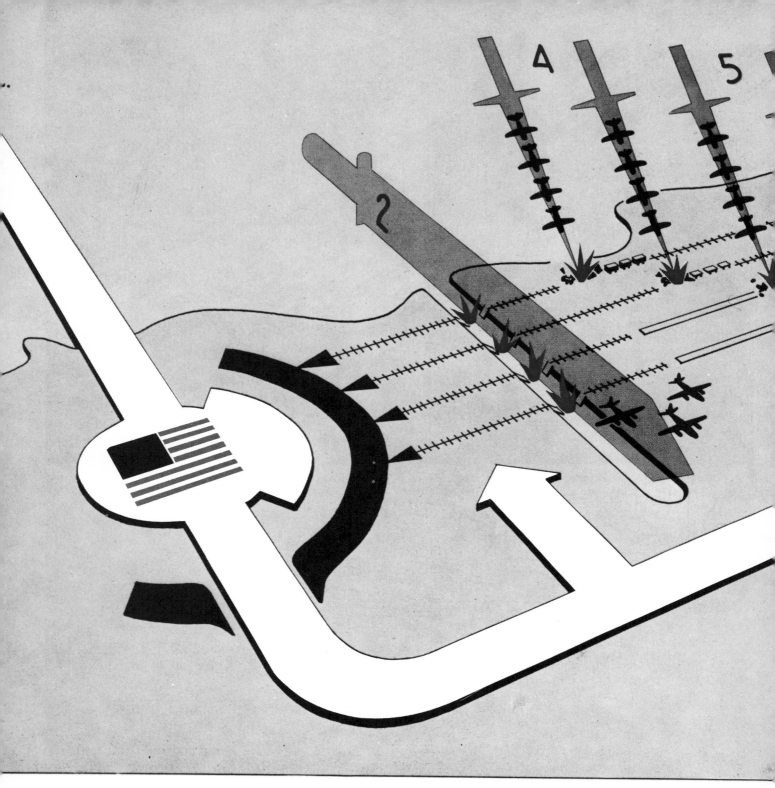

INTERDICTION

How Air Can Perform the Enormous Task of Isolating a Battlefield

Allied invasion plans were based on the theory that, once the Luftwaffe's back had been broken, a heavily defended coast could be breached by isolating the projected landing area through air attack directed against the enemy transportation facilities servicing that area. How this works, even when the troops and fortifications in the area are maintained by a rail network as formidable as that in northern France, is shown in the diagram above.

First step is to saturate rail yards, lowering operating efficiency and forcing the diversion of men and equipment to keep the system open for military traffic.

Second, a line of interdiction is set up by cutting all rail

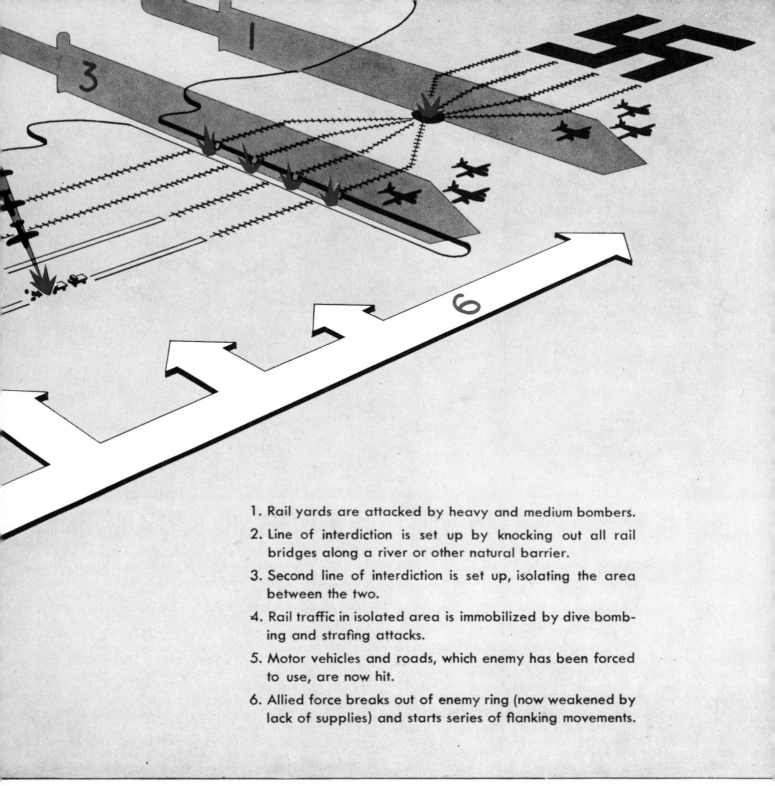

1. Rail yards are attacked by heavy and medium bombers.

2. Line of interdiction is set up by knocking out all rail bridges along a river or other natural barrier.

3. Second line of interdiction is set up, isolating the area between the two.

4. Rail traffic in isolated area is immobilized by dive bombing and strafing attacks.

5. Motor vehicles and roads, which enemy has been forced to use, are now hit.

6. Allied force breaks out of enemy ring (now weakened by lack of supplies) and starts series of flanking movements.

bridges across a natural barrier such as a river. This further hampers the flow of supplies by forcing the enemy to stop his trains at the river, unload into trucks or boats, and then load into different trains on the opposite side.

Third, another line of interdiction is established, forcing a double train-to-truck-to-train transfer, and creating a zone from which the locomotives and cars inside cannot escape, nor those outside get in.

Fourth, the irreplaceable rolling stock isolated in the zone of interdiction is clogged at certain points by bombardment, and then depleted by fighter attacks until the enemy is driven to road transport. This is undesirable from his point of view because trucks are less efficient than trains, because they are more vulnerable to strafing attack, but mostly because of the shortage of trucks, tires, and gas created by strategic bombing.

Fifth, the fighter attack shifts to the roads, forcing the enemy to operate only at night, in widely dispersed motor convoys, under rigid blackout conditions, all of which reduces the flow of supplies to the coast still further.

Sixth, a landing having been made, consolidated, and ground strength built up faster than the enemy's, all with the help of the transportation snarls described above, a series of end runs is undertaken to flank the enemy and annihilate him. To see how this actually worked in France, turn the page.

Continued on next page

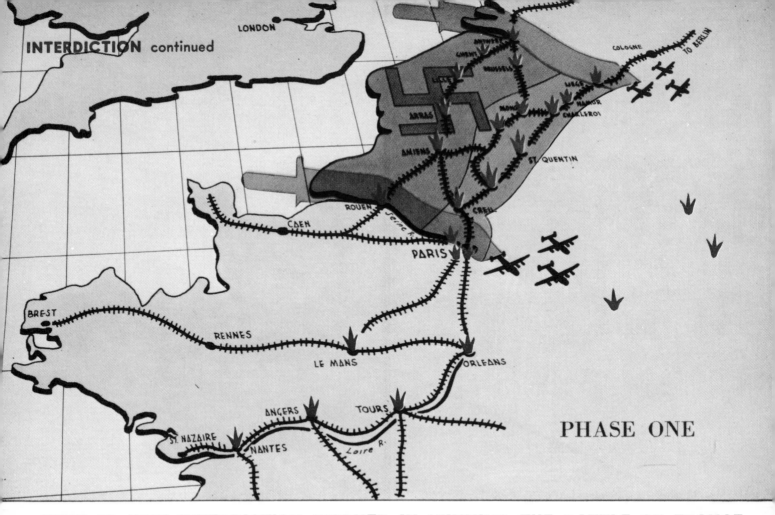

LONDON · COLOGNE · TO BERLIN · ANTWERP · GHENT · LILLE · BRUSSELS · LIEGE · MONS · NAMUR · CHARLEROI · ARRAS · AMIENS · ST. QUENTIN · ROUEN · Seine R. · CREIL · CAEN · PARIS · BREST · RENNES · LE MANS · ORLEANS · ANGERS · TOURS · ST. NAZAIRE · NANTES · Loire R.

PHASE ONE

HERE IS HOW INTERDICTION WORKED IN WINNING THE BATTLE OF FRANCE

As in the theoretical example on the previous page, the invasion of France posed to Allied planners the problem of landing on a coast bristling with fortifications, and strongly garrisoned with troops which could rapidly be concentrated at any point through use of the densest rail system in the world.

Phase One (D minus 90 to D-Day). Air's first task was to prevent the movement of German troops from the Calais coast to Normandy as the invasion developed. The map above shows how the campaign began with bombardment of *all* the rail centers servicing these areas. This achieved the double purpose of improving our chances of securing a foothold without betraying where the attempt would be made. Next a line of interdiction was established between Paris and the sea by cutting bridges across the Seine river. Another such line was then set up along the Albert Canal and Meuse river. Purpose of this was to create a zone of interdiction between the two, and, by a further concentration of attacks within the zone, to heighten the impression that our landing would be made there. A glance at the map will show that the stage was now set. The bulk of the German forces was bottled between two lines of interdiction (shaded area around swastika) which at the same time cut off the real landing area from all directions except the south.

Phase Two (D-Day to D plus 55). Under heavy air cover landings were made, consolidated, and the Cherbourg peninsula captured in due course. However, a ring of enemy troops was thrown around our perimeter, successfully containing it for a period of weeks. The next job therefore was to build up sufficient force to break out, preventing at the same time a similar buildup by the enemy. Accordingly, another interdic-

tion line was established along the Loire river, linking up with the Seine line west of Paris and completely sealing off the battle area. A fourth line was set up east of Paris, extending (dotted red line) to the Loire line at Orleans. Meanwhile, a heavy war of attrition was being waged on the perimeter. We could afford it. Germany could not, as she had by now abandoned all attempts to move by rail, and her efforts at resupply and reinforcement by road (dark arrows) were subjected to devastating fighter and bomber attacks. Finally on 25 July a superior Allied force broke through the east end of the perimeter on the heels of a heavy aerial barrage.

Phase Three (D-plus-55 on). Once through the German ring, Allied armor poured into the vacuum behind it, forming a pocket at Falaise which was largely annihilated by air and ground attack. (Brittany, where a strong FFI movement aided by parachuting agents secured our flank, could largely be ignored.) No enemy stand was made at the Seine, the dangers of a second pocket being too apparent. Instead, the enemy retreated across it in good order despite a terrific jam-up and heavy losses on the banks of the river, whose bridges were still down (see picture on next page). Meanwhile the situation was further exploited by the brilliant and incredibly energetic flanking operations of our tank commanders, who were able to proceed day and night at top speed, aided by air cover and air supply (large red arrows), over roads less damaged than those being used by the enemy. A parallel advance by British and Canadian armies nearer the coast completed the undermining of the whole German defensive system in Northern France. Leaving garrisons at the principal ports, the Wehrmacht pulled out, shedding men and equipment at every step.

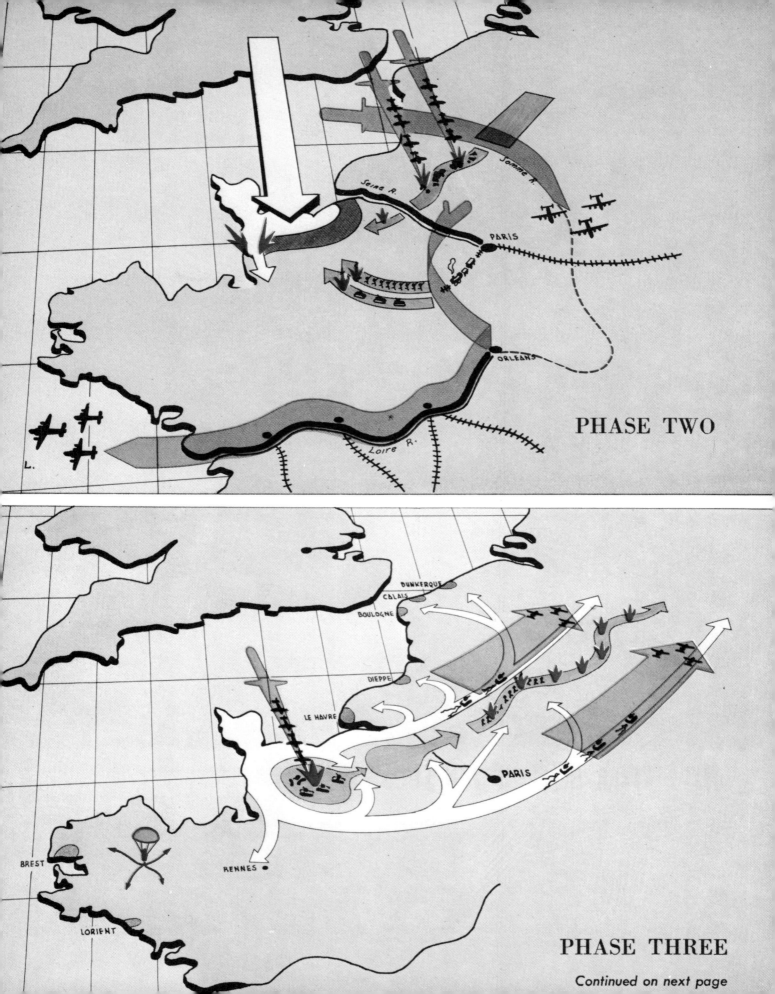

PHASE TWO

PHASE THREE

Continued on next page

SEINE RIVER INTERDICTION LINE

Just north of Paris at Conflans is situated the first of seven rail bridges which cross the Seine river, linking Brittany and Normandy with the great industrial areas of Eastern France, Belgium and the Ruhr valley. Attempts to establish a line of interdiction here were begun in May by the U. S. Ninth Air Force and the British Second Tactical Air Force. By 12 June each of these bridges was down, as shown by the pictures on the opposite page, also each of the thirteen road bridges which cross the Seine between Conflans and the sea. This formidable barrier not only enormously increased the difficulty of transporting German troops and equipment into the invasion area,

but it also made it almost impossible for those who escaped the Falaise pocket to get back without enduring withering attacks from the air while packed against the river bank and waiting to be taken across in boats.

Aircraft operating against the Seine bridges were almost entirely B-25s, B-26s, A-20s, P-47s and Typhoons, engaging in precision bombing, dive bombing and minimum-altitude attacks. Credit was shared about equally between bombers and fighters. An operational analysis found that dive bombing was about one-third as effective as minimum-altitude attack, but considerably less dangerous. For the latter to be successful, the bridge had to offer soft abutments, wooden scaffolding, or some other structure in which the bomb could stick while it exploded. Correct fusing is vital in all bridge attacks.

Continued on page 18

Confidential

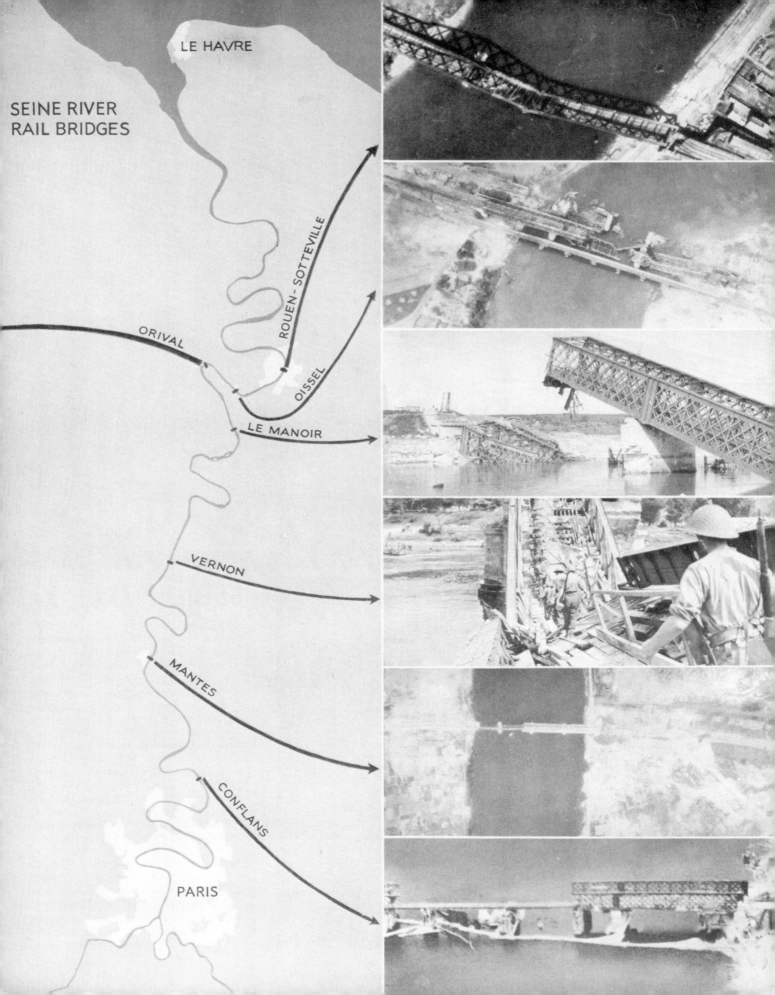

SEINE RIVER
RAIL BRIDGES

LE HAVRE

ORIVAL

ROUEN - SOTTEVILLE

OISSEL

LE MANOIR

VERNON

MANTES

CONFLANS

PARIS

No road safe for the Wehrmacht

GERMAN TANKS, M/T

Once the battle for the Normandy beaches was over and the galloping epidemic of Allied ground strength had begun to spread east and south, exploiting the enemy weaknesses created by the interdiction campaign, it became the mission of these armies to surround and destroy German military power in northern France before it could escape and reorganize itself. Occupation of further territory had become a secondary consideration. These pictures give a clue to what happened to the German 7th Army after it had been enclosed in the Falaise pocket. Hemmed in from the north by British and Canadians approaching Falaise, and from the south by Americans approaching Argentan, its only avenue of escape lay in the 13-mile gap between these towns. Interdiction, as shown on the preceding pages, had already paid enormous dividends in helping to set up this trap. The final task of air was to help kill the animal inside. This was done by the closest kind of

WERE CUT TO PIECES

For us, bumper to bumper and perfectly safe

coordination between ground and air. Constant patrols provided reconnaissance for our ground commanders, allowing them to bring up superior force against any reported enemy concentrations. These were then dive bombed and strafed, and Allied armor, still in communication with the fighter planes, would move in for the kill. As the pocket became smaller and smaller, the congestion within became more acute, and Allied fighters worked the area over with increasing effectiveness. By 20 August, when all resistance collapsed, the entire pocket was carpeted with blasted guns, tanks and trucks.

The size of our air effort is shown by the 11,886 AEAF sorties flown on 18-20 August. German air activity during this period was microscopic. Allied vehicles could jam the roads by day with impunity, as the picture at the right (taken near Valognes on 24 August) graphically illustrates.

Continued on next page

BELFORT YARD BATTERED

One of the great natural barriers of Europe is the chain of the Vosges and Jura mountains which separates central France from southern Germany. Only passage through it is the Belfort Gap, where there is a confluence of rail lines and highways. Thus, the Belfort rail yard is an example of a perfect rail interdiction target. The Eighth Air Force hit it on 11 and 25 May, 17 July and 11 August. Two stages of the last attack, during which 76 heavies dropped 187 tons visually from 19,500 feet, are shown above and below. Cumulative results, right, show locomotive shops almost totally destroyed, transshipment shed and station shattered, all through lines cut.

LETHAL BLACK WIDOWS IN COMBAT GARB SEARCH SKIES OVER FRANCE FOR UNWARY JERRIES

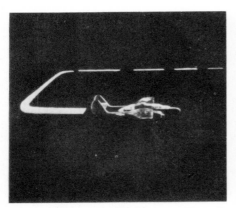

1. ON NIGHT PATROL over France P-61 flies rectangular search pattern.

2. GROUND CONTROL reports "trade" at 9,000 ft., vectors P-61 in.

3. Ju-88 ZIG-ZAGS gently on course o 280° at 190 mph, altitude 9,000 ft. P-6

4. LONG BURST knocks fragments from Ju-88 which drops window and peels off sharply to port, diving to about 5,500 feet. P-61 loses its visual contact here.

5. CONTACT REGAINED at 7,500 feet o same vector of 280°, P-61 opens fire fron

THE WIDOWS BEGIN BITING

Two things have contributed to the development of the modern night fighter. One was the necessity, first for the British and later for the Germans, to defend against night bombardment missions which were saturating their cities. The other is radar, whose development to a point where it was really reliable in interception did not come until after the war had started. Accordingly, *existing* aircraft were radar equipped. In Britain the Beaufighter and later the Mosquito were so used, and proved big factors in making German night penetrations so expensive that they finally shrank to an insignificant dribble. When the ponderous RAF night missions began to roll, the Germans equipped interceptors—notably Me-110s and Ju-88s—with radar, causing an increase in RAF losses, which reached a climax over Nuremberg on the night of 30-31 March, 1944, when 66 RAF heavy bombers were shot down by German night fighters. For the past two years, the Battle of Radar has see-sawed with the Allies and the enemy developing new equipment and countermeasures.

Because our need has not been so urgent, the AAF has not concentrated on the development of night fighter organizations on a scale comparable to those of the British and Germans. Now, however, we have in operation in both Europe and the Pacific the first airplane specifically designed for night fighting—the P-61 "Black Widow." In addition, we have developed an efficient new radar ground control setup, the MEW (Microwave Early Warning). It has been the major radar reporting and control equipment since it first went to work covering the Normandy D-Day.

With an efficient height finder, MEW can pick up hostiles at considerable ranges and vector a P-61 (or any night fighter) to them. Under good conditions, this can bring in a P-61 close enough for it to establish a visual. More commonly it would simply get the fighter to a point where its own airborne radar (SCR-720) could take over. As soon as the kill is made, ground control can take over again, either vectoring the fighter back to base or putting it onto a new hostile.

(Functioning of SCR-720 was described in IMPACT, Volume 2, Number 5. For detailed operational information on MEW, see RADAR Magazine, Number 3 and Number 5.)

The P-61, an aircraft considered far superior to the night fighter version of the A-20 which it supplants, faces a particularly busy future in the war in the Pacific. As we move nearer Japan we must be prepared for the possibility that the enemy may muster more effective air assaults than he has been capable of recently. Part of our preparation is the P-61. How this aircraft goes about an interception is illustrated in the model sequence below showing a Ju-88 killed by a P-61 over Normandy on 6 August. Distances between planes have been shortened because of space limitations.

makes a visual contact from 1,000 feet away and closes rapidly to a range of 400 feet.

500 ft. 5° below and dead astern. Short burst scores several direct hits on the Ju-88.

6. ENEMY MUSHES completely out of control to port and explodes in a burst of flame. Burning parts fell into the overcast below; nobody was seen to bail out.

P-47 STRAFES A WINDING MOUNTAIN HIGHWAY IN SOUTHERN FRANCE

P-38's NOSE-BORNE CAMERA RECORD

THUNDERBOMBERS

P-38 "Droopsnoot" Photo Plane Follows MAAF
P-47s To Obtain Striking Low-Level Obliques

The three pictures shown here were take
from a special "droopsnoot" P-38, rigged up b
the MAAF to obtain the rarest thing in aeria
combat photography—good, clear shots o
dive bombing and strafing. The pictures sho
attacks by the MAAF's favorite aircraft fo
rough work at low level, the P-47, dubbed th
"Thunderbomber" in the theater. Thunde
bombers have seen very heavy action recent
in Northern Italy and Southern France. I
June, Thunderbombers of the Mediterranea

STRAFING OF RAIL YARDS IN ITALY

CAUSEWAY AT VIRGIL'S HOME TOWN, MANTUA, IS "THUNDERBOMBED"

Allied Tactical Air Force flew 5,001 effective sorties, dropping 2,931 tons of bombs; in July, 4,593 effective sorties, 1,929 tons; in August, 7,737 effective sorties, 2,516 tons. During these operations, the Tactical Air Force lost 120 planes and 118 were damaged. There were 23 enemy planes destroyed plus three probables. M/T columns, trains, marshalling yards and, during the Southern France invasion, gun positions and radar stations, have been priority targets.

The MAAF modification which has made a P-38 into a whirlwind photo plane that follows P-47s in their dives, is a plate glass nose resembling that of a B-17. Extending back as far as the camera and the battery plumbing station, this nose is equipped with a photographer's seat and the usual instruments for a bombardier. The camera is an AK 22 with a twelve-inch lens. The "droopsnoot" stays about 1,000 yards behind the combat planes and comes to the IP at an altitude of about 13,000 feet. The photo plane dives just as the last bomb-carrying fighter releases its load: The P-38 goes in lower than the P-47s, usually to 600 feet (with I.A.S. at about 550). This is dangerous above a target strongly defended by flak. One such P-38 was hit near Turin. It crash-landed behind the Allied lines. Pilot and cameraman were unhurt.

BURNING PLOESTI

These captured German films recorded what went on (in daylight) under those great, mushrooming smoke columns so often shown in aerial photos taken during AAF attacks on Ploesti's refineries. The films do not identify individual refineries.

P-47s TAKE FIRST CARRIER RIDE INTO COMBAT

P-47s WITH PILOTS AND CREW CHIEFS STAND INSPECTION AT OAHU, HAWAII, BEFORE LONG TRIP TO SAIPAN

BEING HOISTED ABOARD deck of escort-type carrier at Ford Island, Pearl Harbor, this is one of the 71 P-47s that took the trip.

From Hawaii to Saipan They Went to Hit Japs

One more example of AAF-Navy cooperation is the case of the 71 P-47s ferried to Saipan last June for 7th Air Force operations against the Japs on Saipan, Tinian and Rota. The secret nature of the operation has made it impossible to tell the story until now. It was the first time P-47s were thus used in the Pacific and also the first time, so far as is known, that P-47s were catapulted from carriers.

Preparations for this historic trip were completed in Hawaii at Bellows Field, Oahu, where the land birds were given a final preening for their ocean migration. With machine guns installed, and motors checked, on 16 May they were lined up for inspection by the Commanding General. At the same time, maintenance equipment and supplies were sent by truck to Pearl Harbor for subsequent shipping to Saipan. The planes themselves were flown the short distance to Ford Island naval base, and hoisted aboard two escort-type aircraft carriers.

With planes lashed firmly to their decks, the carriers embarked on 5 June, stopping at Eniwetok for refueling. Despite a Jap attack, the voyage was made without mishap, except that a motion picture screen accidentally fell and injured the prop of a P-47. A Navy TBF from a friendly base flew in a replacement. Mechanics made frequent checks on the planes to keep them in shape for the coming takeoff.

On 23 June, near the coast of Saipan, all planes were successfully launched. It took less than two minutes to launch each plane.

Continued on next page

DURING ATTACK BY FOUR JAP PLANES, BOMBS SPLASH PERILOUSLY NEAR CARRIER WITH LOAD OF P-47s

DESTINATION REACHED, THIS P-47 ON CATAPULT DECK IS READY FOR LAUNCHING FROM THE CARRIER

CARRIER CREWMEN CROUCH TENSELY AS P-47 GETS AWAY SUCCESSFULLY OVER A GLITTERING OCEAN

CARRIER IS BUZZED IN FAREWELL SALUTE AS THE P-47s HEAD FOR THEIR NEW LAND BASE ON SAIPAN

MEN OF THE 21st WATCH HOMECOMING PLANE

HAULING WATER, this coolie replenishes tanks that supply a 21st Photo Squadron laboratory at an advanced base in China.

FAR-FLYING 21s

In the field of aerial sleuthing the 21st Photographic Squadron does a job that in earthbound detective circles would tax the talents of Sherlock Holmes and Perry Mason combined. For its beat, the 21st has nearly four million square miles of Far Eastern territory, shown below. Most of it is Jap-held. Upon clues furnished by the 21st, a good part of our battle strategy against Japan is based.

This outfit was activated on 19 December 1942 at Peterson Field, Colorado Springs. Each department — Laboratory, Camera Repair and Engineering—went through its paces as near to field conditions as possible. By 1 July, 1943, the 21st, joined by its planes and pilots, had reached India. For jumping the Hump, supplies were divided into three parts, in case one cargo plane failed to get through. But no supplies were lost.

In China, the Squadron was divided into three flights, and later into four. "A" Flight absorbed the 9th Photo Squadron which had been stationed there for some seven months, and at Kunming set up headquarters for the entire outfit. "B" Flight was set up at Kweilin, and covered the Canton-Hongkong, and Hankow-Wuchang area, with occasional runs to Shanghai. In October 1943, when it became necessary to get regular cover on Formosa, a smaller forward base was established at Suichwan, known as Flight "C." From there, also, the Squadron's first extremely long mission was flown, covering Sasebo and Nagasaki in the Jap homeland—a hazardous roundtrip of about 2,200 miles.

Next spring "C" made its historic mission to Corregidor (page 37)—the first time it had been covered since the dark days of 1942. The flight lasted nine hours. On 17 April a fourth flight, "D," was located at Liangshan to cover Northeast China, as well as Mukden (pages 34, 35). "D's" runs are long and rugged, often staged from primitive forward fields where planes are laboriously refueled from five-gallon cans.

AREA COVERED by 21st is shown below, along with original locations of its four Flights, indicated by AAF plane insignia.

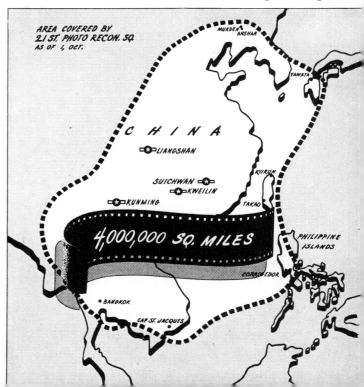

SQUADRON MAKES RECON HISTORY

WATER-HAULING FROM A RIVER IS ANOTHER STEP IN KEEPING 21st LABS RUNNING OVERTIME IN CHINA

EXCELLENT PROTECTION, even for jeeps, against enemy planes is afforded by limestone caves at one base.

PHOTO LAB at forward base, handy to water supply, is located against one of the jagged limestone hills typical of the area.

Confidential

Continued on next page

21st SQUADRON continued

GASOLINE TRUCK waits to refuel a plane of the 21st, as camera repairmen complete work. In background are ruins of headquarters from which Japs were driven by Flying Tigers.

FLIGHT LINES for both charting and reconnaissance photography are carefully drawn during briefing to permit the pilot to obtain maximum coverage with minimum time over the target.

INSTALLING MAGAZINES of film on F-5, "Frantic," camera repairmen get plane ready. The "Frantic" flew long range mission to Yawata, has flown more than 100 combat missions.

READY FOR TAKE-OFF, is Major G. H. Fulcher, former operations officer, and now Commanding Officer of Squadron. This particular mission was flown over Canton and Hongkong.

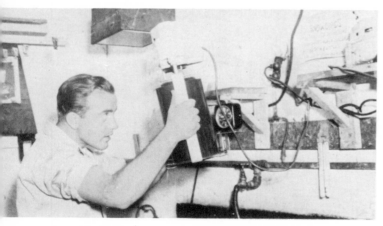

AFTER MISSION, developer checks negatives during washing process. Below: Squadron S-2, Major W. Nicholls, interrogates Lt. Col. John C. Foster on his return from Saigon mission.

FOR RUSH PRINTING, pilot and S-2 Officer watch as P.I.'s pick negatives. Below: Personnel of photogrammetry section complete essential charts from trimetrogon photographs.

FRUITS OF THEIR LABORS — MUKDEN TO MANILA

Like a big game hunter bringing home a hide is the photo reconnaissance pilot bringing home his film. It is the trophy of his kill. More than that, it leads to bigger kills. It may save his comrades' lives, and is vital to the progress of war. Here, and on the next four pages, are some of the prize pictures taken by the 21st Squadron whose hunting ground includes Burma, Thailand, French Indo-China, Philippines, Hainan, Formosa, Japan, Korea, Northern and Eastern China.

The outfit which produces this coverage certainly justifies the term "far-flung." From Flight "A" to Flight "B" is 500 air miles, to Flight "C" 800 miles, to Flight "D" 900 miles. Each Flight operates independently under a Flight C.O., but is closely coordinated with Flight "A" which is Squadron Headquarters. Each Flight flies tactical missions as requested by the Wing to which it is attached for operations, and at the same time, flies strategic missions requested by the 14th AF. All laboratories take great pride in their work, the "A" lab working 24 hours a day on three shifts. From 12 July 1943 to 12 July 1944, the Squadron for all flights ran 549 missions of which only 4.5% were duds due to engine or mechanical failure, and 17% due to bad weather. Making the above record, only one pilot was lost, on a non-combat mission.

TAKAO This Formosa harbor is a major staging point for Jap convoys, and was a target of big U. S. Naval attacks in mid October. Ships here are (1) suction dredger, (2) tanker 400'/500', (3) M/Vs 200'/500', (4) M/Vs 200'/400'.

Continued on next page

NORTH MUKDEN Buildings here had been reported as a fuselage and assembly plant. But on 19 June this valuable photo revealed that plant is for modifications and repairs. Key: (1, 11) administration, (2, 3, 6, 7) hangars—some under construction, (4) workers' quarters, (5) power, (8, 9) workshops, (10) probable foundry, (12) boiler house. Lower left: ancient Manchu tomb. Round trip for this mission was 2,150 miles, all but 90 of them over enemy territory.

MUKDEN
EAST
AIRFIELD

EAST MUKDEN Also taken on 14 June, this area is near North Mukden airfield. Key: (1) AA battery, (2) Manchuria Airplane Mfg. Co.—A/C assembly, (3) Mukden arsenal, (3a and 3c) explosive storage and probable shell loading, (3b) probable components loading plant, (4) Manchuria Iron Works, (5) machine tool plant, (6) ceramics plant. Aircraft count here exceeded any photographed at any single field by the 21st Squadron in Asia. They numbered 126.

Continued on next page

OKAYAMA Taken on 25 August, this covers a major Formosa target hit later by 20th Bomber Command B-29s. On first mission on 14 October, 106 B-29s hit Okayama A/C plant with 785.46 tons. All air strips in area were inoperable due to bomb damage, at least 50 aircraft on ground were destroyed or damaged. On second mission two days later Heito and other Formosa targets were hit by 69 B-29s. Of these, 32 hit Okayama, had no losses. Of 34 major buildings at target, all but two have now been destroyed.

TARGET AREA NO1
AIRCRAFT PLANT

SOUTH HANGAR &
BARRACKS AREA

EAST HANGAR
& ADMIN. AREA

UNDERGROUND
STORAGE

TARGET AREA NO. 2
OKAYAMA AIRDROME

1000   0   1000   2000

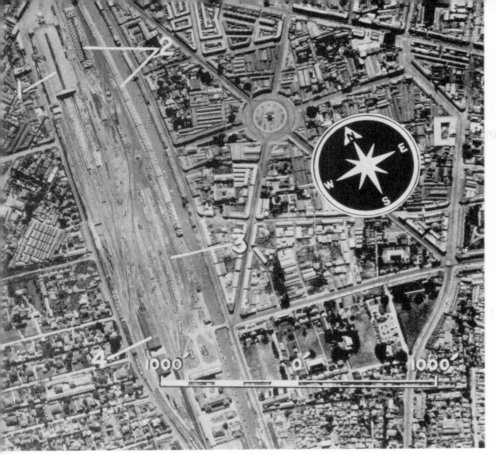

BANGKOK Above, excellent coverage of railyards in Thailand's capital shows (1) terminus station, (2) freight sheds, very poorly camouflaged in comparison to German methods, (3) railroad sidings, (4) locomotive sheds.

CORREGIDOR Below, first coverage of Philippines since 1942 shows on 12 May 1944 (1) Corregidor, (2) Caballo island, (3) Caballo bay, (4) Kindley Field, (5) Seaplane base, (6) north channel, (7) Bataan.

CAP ST. JACQUES Above, near Saigon in French Indo-China, this harbor was hit by 14th AF Liberators, four days before this picture was taken on 3 March. Big tanker is still burning from the attack.

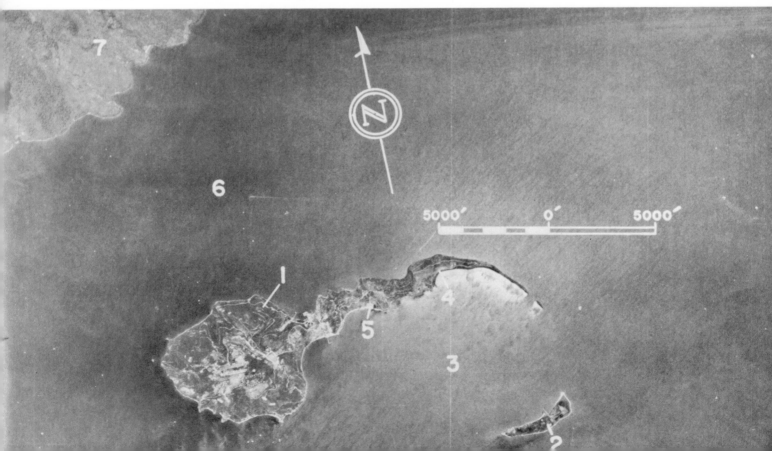

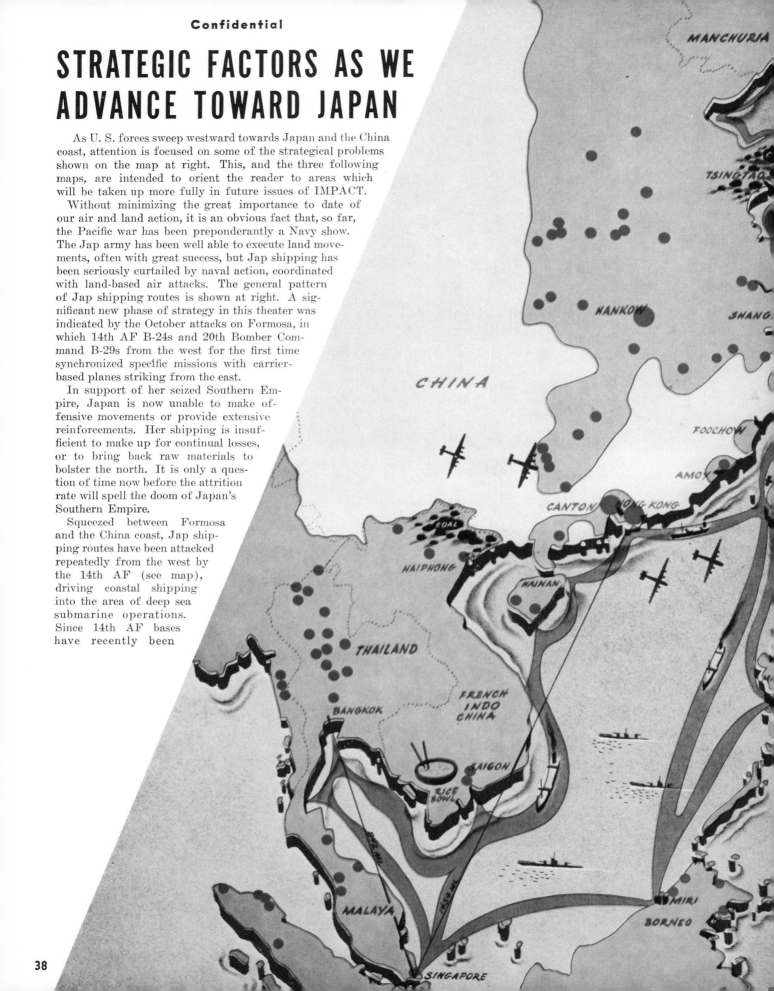

STRATEGIC FACTORS AS WE ADVANCE TOWARD JAPAN

As U. S. forces sweep westward towards Japan and the China coast, attention is focused on some of the strategical problems shown on the map at right. This, and the three following maps, are intended to orient the reader to areas which will be taken up more fully in future issues of IMPACT.

Without minimizing the great importance to date of our air and land action, it is an obvious fact that, so far, the Pacific war has been preponderantly a Navy show. The Jap army has been well able to execute land movements, often with great success, but Jap shipping has been seriously curtailed by naval action, coordinated with land-based air attacks. The general pattern of Jap shipping routes is shown at right. A significant new phase of strategy in this theater was indicated by the October attacks on Formosa, in which 14th AF B-24s and 20th Bomber Command B-29s from the west for the first time synchronized specific missions with carrier-based planes striking from the east.

In support of her seized Southern Empire, Japan is now unable to make offensive movements or provide extensive reinforcements. Her shipping is insufficient to make up for continual losses, or to bring back raw materials to bolster the north. It is only a question of time now before the attrition rate will spell the doom of Japan's Southern Empire.

Squeezed between Formosa and the China coast, Jap shipping routes have been attacked repeatedly from the west by the 14th AF (see map), driving coastal shipping into the area of deep sea submarine operations. Since 14th AF bases have recently been

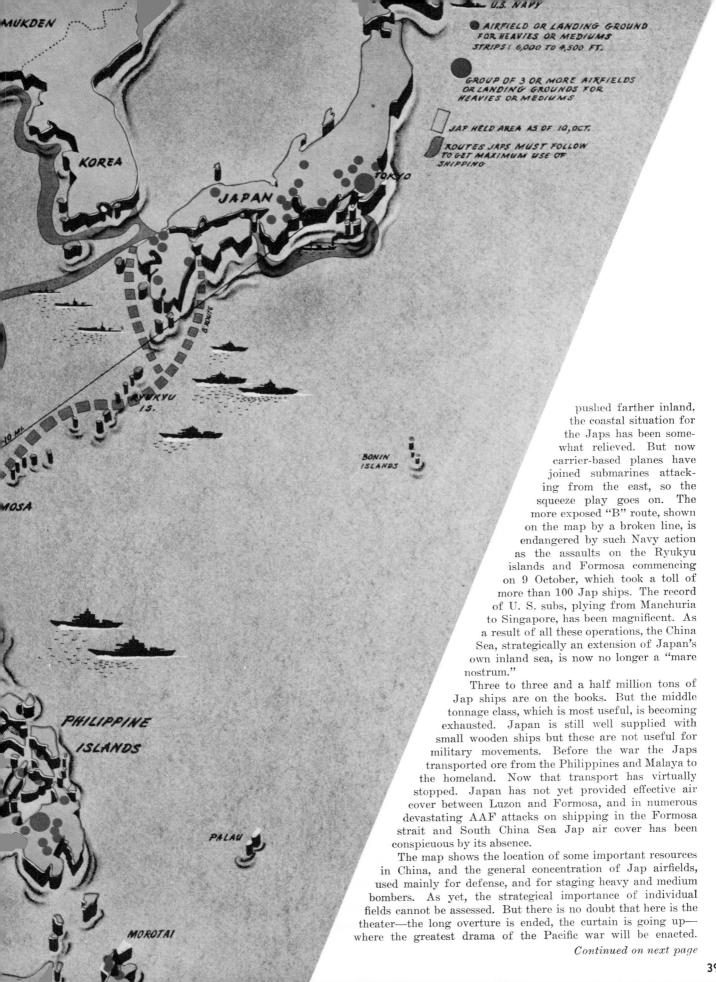

U.S. NAVY

● AIRFIELD OR LANDING GROUND
FOR HEAVIES OR MEDIUMS
STRIPS: 6,000 TO 4,500 FT.

● GROUP OF 3 OR MORE AIRFIELDS
OR LANDING GROUNDS FOR
HEAVIES OR MEDIUMS

☐ JAP HELD AREA AS OF 10, OCT.

▪ ROUTES JAPS MUST FOLLOW
TO GET MAXIMUM USE OF
SHIPPING

MUKDEN

KOREA

JAPAN

TOKYO

10 MI.

B ROUTE

RYUKYU
IS.

FORMOSA

BONIN
ISLANDS

PHILIPPINE
ISLANDS

PALAU

MOROTAI

pushed farther inland, the coastal situation for the Japs has been somewhat relieved. But now carrier-based planes have joined submarines attacking from the east, so the squeeze play goes on. The more exposed "B" route, shown on the map by a broken line, is endangered by such Navy action as the assaults on the Ryukyu islands and Formosa commencing on 9 October, which took a toll of more than 100 Jap ships. The record of U. S. subs, plying from Manchuria to Singapore, has been magnificent. As a result of all these operations, the China Sea, strategically an extension of Japan's own inland sea, is now no longer a "mare nostrum."

Three to three and a half million tons of Jap ships are on the books. But the middle tonnage class, which is most useful, is becoming exhausted. Japan is still well supplied with small wooden ships but these are not useful for military movements. Before the war the Japs transported ore from the Philippines and Malaya to the homeland. Now that transport has virtually stopped. Japan has not yet provided effective air cover between Luzon and Formosa, and in numerous devastating AAF attacks on shipping in the Formosa strait and South China Sea Jap air cover has been conspicuous by its absence.

The map shows the location of some important resources in China, and the general concentration of Jap airfields, used mainly for defense, and for staging heavy and medium bombers. As yet, the strategical importance of individual fields cannot be assessed. But there is no doubt that here is the theater—the long overture is ended, the curtain is going up— where the greatest drama of the Pacific war will be enacted.

Continued on next page

AS SHIP LOSSES MOUNT, JAPS RELY ON CHINA'S RAIL SYSTEM

With ship losses soaring, the Japs are forced to depend more on the rail system shown above to transport troops and supplies to armies in China, and to send home raw materials. Major rail arteries are shown by heavier tracks. These connect Manchuria, home of the Kwantung Army and its arsenals, with the vital Yangtze river route and with the iron and coal of North China. Another major line goes through Manchuria, down to the Korean port of Fusan, enabling Japs to use the relatively safe, short route across the Korean Strait to the homeland. Bomb bursts on map show how 14th AF has been ripping up rails in Southeastern China and blasting river traffic. As a result, many Jap troops have had to go by truck or by foot to fighting zones. Thus, the battle of supply lines in China, as in Europe, becomes a crucial part of our war strategy.

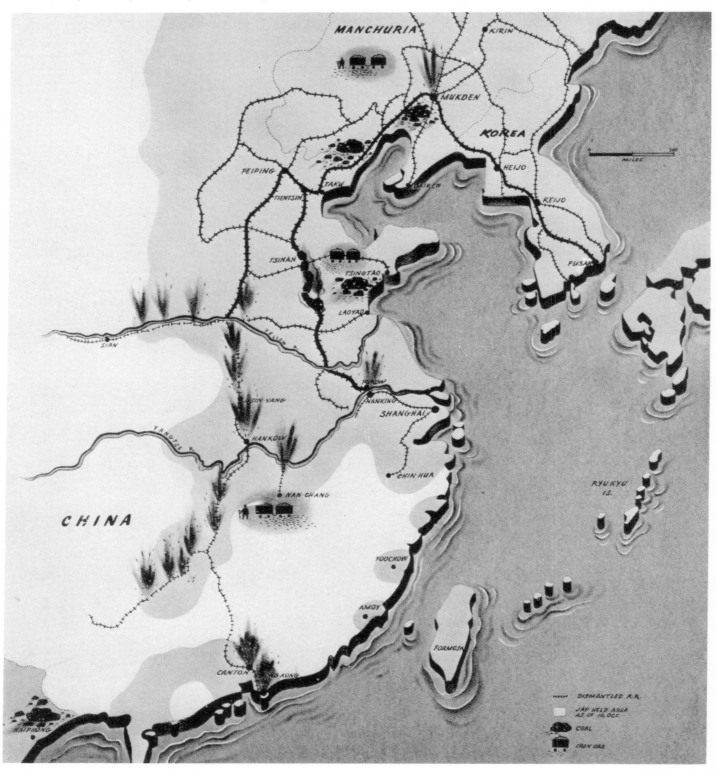

INDUSTRY MAY ROT FOR LACK OF MATERIAL

Above are indicated some principal Japanese industries, and three main areas where they are located. These may soon be rendered impotent, both by AAF bombs and because Jap shipping losses are depriving them of raw materials. Also, contributing to Japan's transportation nightmare is the fact that she depends heavily upon one major, over-burdened rail route, shown above. This tenuous backbone of land transport links coal and steel areas of the north and south with the big industrial and population centers of central Japan. It also serves ports of entry from the mainland, and via car ferry, connects with the northern island of Hokkaido, rich in coal and lumber. Coastal vessels carried the bulk of this traffic until Japan diverted ships to supply her crumbling empire.

FORMOSA: JAP BASTION AND SUPPLY BASE

Formosa is prized by the Japs as a supply base, as an aircraft staging and training center, as a bastion guarding Jap shipping lanes, as an air base for defense of China and the Philippines, and for its own natural resources. It produces, roughly, one-third of Japan's sugar, nine per cent of her copper, 15 per cent of her aluminum. Its harbors at Kiirun and Takao are useful to convoys for assembling and fueling.

For all these reasons, Formosa was pasted by B-29s and carrier-based planes in adroitly coordinated attacks in mid October. Main targets, and type of attack, are shown at right. Greatest damage was done at Okayama (page 36). But the No. 1 reason for blasting Formosa was to help isolate the Philippines in preparation for the historic event of 20 October.

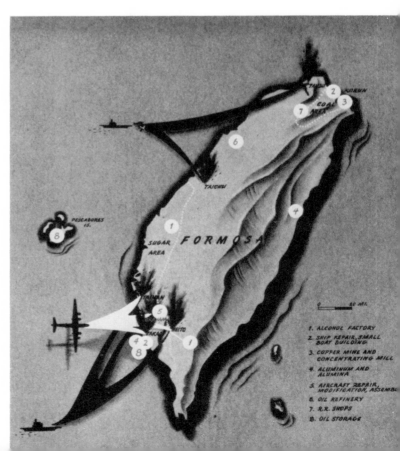

1. ALCOHOL FACTORY
2. SHIP REPAIR, SMALL BOAT BUILDING
3. COPPER MINE AND CONCENTRATING MILL
4. ALUMINUM AND ALUMINA
5. AIRCRAFT REPAIR, MODIFICATION, ASSEMBLY
6. OIL REFINERY
7. R.R. SHOPS
8. OIL STORAGE

MAP SHOWS WHERE PHILIPPINES TOOK PRE-INVASION POUNDING

GRAND STRATEGY UNFOLDS—WE ARE IN PHILIPPINES

The significance of strategic factors discussed on preceding pages was illuminated on 20 October when the latest step in our Far East strategy placed us back in the Philippines. Here was the pay-off for a series of seemingly unrelated operations: the neutralizing of Formosa by coordinated carrier-based and 20th Bomber Command attacks; the relentless war on Jap shipping by the 14th AF, FEAF, and the Navy; the attacks on Jap industry from Manchuria to Yawata. All of this, to be sure, was directed towards the final conquest of Japan. But at the same time these operations contributed definitely to the Philippine invasion.

For at least six weeks before the landing at Leyte, combined AAF and Naval action was concentrated specifically on pounding the Philippines. At left are shown the general areas where most of these attacks occurred. Planes and carriers are used on the map only to symbolize the type of attack (land- or carrier-based). All carrier-based attacks are by the Third Fleet, unless otherwise designated, and no action after 21 October is indicated. Numbers are keyed thus:

1. 1-6 Sept. Philippines on 1 September were bombed for first time since 1942 by 57 5th AF heavies of the FEAF, hitting targets in Davao area (IMPACT, Vol. 2, No. 10). Attacks were continued daily until 6 Sept., and thereafter intermittently. Attacks on Buayan airfield by B-25s began on 6 September.

2. Through September Jap shipping was continuously bombed near these targets by PBYs and FEAF B-24s.

LANDING BEACH AT LEYTE, NORTH OF DULAG, SHOWS TYPICAL JAP INSTALLATIONS. KEY: ABOVE, RIGHT.

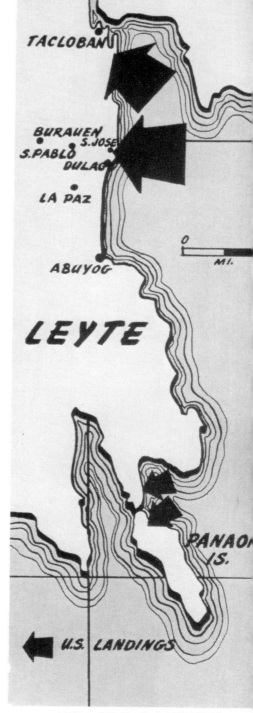

AREA OF U. S. LANDINGS

LANDING AREA at Leyte was photoed 14 to 16 September. By 25 October U. S. forces had won 25 miles of coast, and three airfields, at Tacolban, Dulag, and San Pablo.

3, 4. 12-14 Sept. At Catabato, Leyte and in the Visayas 486 Jap planes were destroyed —164 in the air, 322 on ground. Navy reported, "Enemy's non-aggressive attitude at Mindanao is incredible."

5. 20-21 Sept. Heavy attacks on Clark and Nichols fields, Manila harbor, and Cavite naval base, destroyed warehouses, railroad equipment, oil storage, harbor installations. More than 50 classified ships and one sub were sunk. 169 planes were shot down, 180 were damaged on ground.

6. 11 Oct. At Appari 10 to 15 aircraft were destroyed on ground. On 18 October 15 destroyed on ground at Laog.

7. 15-18 Oct. Our planes were aggressively intercepted by Zekes, Oscars and Tonys of which 80 to 90 were destroyed in air, 60 to 70 on ground. An extra 30 planes were shot down in the vicinity.

8. 20 Oct. FEAF, RAAF, units from 3rd and 7th Fleet, and Australian Naval Squadrons covered the Leyte assault.

9. 17-21 Oct. Striking first in the Luzon area, and then coming down to cover landing operations at Leyte, our planes shot down 77 enemy aircraft in air, and 117 on ground. 7th Fleet units at Leyte, Cebu and Panay also shot down six enemy aircraft on 20 October.

─────── **KEY TO ANNOTATIONS BELOW** ───────

⌀ AUTOMATIC AA POST (EMPTY)	ơ MACHINE GUN		ǫ OBSERVATION POST
⊾ ARTILLERY EMPLACEMENT	↙ RIFLE PIT OR FOXHOLE		⚓ AMMUNITION STORAGE
☗ COVERED ART. EMPLACEMENT	▣ COMMAND POST		⊞ TRENCH
◮ PILLBOX	⬱ SEARCHLIGHT		⏧ ANTI-TANK TRENCH

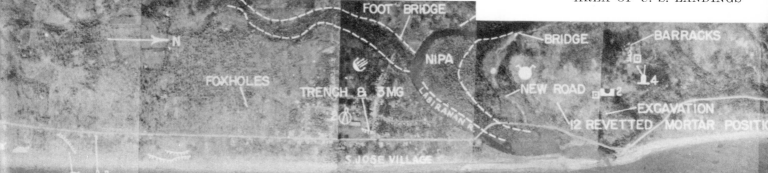

EACH OF BOTH LANDING AREAS COVERED ABOUT THREE MILES OF COAST. DATE OF PHOTO, 14-16 SEPTEMBER

IWO JIMA

While other air forces and the Navy make history elsewhere in the Far East, the 7th AF has concentrated on neutralizing the Bonins. One of its main targets is Iwo Jima, only 670 miles from Tokyo, and the only major air base between the Mariannas and Japan. After Navy air attacks in July, Iwo Jima on 10 August was hit for the first time by the 7th AF, which since then has bombed it almost daily. A 7th AF Intelligence officer comments, "If our B-24s were on Iwo Jima, they could blast Hirohito himself, and the Japs know it. On no other islands has there been such concerted effort to repair bomb damage. Since 1891, bats and Japs have been the only animals of any size on Iwo Jima. The bats got there first and will undoubtedly remain there last." Between 10 August and 19 September, to take a typical period, 288 sorties were flown over Iwo Jima and 627.46 tons dropped. Result: Iwo Jima is no longer an effective base.

JAP PLANES BURN ON IWO JIMA AIRFIELD DURING 7th AF ATTACK

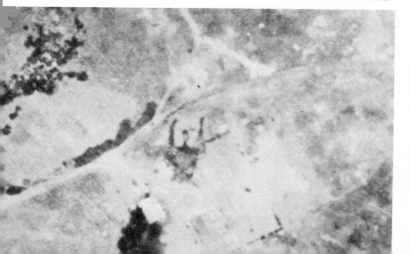

RADIO STATION was not only off the air but almost off the earth after bombing attack (below). B-24s met moderate but consistent fighter opposition from Iwo Jima's two airfields.

FUEL TANKS, storage area, and Jap planes north of Airfield No. 1 presented this tempting target for 7th AF bombs. Below: after attacks the same area is almost entirely obliterated.

BALL NOSE TURRET IS SET UP IN B-24 WITH CANVAS BAG FOR EMPTY CASES AND LINKS UNDERNEATH

B-24 GETS NEW NOSE

Future B-24s will have an Emerson 128 ball nose turret that will reduce maximum weight, provide better visibility for bombardier and navigator, and improve the plane aerodynamically. As a result of tests at Eglin field and recommendations by the AAF Board, first installations will be in airplanes going into production early in 1945.

During the recent tests at Eglin, several Liberators were rigged up with various nose-armament fixtures. One even had a B-17 nose built into it. The tests demonstrated the superiority of the Emerson 128 ball turret, electrically driven and mounting two .50 BAM guns, in the nose position of a B-24G. The cone of fire is 120°, and while this is slightly less than the present radius, it is regarded as sufficient. The gunner's field of view from the new turret is considered satisfactory, and he has room to wear winter flying equipment without discomfort.

An automatic centering device has been developed in the Emerson 128 which enables the pilot or co-pilot to return the turret to center position if gunner is injured. The gunner may then be removed and the guns fired by pilot or co-pilot.

The new armament reduces the weight of the plane by about 225 pounds. The ball turret increases navigator and bombardier visibility by making possible the new side windows seen in the picture above. The new nose turret contributes to better flight performance because it is aerodynamically cleaner than the older style A6B and A15 nose armament; its smooth curve permits better airflow around the nose, and there is no turbulence at the juncture of nose and fuselage, removing the necessity for bulkheads behind turrets. Normal cruising speed of the bomber is stepped up 10 miles per hour.

HEAD-ON VIEW shows flat-head screws which replace round type, cut down friction wear on felt-covered rubber wind seals.

1. **DIVING DOWN** in a coordinated attack on a B-29 are two Jap Tojos at Anshan, Manchuria. Here one Tojo com- ing in from two o'clock high and another from eleven o'clock high open fire simultaneously from approximately 1,000 yards.

2. **TOJOS CLOSE IN** to 300 yards, firing all the way. Ten per cent of the Jap attacks on this mission were coordinated, more than on all previous missions.

3. **BREAKAWAY** of Tojos is by sharp power dives, as B-29 continues on undamaged. On this mission most of the Jap attacks came from high frontal positions.

Superforts vs. Nips

With the 20th Bomber Command's B-29s becoming seasoned veterans, one thing is obvious: Jap fighters have as yet found no really effective method of attack. On the 21 August mission to Yawata, first time the Superforts met major opposition, 50-60 enemy fighters attacked from all directions with a low, frontal approach preferred. Only 72 per cent of the passes resulted in Jap gunfire, showing that Jap pilots were misjudging the B-29s' high speed and being thrown off by the bombers' evasive tactics. One B-29 was destroyed apparently by an air-to-air bomb, two more in a three-way collision with a Jap.

On the 8 September Anshan mission, and those subsequent, no B-29s are known to have been lost to enemy fighters. The two model sequences shown here are based on engagements during the 26 September Anshan mission in which an increase in coordinated and *high* frontal attacks was reported. On this mission, the enemy was able to fire in only 52 per cent of his passes.

1. **ANOTHER TYPE** of coordinated attack was by two Tojos, which are seen attacking from two o'clock low in trail.

The enemy pilots opened fire at 800 yards, the B-29 returned fire, but Jap planes failed to show any evidence of damage.

2. **ATTACKS PRESSED** to 50 yards by bold Japs, scored hits on the B-29 fuselage behind the radio operator's position.

3. **AS B-29 FIRES,** Tojos go into fast diving turn. The Japs make good use of cloud banks in many of their breakaways.

DRAMATIC RESCUE METHOD TESTED

AWAITING HOIST on 7 October 1944 is Pvt. Constantine Stiakatis. Pilot of plane was Lt. Norman S. Benedict. Electric winch in plane that plays out elastic rope according to pressure, reduces "g" force on the man being raised.

An agent who has been casing enemy positions on the ground in a Baltic forest or Pacific jungle keeps a rendezvous with a plane in a cleared space. A kit is dropped to him and he takes two telescopic poles out of it and sets them up, stringing a nylon loop between the tops. He snaps his special back-type chute harness to this loop and sits down, curling up like a hedgehog.

This man is now ready to be lifted into a plane by a new AAF technique for rescuing agents, prisoners, and stranded fliers. These photographs were taken during recent tests of the technique in this country.

The plane comes in for contact at 130 mph. Ten feet below and behind the wheels it trails a hook at the end of a wooden pole. This pole guides the tow-rope hook into the pick-up loop. The hook mechanism latches to the pick-up loop and then swings free of the guide pole on its elastic nylon rope, drawing the new passenger skyward as the plane pulls up at 35° angle. Two minutes and 45 seconds later, an electric winch has hauled him into the plane.

HE'S OFF, and no bouncing. Stiakatis was "guinea pig" in most recent of four tests with human beings. Weighted dummies and sheep were tried first. Ground observer says: "Subject at takeoff looks as though some strong man had suddenly lifted him in a chair four feet straight off the ground. Then suddenly he sails away and upward much as a glider does."

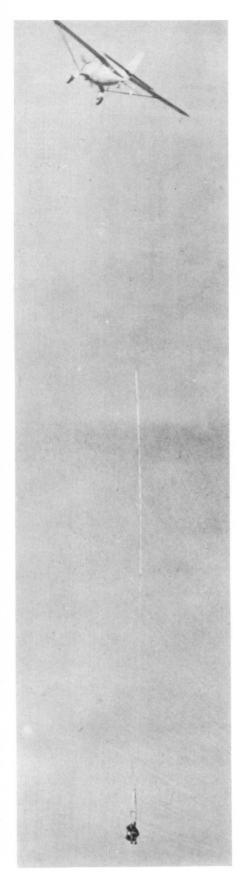

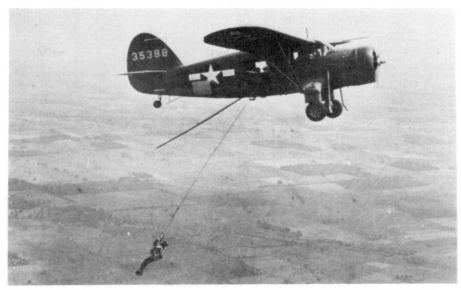

PREVIOUS TEST shows S/Sgt. H. C. Conway being reeled up to C-64. IMPACT cover photo shows earlier phase of Conway's test, at exact moment plane hooked into pick-up loop and a split-second before he was pulled upward.

CONWAY SHINNIES up guide pole, through slipstream, to plane. J-edged blades in front of fixed landing gear cut loop if plane is too low on pick-up, so plane's landing gear cannot get tangled in loop and cause injury to man waiting.

LEG STRAPS are still fastened. In a moment Stiakatis will undo them, wave arms and legs to reassure onlookers.

INTO PLANE at last, Conway is unhurt, unjarred, like other four human pick-ups. Project has been developed chiefly by Equipment Laboratory, ATSC, Wright Field, assisted by Aero Medical Lab., Parachute and Glider Branches.

NIGHT ATTACK ON U-BOAT

Dropping flares, an RAF Coastal Command plane, attacks a German sub from 75 feet. Depth charge can be seen exploding near the center of the picture.

IMPACT

ZEKE POKES AT 14th AF
B-24s OVER HONG KONG
See p. 10

DISTRIBUTION:
SQUADRONS

OFFICE OF THE
ASSISTANT CHIEF OF AIR STAFF, INTELLIGENCE
WASHINGTON, D. C.

Vol. 2   No. 12
DECEMBER, 1944

BALIKPAPAN — PLOESTI OF THE EAST INDIES, see p. 15

IMPACT
Contents
December, 1944

Confidential

During fire bomb attack on Isle de Cezembre near St. Malo on 31 August, a tactical reconnaissance plane of the 9th AF skims above towering smoke columns which indicate hits. Note fiery burst from bomb dropped by P-38, top, right.

FIRE BOMBS

Napalm fire bombs, first used in active combat in July, are now a standard and very successful AAF weapon in both European and Pacific theaters. Shown here are some of the most effective photographs yet obtained of fire bombs in action near St. Malo. (As discussed in IMPACT, Vol. II, No. 9, this bomb is simply a belly tank loaded with standard QM gasoline thickened with napalm jell, and equipped with an igniting mechanism.)

Fire bombs first hit St. Malo on 17 August. From the 9th AF, 36 P-38s, carrying two 165-gallon capacity tanks on each plane, were dispatched to attack the German-held citadel where Colonel von Aulock, "The Madman of St. Malo," tried to establish permanent residence. The Group Leader had just dropped his bombs, when the ground controller sent word that the citadel had surrendered, so the rest of the Group bombed the secondary target, the Isle de Cezembre. This small, heavily fortified island commanded the deep water channel to St. Malo.

Cezembre got its second baptism of napalm on 31 August (above), although meanwhile it had been hit by HE bombs dropped by B-26s of the 9th AF, and shelled by artillery from ship and shore. This time 56 P-38s did the job, and on the next day the island surrendered.

They Helped Blast Germans from the Isle de Cezembre guarding St. Malo

Investigation revealed that the island was provided with a series of underground shelters, magazine, command post, and control points. Dug into the rock, these were lined in some cases with reinforced concrete. They resisted penetration and there was no evidence of damage to walls or contents by HE bombs. The contents of one shelter were burnt out by napalm seeping through. About 300 prisoners were taken. They told their captors that the combined effect of the bombing was terrifying, especially the napalm. When the napalm invaded the shelter, they made no attempt to put out the fire, but evacuated. Every means of defense larger than machine guns was completely destroyed, and the island could easily have been taken by a landing party.

A report from the theater states, "It is felt that the Fire Bomb accomplished a certain definite portion of damage to personnel, equipment, and morale that was not accomplished by the use of HE. It is not to be construed, however, that this indicates the Fire Bomb would have accomplished this alone. Experience indicates that the Fire Bomb has a definite place when used in conjunction with HE, or on rubble and damage that is a result of HE bombing."

At right, sequence of four pictures shows development of napalm hit on Cezembre, 31 August. Note P-38 in top view.

Continued on page 4

Cezembre is a Dead Duck after Attacks

These two pictures show how Cezembre looked after combined AAF attacks. Above, still smoking from a napalm attack, is the crater-covered island, lying two miles off Dinard. At right is all that remains of one of six old, large French guns that were Cezembre's main defense. The other five were also destroyed. There were said, too, to be three AA guns. The mount of one was found in the valley. Apparently the Germans depended on these and on machine guns for defense against landing, as the big guns probably could not be depressed enough to cover a landing. There seemed to be no demolition of guns—it being hardly necessary, though the Germans did destroy papers, radio, stores.

4   **Confidential**

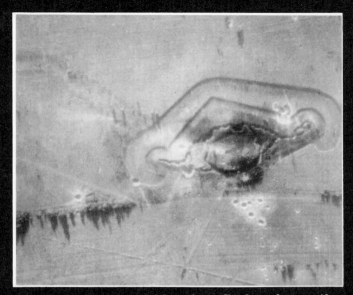

Fire bombs dropped by 9th AF P-47s on 28 September sear bomb-scarred Metz fort. Right, after strike.

Forts on Siegfried Line, 50 miles east of Metz, are bombed on 9 October by B-26s. Right, after strike.

METZ

How 9th AF fighter-bombers and bombers worked in close cooperation with General Patton's troops pushing towards Metz is shown above. These fortified positions have seen many sieges. Fortified by Romans, sacked by Attila, rebuilt for Louis XIV, and for Napoleon III, they now have been battered by a potent combination of napalm and HE bombs, and are falling one by one to U. S. forces.

German troop train met five 8th AF P-47s on curve at Gisors, France.

IN THE WAKE OF

"The enemy has succeeded, by concentrated and ceaseless attacks from the air, in disorganizing our supply to such an extent and to cause such losses of railway rolling stock and vehicles that supply has become a serious problem."

In a memorandum to his troops last June, Field Marshal von Rundstedt, German commander-in-chief in the West, thus described the tremendously effective role that fighter-bombers play in isolation of a battlefield. The pictures from France on these two pages are further evidence of the great work that has been and is being performed by 8th, 9th, 12th and 15th AF fighter-bombers.

Aftermath of the attack at Gisors 18 Aug., shown at left and below, on a German troop train, is a classic example of effective dive bombing and strafing. Here the target was protected by a deep curving cut through a hill and in addition was well camouflaged by a thick covering of branches and straw. Yet all bombs were accurately

Camouflage with branches didn't fool P-47 pilots.　　*Ten 500-lb. bombs and fancy strafing did the job.*

Searchlights on the train were demolished also.　　*Fire completed devastation after fighters departed.*

FIGHTER ATTACKS

placed; strafing only polished off the job.

Imagine 400 Hun fighters racing up and down the Pennsylvania Railroad between Trenton and Philadelphia, completely unopposed by U. S. interceptors, and shooting up everything in sight. On 24 Oct. P-47s and P-51s of the 8th AF did just exactly this in the Brunswick-Hanover area when they beat up 150 locomotives, destroying 61, and in addition accounted for 346 railway cars destroyed and 119 damaged. In another dissection of the German rail system, on 9 Nov. near Saarbrucken 8th AF Mustangs knocked off 61 more locomotives and 227 railroad cars of the rapidly dwindling Nazi supply.

Fighter-bombing is highly dangerous due to the accuracy and concentration of German automatic weapons and small-arms fire. Losses are not light. Therefore, the achievement of pilots who must pound in there at low level day after day, certain they'll be shot at, is a truly heroic one.

8th AF P-38 strafers blew munitions train off face of the earth here.

Marshaling yard at Compiegne, France, was of small value to the Germans after visit by 8th AF P-47s.

CHINA AIR BASE RETREAT

The vigorous Japanese advance through Hunan and Kwangsi provinces which began last spring and inexorably keeps pushing the Chinese armies back, has compelled the 14th AF to demolish and evacuate several of its important bases in that region. Fighters and bombers carry on with their missions as the installations are being destroyed: the planes land by the glare of burning buildings, take off through rolling black smoke, and fly over roads choked with refugees for one more thrust at the Jap lines before the final retreat to another base. Airstrips are blown up last.

This has been the story at station after station: it began with Hengyang and Lingling last summer, continued with Kweilin and Tanchuk early in the fall, and with Liuchow in November. Photos on this page show destruction of installations at two of the three Kweilin airfields in mid-September (the third remained in use till the Japs crowded painfully close in October). On the opposite page is an unusually graphic picture of Tanchuk after it was evacuated.

Above, Chinese prepare to bury bomb in runway.

Good earth is gouged deep by 1,000-lb. G.P. bomb.

Incendiary bullet is fired at gas drum inside building.

Kweilin hostel after incendiary bullet treatment.

Tanchuk air base, West river, Kwangsi Province, photographed by 21st Photo Reconnaissance Squadron after 14th AF evacuated airfield in September. Following ground demolition process, base was bombed by departing planes.

SHIPS BURNING

Smoke pours from Kowloon docks and Jap shipping burns in Hong Kong harbor during 16 Oct. attack by 14th AF.

14th HITS HONG KONG AND JAP BRIDGES

Japanese merchant ships were crowded into Hong Kong harbor on 16 October, a time when the waters of the South China sea were too hot for the comfort of enemy vessels. Then the 14th AF suddenly made Hong Kong harbor hot: 28 B-24s and 12 B-25s came roaring in to bomb Jap shipping and the great Kowloon docks.

The picture above, like the one on IMPACT'S cover and the three at the top of the next page, testify to the success of the attack. The Kowloon docks are among the largest in any part of the Pacific, and those selected for the 16 October mission (on the smoking peninsular spur in the photo above) consist of three drydocks with respective dimensions of 680' x 90', 435' x 60' and 265' x 40', two repair slips 225' x 30', four building ways 450', launching slip 175' x 25', six cranes, and miscellaneous buildings. These drydocks can be used for all types of repair and refitting, and for the building of ships up to 10,000 tons. The

Liberators dropped 294 x 500-pound G.P. bombs from 17,000 feet, 77 percent of them in the target area (see photos at top of next page). The B-25s came in at low level and hit the harbor shipping (observe boats on fire in picture above). Two vessels confirmed as sunk totalled approximately 8,600 tons, while eleven more ships visibly damaged represented some 40,000 additional tons. These figures do not include the dock area, where bombs sent a 270' ship under water and probably damaged several others, among them three 190' ships. Thirty-five fighters, P-40s and P-51s, served as escort and met with little opposition.

The 14th again effectively attacked Kowloon docks several times in November, and has continued to hammer Jap targets at widely dispersed points on the Asiatic mainland. The two pictures at the bottom of the next page show attacks in French Indo-China, where the 14th has repeatedly cut the vital railroad line from Saigon to the north.

Confidential

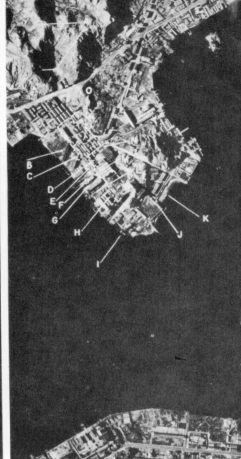

270' SHIP SUNK BY DIRECT HITS

NEAR MISSES ON 420' PASSENGER CARGO SHIP

Kowloon attack effectiveness is revealed in three photos above. First shows strike on 16 October. Second is an earlier picture with bomb plot overlaid subsequent to the attack. Third picture, made on 17 October reconnaissance, indicates damage as follows: (a) no damage by 10 bombs 2,000' off target, (b) probable damage to 400' vessel in westernmost drydock, (c) middle section of pattern shop smashed, (d) pattern shop building almost totally destroyed, (e) direct hit on east end of boiler shop, (f) middle part of storage building nicked, (g) probable damage to 175' vessel in dry-dock, (h) machine shop slightly damaged, (i) 270' cargo vessel sunk beneath crane, (j) 35' section of wall knocked out, (k) probable damage to 280' beached hulk, (l) black-smith shop hit and forge shop destroyed, (m) corner of pattern shop crushed, (n) direct hit on west end of foundry, (o) several buildings destroyed in the barracks area.

Railroad bridge over Dai Giang river in northern French Indo-China is neatly pinpointed by 14th AF Liberators.

Three Libs of 14th AF, bombing at 200 ft., destroyed one pier of bridge on 8 Sept. attack at Hué, French Indo-China.

Captured Oscar MK. I

No matter how much Allied fighter pilots learn from actual combat, they gain an even greater advantage over the enemy if they have the opportunity to fly captured pursuit planes in mock combat trials against our front-line fighters. In the model sequences shown on these pages it is possible to observe some of the results of preliminary combat trials flown in Australia between the type 1 F Oscar 2A and a P-47D-23. *(Distances between planes in these photos have been reduced because of space limitations. Results of the maneuvers demonstrated were essentially the same at altitudes of 10,000 feet and below.)*

The trials were made at 5,000′, 10,000′, and 20,000′. The Oscar was flown by Lt. C. F. Whistler, and the P-47 at altitudes of 5,000′ and 10,000′ was flown by Lt. A. V. Jackson who has had experience with Japanese fighters. Lt. W. H. Strand, with 450 combat hours in P-47s and experience against Jap pilots, flew the Thunderbolt at 20,000′.

Of the trials Lt. Whistler, pilot of the Oscar, reports:

"On takeoff I got 38″ Hg. and 2,600 rpm with the prop control a little back of full forward. The fuel pressure flickered back and forth as it always does on takeoff. It had little tendency to swing to the left and was easy to correct with slight rudder pressure.

"At both 5,000′ and 10,000′ I pulled up in a hammerhead stall and the set-up was the same for both altitudes. The airspeed was below 50 mph at the time I fell off to the right and the P-47 overran me and I could drop on his tail for a short burst before he could dive away.

"At 10,000′ I intended to loop at about 190 but I kept waiting for the P-47 to close up until I was doing 240 mph in a slight dive before I started my loop. I came out doing about 200 mph within firing range of the P-47. If he had not followed me so far into the loop, I think he could have been out of range before I completed the loop."

Of the same maneuver the P-47 pilot, Lt. Jackson, says:

"If the P-47 pulled up firing until 200 mph was reached,

1. **Oscar pulls up** into a hammerhead stall from 190 IAS while P-47 holds him in sights long enough to hit him.

2. **P-47 overruns** Oscar as Jap plane's airspeed falls off to 50 mph. Thunderbolt kicks off to right to regain speed.

3. **Complete advantage** then is held by Oscar as he drops onto P-47's tail to get in burst before making breakaway.

1. **Oscar loops** at 240 mph, P-47's cruising speed. Thunderbolt pulls into vertical stall, unable to follow through.

is Flown against P-47D

then dropped its nose and ran away, it could be away from Oscar before he could pull up into a firing position within range. In the P-47's loop it pulled away on the dive and looped far above the Oscar. It seemed that the Oscar could not follow in the large arc of the P-47's loop."

Characteristic of almost all Jap pursuit planes, the Oscar has a terrifically sharp rate of turn at low and medium altitudes. Lt. Whistler states, "The P-47 could fire at me but would have a big deflection shot. On the second pass by the P-47 I turned to the right. My turn didn't seem as tight as ones to the left, but the Oscar's advantage is as good in the right turn as it is to the left. My airspeed dropped off to about 140 mph during these turning maneuvers."

Discussing the same tight turns at 20,000' the Oscar pilot says that at an IAS of 175 he started a steep turn to the left with the P-47 about 250 yards astern. By tightening his turn more as his airspeed dropped, he caused the P-47 to pass the Oscar by the time it had turned only 150°. Lt. Whistler reversed his turn in the Oscar as the P-47 continued to turn, pulled up, and would have barely been able to get in a head-on shot at the Thunderbolt.

Lt. Jackson flew the Oscar at 20,000'. He reports:

"The Oscar and P-47 aren't in the same league at 20,000'. The P-47 with its 230 mph cruising speed, moves rapidly away from the Oscar's 170 at that altitude.

"The Oscar is practically hopeless at 20,000' or above."

Of the trials at 20,000', Lt. Strand, in the P-47, reports that the Thunderbolt is much faster than the Oscar. He recommends use of high IAS on the P-47 in order to gain an altitude advantage over the Oscar, because the P-47 can climb right away from the Jap plane with a shallow rate of climb. At 20,000' the Oscar begins to lose its airspeed, and the P-47 is just beginning to get its maximum qualities. Lt. Strand does not recommend looping the P-47 with an Oscar in combat, because the Jap will complete his loop at such low airspeed that the P-47 cannot follow him through.

1. **Oscar cruises** at 25" Hg. with 2,050 rpm at 185 IAS as P-47 starts run from 1,000 yds. above and behind.

2. **Diving** slightly to a position about 400 yards behind Oscar, P-47 has Jap plane squarely in sights briefly.

3. **90° of bank** is obtained by Oscar before P-47 can start turn giving only 1½ seconds lead at extreme deflection.

2. **Thunderbolt stalls,** falls forward to recover as Oscar continues around on arc of loop, bores in towards P-47.

3. **Before P-47** can regain speed, Oscar pulls onto his tail within range. P-47's loop has far greater arc and speed.

GORONTALO SURPRISE
5th AF Bombs Celebes Harbor

Typical of the day by day destruction of Jap shipping and shore installations in the N.E.I. is the attack on Gorontalo on the northern neck of the main Celebes island, illustrated here in a sequence of three pictures. The attack was made on 16 September by 14 B-25s escorted by 11 P-38s of the 5th AF. Striking swiftly at low level, the Mitchells achieved complete surprise.

Not a shot was fired from the ground. No enemy planes intercepted. Terrific explosions resulted. The entire area was left in flames which were still burning after midnight with smoke to 9,000 feet and explosions still rocking the area. Targets across the river from the warehouses were further bombed and more fires started during a mission that night by two B-24s and a PBY.

Over Gorontalo warehouses a B-25, followed by another, drops 2 bombs.

Warehouses are left in flames. Below, two of the attackers turn homeward, leaving a smoking Jap tanker.

EAST INDIES OIL

Liberators of 13th and 5th AF fly through inferno caused by 10 October strike on Balikpapan refineries.

OPENING BLOWS ARE AIMED AT A MAJOR SOURCE OF JAP FUEL

In terms of estimated 1944 consumption, the East Indies supply more than 85 percent of Japan's aviation gasoline, and more than 75 percent of her fuel oil.

These figures explain why since 30 September oil targets in the Netherlands East Indies have begun to receive some of the same concentrated AAF hellfire that reduced German liquid fuel output by more than 75 percent in six months.

Japan's need for N.E.I. fuel oil is particularly acute. Total 1944 Jap requirements are estimated at forty million barrels, and the total production is forty-two million. Only ten million are produced in Japan's Inner Zone, the balance coming from the Netherlands East Indies.

"In this tight situation," quoting directly from an August report prepared by AC/AS, Intelligence, "eliminating N.E.I. fuel oil would curtail operations of the Japanese Navy and part of the Japanese merchant fleet. Any serious curtailment of N.E.I. fuel oil could be expected to have direct effects, though such effects would not be critical until there had been a serious curtailment of a fuel oil stockpile currently estimated at eight months' supply."

On the next two pages is an account of the first heavy AAF blows at East Indies petroleum production, aimed at Balikpapan, one of five main N.E.I. production areas and source of an estimated 35 percent of Jap fuel supply.

Ground view of Balikpapan taken in 1940 shows harbor and view over greater part of refinery.

LONGEST B-24 MISSIONS IN SWPA SMASH OIL PLANTS AT BALIKPAPAN

On at least two counts the 13th AF mission against Balikpapan on 30 September was history-making. It was the first heavy strike against strategic Jap targets in the South Pacific. It was the longest SWPA mission—2,500-mile round trip—ever flown by Liberators in formation.

Called the "Ploesti of the East Indies," Balikpapan bears much the same relation to Japan as the great Rumanian oil refinery did to Germany. Balikpapan is Japan's largest refinery in the N.E.I., with a capacity of roughly four million barrels of crude oil. Now it is believed to be the only N.E.I. refinery for lubricating oils, and it supplies much needed aviation gasoline for the Jap air force in the SWPA. Crudes from SE Borneo, Taraban, Boela and East Java are processed here, stored in the big tank farm, or shipped by tankers. Destruction of this plant would have not only an almost immediate effect on Japan's operations in this theater, but would seriously weaken her entire Philippine and Empire defenses.

Balikpapan's main plants *(see far right)* are the Pandansari and Edeleanu refineries, and the paraffin works. These had been bombed before, but the Japs made quick repairs and work continued, evidently under the assumption that their distance from our bases guaranteed immunity from all except token raids.

This assumption proved to be very wrong.

Our concentrated attacks began on 30 September by 69 Liberators of the 13th AF and 90th Bomb Group in the 5th AF. Fighter interception was "vicious," and continued to be so during later missions. We destroyed seven fighters, with nine probables. Eleven of our Libs were holed, and we lost two.

Japs strafed our crews as they bailed out, even engaging one man with a wing tip.

A second strike by 40 Libs on 3 October scored scattered hits on the refineries, and started huge fires. A theater report states, "Arriving over the target, the planes were met by intense AA and no interception. As the ships turned back, 40-odd Zeros fell on the giant bombers like vultures. Seven bombers were shot down by AA and Zeros. Three more dropped out on the long trip home. We downed three Zeros. Our planes were under fire from the time they reached the coast, over the target, and on the way out. Interception lasted over an hour. It is strictly a suicide run."

But during the next two strikes the picture brightened. They varied from the first two strikes in three respects: (1) employment of two bombing altitudes, (2) *use of fighter escort at extreme long range*, and (3) degree of destruction attained. On 10 October three groups of 5th AF B-24s led the attack from 11,000 feet, and two groups of the 13th AF dropped from about 20,000 feet. The Japs dropped aerial phosphorous bombs, as usual, and made the very rare achievement of a direct hit on a Liberator cockpit, causing it to explode in mid air. The strike of 14 October again was led by three 5th AF groups, followed by two from the 13th. How we licked the Jap fighter problem is best told by the figures for these two missions. We destroyed 76 enemy aircraft, and lost five bombers and six fighters of our own. In addition to a good deal of miscellaneous damage, the paraffin and lubricating oil works were crippled, Pandansaru was disabled temporarily, at least, and the Edeleanu refinery was completely knocked out.

Paraffin Refinery, spewing black smoke, was hit by 75 percent of bombs dropped by 13th AF on its successful 10 October strike.

Cracking Plant, secondary target, was hit on 10 October when smoke from paraffin plant hid primary target, Pandansari.

N

BARRACKS
(POS 25MM)

B

B

KG. BAROE

B

B

B

B

CABLE OR
PIPE LINE

R-2

POSSIBLE GUN
POSITIONS U/I

BLDGS.
DESTROYED

LOGS

PANDANSARI
REFINERY

SAWMILL

PIER 8

F/P BASE

2-0

4-0
U/C

BALIKPAPAN

2 F/P'S

NEW
ROAD

EDELEANU
PLANT

NEW JETTY
7A

PANTJOER
TANK FARM

BAY

PIER 7

PIER 6

PARAFFIN
REFINERY

PLATEAU

TANK

PIER 5

FOX TARE ABLE
(6360 G.T.)

TANK
FARM
NEW

NEW JETTY

WORKSHOPS

CAMOUFLAGED
LOG

NEW

NEW JETTY

NEW

PIER 4

OLD WRECK

OLD
REFINERY

PIER 3

PIER 2

PIER 1

K.P.M. WHARF
(REPAIRED)

CRACKING
PLANT

CLEARED &
REPAIRED

2-2

ROAD

B

6-6

P. BABI

Okayama gets concentrated bombing by B-29s 14 Oct.

B-29 FIELD DAY
Japs Lose Big Formosa Aircraft Plant

At right is blunt proof, if any is needed, that our B-29s now hit hard and heavy. It is the big Jap aircraft assembly, modification, and repair plant at Okayama on Formosa taken a few days after three coordinated attacks: one by the Navy, which concentrated on the aircraft and hangar area, and two on the main plant area by the 20th Bomber Command. These 20th B.C. attacks, closely timed with carrier-based strikes, helped pave the way for the Philippine invasion in mid October.

Following on the heels of the Navy strike, 103 B-29s from the 20th B.C. struck at the big target on 14 October. No fighters intercepted, and we lost no planes to enemy action. A follow-up attack of only 33 planes over the target on 16 October was enough to finish the job. This time about 35 Jap fighters showed up, attacked 26 of our planes, but did not shoot any down. Nine aerial attacks with phosphorus type bombs were made by the enemy without damage to our aircraft. Total tonnage dropped on both missions was about 850 tons of HE and incendiary bombs. Now Okayama's plant, with some million square feet of floor space gutted, is no longer a key unit in enemy operations south of Japan.

At Okayama aircraft plant, 43 out of 80 buildings were destroyed by B-29 attack on 14 October. Two days later, after second attack, only six small buildings remained intact.

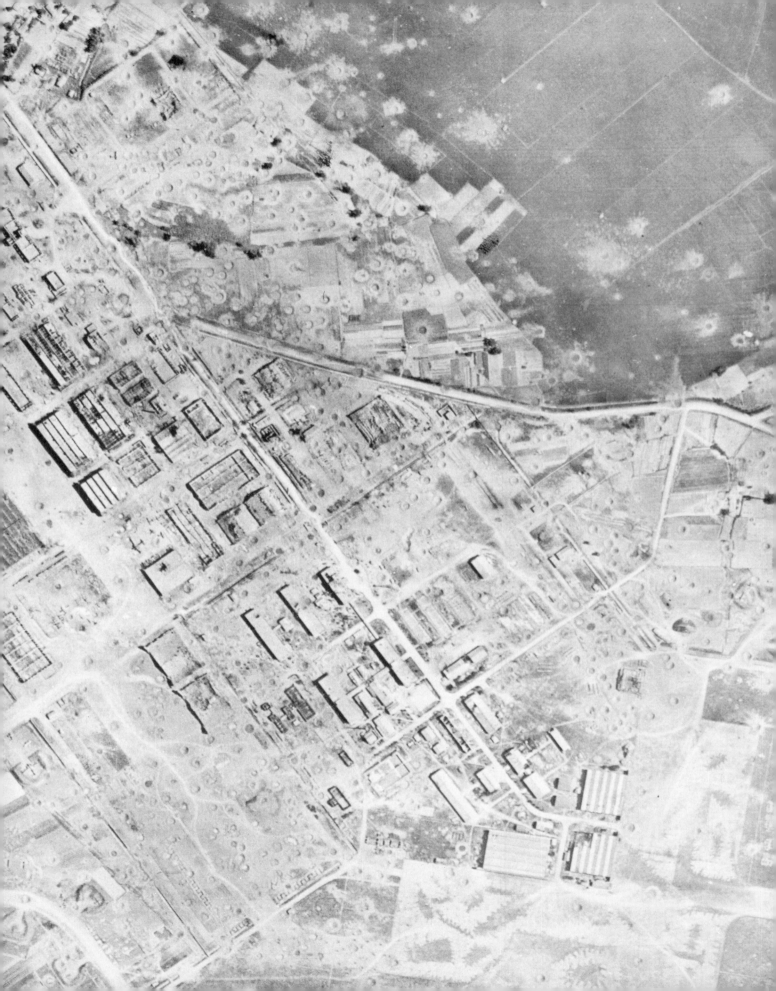

Over Debrecen, Hungary, on 21 Sept., this B-17 received a direct hit by heavy flak during bomb run on military traffic

ALMOST CUT IN TWO, FORT GETS HOME
Pilot on First Mission Flies It 520 Miles without Controls

"The-Swoose-Cannot-Fly?" was the name of a B-17 famous early in the war. Here are pictures of another Fort, equally deserving of fame, whose name could well be "How-in-Hell-Can-It-Fly?" Yet, fly it did, all the way from Hungary back to its base in Italy where it landed successfully.

In a bit of piloting that would have done a veteran proud, the landing was accomplished by 2nd Lt. G. M. Miller of the 2nd Bomb Gp., on his first mission as first pilot. He had previously flown 22 combat missions as co-pilot. Here is what Maj. Gen. Nathan F. Twining, Commanding 15th AF, says about it:

"While over the target, a direct hit by heavy flak exploded in the waist and almost blew the aircraft apart. One waist gunner and tail gunner were killed, the radio operator and other waist gunner were wounded. As the rudder cables were severed and the elevator controls hopelessly damaged by the explosion, the B-17 immediately went out of control and lost altitude into the clouds. Recovery was effected and flight continued in the clouds to avoid losing further altitude. Directional control was maintained by use of the outboard engines and altitude was controlled by increase or decrease of engine power.

"Lt. Miller flew the B-17 520 miles over enemy territory and across the Adriatic sea to its home field. While coming in for a landing, an engine began to cut out at an altitude of 300 feet, but Lt. Miller managed to retain control and a perfect landing was made on a crash strip beside the runway. In spite of a smooth touchdown, the fuselage crumpled and fell apart at the waist before No. 38078 could be brought to a stop and taxied to its position on the line.

"This is an outstanding example, not only of the ability of our heavy bombers to withstand battle damage, but also of the skill and presence of mind of our air crews in carrying through their missions to a successful conclusion in the face of opposition, casualties, and difficulties in the air."

Incredible damage is seen below, at left.

This One Got Back, Too

A direct hit by flak clipped off the nose of this 8th AF B-17 over Cologne, Germany, on 15 October, killing the bombardier. The pilot's account follows:

"As soon as I recovered from the shock of the explosion I found all four engines running and flight controls operating satisfactorily. Numbers 2 and 3 props were hitting the dangling nose guns, but this soon ceased.

"Upon making our base, because of damage, I made a high approach, power on with partial flaps. This killed excess airspeed, making it possible to land reasonably short. I applied brakes when speed had slowed sufficiently and when the brakes did quit, we stopped safely just off runway."

AAF COMES UP WITH SINGLE-TAIL B-24

XB-24N is Lighter, Has Improved Stability and New Armament

A close look at the pictures on these two pages will show you that the B-24N, going into production early in 1945, is not just an old-type Liberator with a new tail, but an entirely redesigned airplane. With the new features, the AAF expects to increase operational performance by a reduction of weight and drag. Pilot, navigator, and bombardier will have far better visibility, an additional 600 horse power will be available for take-off, and armament revisions will greatly improve effectiveness of the plane's fire power.

This aircraft is the result of three years of experimenting with variations of the Liberator. It has long been realized that the twin-fin empennage lacks sufficient directional stability in the event of power failure on one side. After numerous tests, a satisfactory single-fin tail assembly was developed. A variation of this was adapted by the Navy for the PB4-Y2.

The major design changes in the B-24N incorporate the Emerson 128 nose turret (shown in last month's IMPACT), the model A-3F lightweight upper turret, and a lightweight version of the Motor Products -5 tail turret. The plane will also probably utilize one of several proposed barbette gun mounts, designed to replace the lower ball turret and the hand-held waist gun. The Motor Products proposal illustrated in the lower right hand picture on the opposite page consists of hydraulically operated, remotely controlled barbettes; the gunner's sighting station (also shown in the photo) is located at the present waist-gun position. The installation, which would reduce the drag and effect a saving in weight of approximately 700 pounds, covers the fields of fire now in the range of the guns to be replaced.

The R1830-75 engines provide 150 additional horse power apiece and, with the turbo flight hoods, should account for a definite increase in speed and operational ceiling, plus a greater margin of safety on the take-off. Simplified communications equipment will reduce the over-all weight about 200 pounds. A thermal de-icing system for wings and empennage also provides cabin heat. The instrument panel and control pedestal have been completely redesigned, and the pilot's canopy has bullet-resisting glass in the windshield. There are emergency escape hatches for pilot and co-pilot and another over the rear bomb bay.

Oblique shows the current type B-24J

Flight picture of XB-24N shows high, single fin of new tail assembly, altered canopy, and Emerson 128 nose turret.

Plane has been undergoing operational performance and suitability tests at Wright Field, soon moves to Eglin Field.

with the familiar twin-fin empennage.   *New XB-24N stands by for contrast with J-type Liberator at the left.*

Tail view of XB-24N shows Bell power-boost mount which will be replaced by lightweight Motor Products -5 tail turret.

Drawing shows proposed barbette gun mount as it would look when installed on each side of new type Lib's fuselage.

V-2

From the day that Allied Intelligence first began to fit together bits of information about the monster German rocket which was to level London, the truth about V-2 has persistently proved more fantastic than the rumors. It has grown in size from a supposed twenty-odd feet to a confirmed 45 feet 10 inches. Its maximum velocity is now known to exceed 3.500 miles an hour. It soars to a height of 58 miles into the lofty calm of the ionosphere, and it can be launched practically anywhere.

The huge sites in the Pas de Calais (IMPACT, Vol. II, No. 9) are now known not to be connected with launching. The typical launching site proves to be nothing more than a widened spot in a road large enough to park a few trucks. A permanent concrete slab is imbedded here, and the rocket brought up on a large dolly which upends it on a low firing table placed on the slab. After lengthy computations and adjustments, the rocket is filled with fuel, and its instruments checked. Everybody then departs to a safe distance and it is started up. wobbling slowly into the air trailing a cloud of smoke.

Although it contains radio equipment, this is believed to be for the purpose of monitoring gyros, which control the flight of the rocket along a preselected trajectory, after it has gathered sufficient speed to fly a true course.

Rocket is launched after being placed in vertical position (left) on firing block and fueled up from tank trucks containing liquid oxygen and alcohol (main fuels) and hydrogen peroxide (fuel for driving turbines).

Continued on next page

V-2 craters average 35 ft. across, 15 ft. deep, but are sometimes 75 by 30 ft. as pictured above and below. Terrific speed at impact causes this.

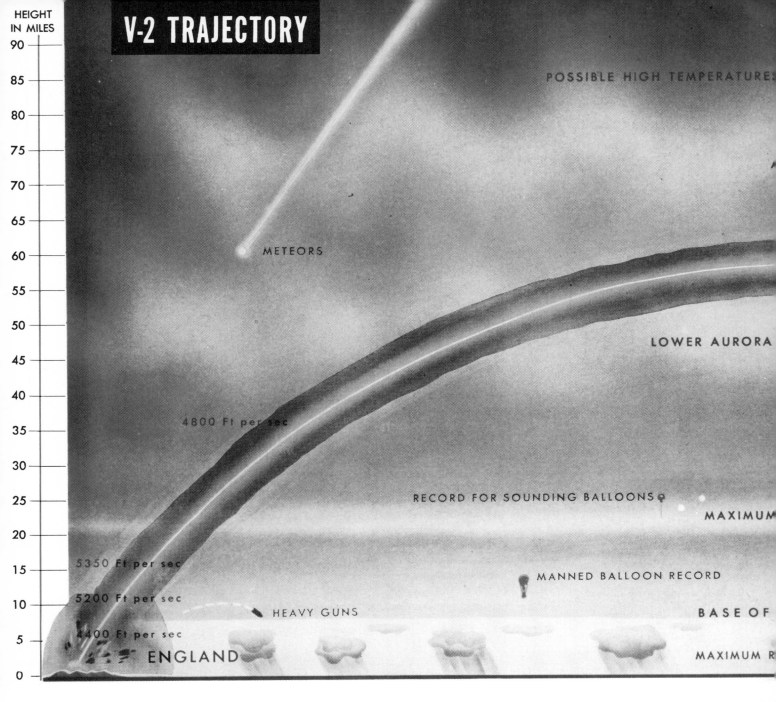

V-2 TRAJECTORY

HEIGHT IN MILES

90
85
80
75
70
65
60
55
50
45
40
35
30
25
20
15
10
5
0

POSSIBLE HIGH TEMPERATURES

METEORS

LOWER AURORA

4800 Ft per sec

RECORD FOR SOUNDING BALLOONS

MAXIMUM

5350 Ft per sec

MANNED BALLOON RECORD

5200 Ft per sec

HEAVY GUNS

BASE OF

4400 Ft per sec

ENGLAND

MAXIMUM R

Elliptical earthwork at Peenemunde is where rockets are tested. Shown are V-2 (A), cranes (B), assembly shop (C).

RANGE, SPEED OF V-2 POSE HUGE PRO

Two things are noteworthy about V-2. First, its awesome size and speed are not true indices of its efficiency as a weapon. Actually, it is comparable to the less spectacular V-1 in destructive power and accuracy. Second, and despite the foregoing, it should not be overlooked that V-2 is a bold and brilliant engineering experiment. Never has man fired a projectile so far, or so fast, or so high. The construction problems alone are formidable, considering the enormous stresses and changes in temperature encountered during flight. Range and directional control are even more complicated. Consider the following. V-2 takes off in an uneasy wobble, quickly gathers momentum, and at the end of burning is traveling about one mile a second. Shortly after launching, it is deflected from its vertical course either

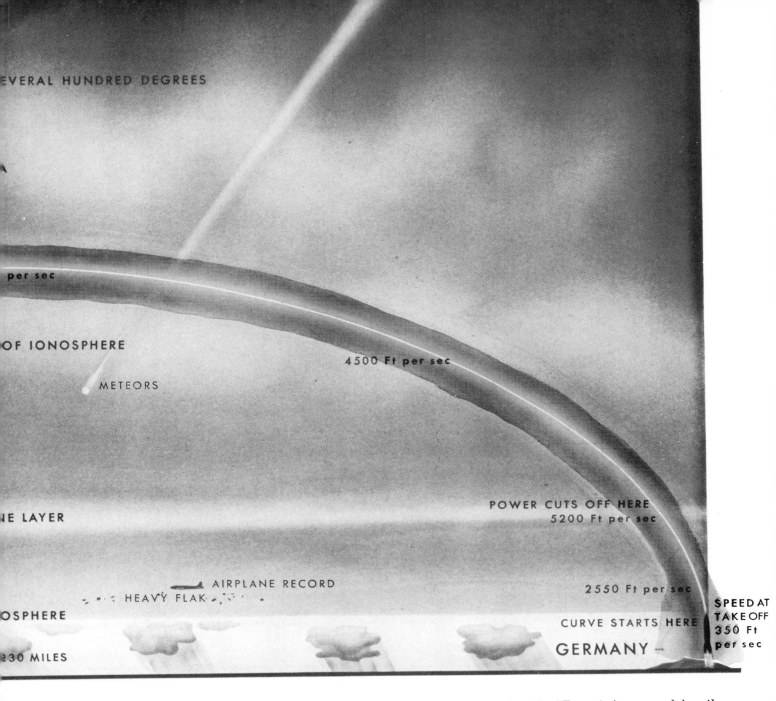

EVERAL HUNDRED DEGREES

per sec

OF IONOSPHERE

METEORS

4500 Ft per sec

NE LAYER

POWER CUTS OFF HERE
5200 Ft per sec

AIRPLANE RECORD

HEAVY FLAK

2550 Ft per sec

OSPHERE

CURVE STARTS HERE

SPEED AT
TAKE OFF
350 Ft
per sec

230 MILES

GERMANY

EMS IN CONSTRUCTION AND CONTROL

Earthwork was hit by 8th AF on 4 August and heavily damaged. Similar works also exist at Friedrichshaven.

by remote control or preset gyro. All this time its weight decreases steadily because of fuel consumption. After power ceases, gravity takes over, and from this point to target, the course is that of a free projectile in space, affected, however, by the rotation of the earth, and by the great differences in air density at different altitudes. At the top of its flight curve speed is reduced (from 5,200 feet per second at the point of power cutoff) to 3,850. Gravity pull during the swoop groundward gradually increases the speed again until a maximum of 5,350 feet per second is reached. By this time the projectile is again traveling through dense atmosphere. It decelerates rapidly during the last fifteen miles of flight, to an approximate 3,000 feet per second on impact, the nose becoming red hot through skin friction.

Extreme accuracy of paratroop drop at Groesbeek, Holland, is aided by compact, flat formations of 9th T.C.C.

CG-4As of the 9th T.C.C. swoop in for landings on the broad flatlands of Holland near Nijmegen. In first five days despite weather American C-47s and gliders delivered 27,419 combat troops and 4,086,235 lbs. of equipment, including 9,385 gallons of gasoline. In contrast to Normandy glider landings, few losses occurred because of terrain hazards.

American paratroopers land west of Grave, Holland, and rush into action to seize key bridge across Maas river.

Holland: Proving Ground for Airborne Operations

The September invasion of Holland, largest in the history of airborne warfare, proved conclusively that daylight paratroop and glider operations over heavily defended enemy positions can be a brilliant success.

For the period D-Day (17 September) to D plus 9 (26 September) British and American troop-carrier pilots flew 5,292 sorties and towed 2,602 gliders into action. Successfully delivered were 39,620 troops and 4,595 tons of military supplies at a cost of only 2.3 percent loss in aircraft.

Great dividends from daylight were gained in the accuracy of paratroop drops, in landing of gliders, and in rapid assembly of troops. Battalion commanders of the 82nd and 101st Airborne Divisions have described operations as the best in the history of their units.

Three factors are responsible for the tremendous success of the operation, despite powerful German defenses:

1. Overwhelming attack air forces knocked out many flak positions before and during airborne operations and protected troop carriers from enemy fighters.

2. Maximum of tactical surprise was attained through able staff work; large forces were placed in a minimum of time and simultaneously.

3. Thorough training of troop carrier and airborne personnel produced almost perfect landings.

American airborne troops captured intact the Maas bridge at Grave, two bridges over the Maas-Waal Canal, high ground between Groesbeek and Nijmegen, the cities of Eindhoven, Beek and Nijmegen, and most important of all, the famous Rhine bridge at Nijmegen. The whole operation, despite the withdrawal of British airborne troops at Arnhem in the face of overwhelming odds of enemy troops and fire power, has been judged highly successful.

Continued on next page

Air Resupply Vital

Air resupply proved absolutely essential in the airborne invasion of Holland. Major General James M. Gavin, Commanding 82nd Airborne Division, reports that even though contact was established by his men with English troops soon after landing, the British did not have necessary supplies available.

The B-24 resupply mission on D plus 1 was the only one flown at proper altitude, due to weather and enemy flak. Considerable dispersion occurred because of variance from release points, but the resupply drop served its purpose even though 20 percent of the equipment fell into enemy hands.

Resupply missions on other days were not so successful, not only because of bad weather but because enemy ground opposition grew more severe once the surprise element was over, as was expected.

Gen. Gavin says, "Parachute resupply is, at its very best, an emergency means of resupply, and I believe to function properly it would require

Upper picture shows flak-damaged C-47 plunging to earth during landing of 1st Allied Airborne Army. Below, crashed transport burns after crew bailed out.

8th AF B-24s drop equipment on D plus 1 to airborne troops in Holland. Mission successfully released 782

in Airborne Attack

about one third of the combat force engaged being used as recovery detail. This is impossible in hard fought situations such as existed in Holland. Troop carrier command pilots made every effort to effect resupply despite enemy interference; and I believe that supplies delivered were an essential contribution to the 82nd's combat success. It is hoped that in future training the problems of resupply missions will be worked out in practice."

Pilots in the CBI theater, though not so accustomed to working with paratroops as T.C.C. units of the ETO, are far more familiar with air resupply problems. Benefits of their experience will be utilized in training in the United States before T.C. units leave for overseas.

In a tribute to the 9th T.C.C. Gen. Gavin says, "The 82nd could not have successfully accomplished any of its missions but for courageous performance of the pilots, which has been the subject of boundless favorable comment by all ground personnel."

American paratroopers plough through fire from German 88s in assault on Arnhem. Flak prior to landings caused few casualties among airborne personnel.

ons of supplies at cost of 16 Liberators.

Dirt and flame spurt as flak-damaged 8th AF B-24 plows into Holland field.

A-26 INVADER MAKES OPERATIONAL DEBUT

Another problem has recently been added to the Luftwaffe's mounting collection of troubles: the A-26 Invader is in combat in the ETO.

Scheduled to replace the B-26 and A-20 as the AAF's principal medium level air weapon, between 6 September and 19 September A-26s successfully flew eight missions over Europe. Targets were heavy gun positions at Brest, the Bath Dike (a rail and road causeway) in Holland, marshaling yards at Duren, Germany, and German defense positions at Nancy and Metz.

The Invader is probably the best medium bomber or attack airplane in the world today. Combat cruising speed of 220-230 IAS, as employed in the ETO, gives maximum range and most efficient performance. To maintain this speed, the A-26 pulls 28" to 34" hg. of manifold pressure with 2,050 to 2,100 rpm's for loads up to 4,000 lbs. The same cruising power settings with normal bomb load give a rate of climb of 400 to 500 ft. per minute at 190 IAS and 205 mph on bomb run with doors open. A constant power setting can be used for climbing, cruising, and bombing.

Radius of action with the formation shown at right and used in the ETO is 450 miles, still maintaining the necessary fuel reserve. Roughly, this gives the A-26 an increase of 75 miles in range over a Marauder and 100 miles over a Havoc. Fuel consumption has been lower than expected, averaging 156½ gals./hr. for the eight missions.

Experience shows that 12,000 feet is the best possible operational altitude for medium level bombardment with the A-26. No low level missions have yet been reported over Germany. In other theaters where the risk from flak is not as great as it is over Germany, the speed and maneuverability of the A-26 will make it highly adaptable to low level bombing and strafing attacks.

To date the Invaders have met no enemy fighter opposition and have encountered flak on only two missions with minor damage. Single engine performance is unquestionably the best of any bomber in operation today.

Potent one-two punch of 75 mm and 37 mm cannon in interchangeable attack nose of A-26 Invader can knock out enemy fortifications and gun positions.

New bubble canopy and raised cockpit of A-26 permits greater visibility.

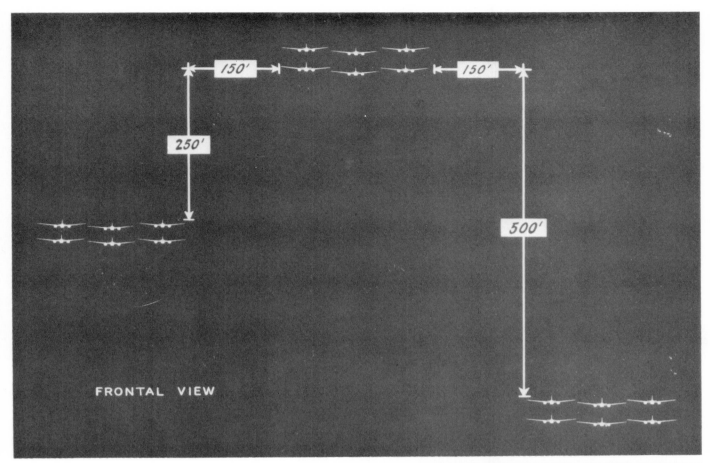

FRONTAL VIEW

Frontal view of A-26 combat formation shows relative positions of the boxes. Wing men fly level with or slightly above lead airplane so that wing tips just clear. Formation is much similiar to that flown by A-20s and B-26s in ETO. No. 2 flight flies 150 feet to the right and 250 feet below lead; No. 3 flight 150 feet to left and 500 feet below.

Side view of Invaders' combat box shows only four out of six planes of squadron because wing men are on the same level. Noses of wing men just clear the tail of lead plane in each element. Second element lead plane flies 20 feet back and 20 feet down. No. 2 flight flies 250 feet below to the right, No. 3 flight 500 feet below to the left.

Plan view—Compactness of formation is easily visible from this angle. No. 2 flight flies 150 feet to right with lead plane opposite tail of first flight. No. 3 flight occupies same position on left, though flights do exchange positions. Formation is highly flexible and well suited for extreme speeds and maneuverability of Invader.

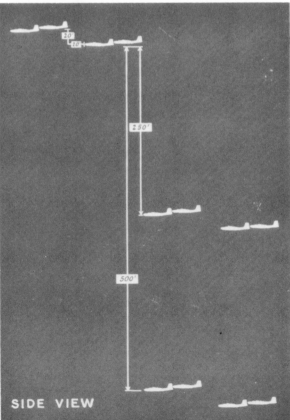

SIDE VIEW

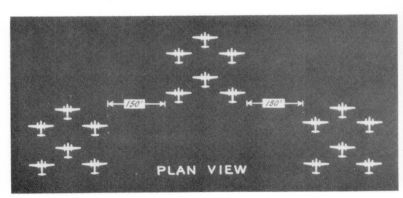

PLAN VIEW

OPENING NAZI "CANS"

Prior to 24 August the only two German destroyers in French waters were the "Elbing" (foreground) and "Seetier" (background) in photo above. Off Le Verdon RAF Beaufighters caught them in rocket and cannon attacks. Returning air crews reported a huge explosion. Next day oil streaks were photographed where strike occurred; neither vessel has since been seen. Below, Beaufighters strafe enemy "M" Class minesweepers in North sea off Holland on 25 August. Twelve airplanes can be counted in the melee. Object that appears to right of photo plane's vertical fin is a barrage balloon.

FACTS ABOUT PLOESTI

Astra Romana, Ploesti's largest refinery, during low-level attack by 8th and 9th AF on 1 August 1943.

DURING the year August 1943-August 1944, Ploesti was subjected to 26 bombing attacks in a campaign to destroy it as Germany's main fuel center. The following 18 pages of IMPACT are devoted to this campaign in the belief that qualified AAF personnel will be interested to examine, through the media presented here, the condition of the first really important strategic target to fall into Allied hands after a long-continued bombardment. It is also felt that a study of the results achieved over this mammoth oil area will be of value to all those concerned with further blows at oil targets, either in Europe or in those areas now owned or held by Japan. No "cost analysis" of the whole campaign has been or should be made here at this time. Nor should final conclusions be drawn regarding the superiority of one kind of attack over another. Ploesti is presented here merely as an historical study of an elaborate tactical problem—solved virtually single-handed by the precision bombardment and tactics of the Fifteenth Air Force.

Continued on next page

WHAT WE DID TO REFINERY PRODUCTION

The importance of Ploesti in the German war economy can hardly be overestimated. It is the largest oil producing area in Axis Europe and contains the largest concentration of refineries. It supplied the Nazis, before it was attacked, with a third of their total liquid fuel requirements, and, more important, with a third of all their gasoline. It is not easy for Americans, who have long lived in an economy of oil abundance, to understand how vital the defense of such a target is to a nation whose oil position is as fundamentally unsound as Germany's. Until Rumania fell into her lap she had been importing crude from this and other European countries to make up the difference between what she produced synthetically at home and what she consumed. Her synthetic production has grown rapidly in the last few years, but (compared with refining crude) the expense and difficulty involved in such production only accentuate how badly she needed a handy natural oil supply of her own.

With this picture of Ploesti clearly in mind, two things about it immediately become apparent: (1) It was certain to be attacked sooner or later. (2) In anticipation of such attacks it was certain to be heavily defended. But, as a corollary to (2), it was probable that the defenses would be rusty if not alerted. Accordingly, when it was decided to attack Ploesti in the summer of 1943, the operation was planned as a one-punch affair designed to achieve maximum effectiveness and surprise at any cost. No preliminary reconnaissance was permitted. The attack was to be made at minimum altitude to insure complete coverage of the target with the relatively small force available. It came off on 1 August 1943. Pictures of it may be seen in IMPACT, Vol. I, No. 6. The elaborate briefing which prepared the way for it is described in IMPACT, Vol. II, No. 2.

At the time of this attack Ploesti was theoretically capable of handling 757,000 metric tons of crude a month, but was actually putting through only 407,000 tons. This was due partly to the fact that Germany was then getting sufficient oil, partly to the fact that the Ploesti fields are gradually drying up, which has had the effect of leaving it with more refinery capacity than crude production. Considering that only 142 tons of bombs were dropped, the damage done on this mission was tremendous. Production for August fell to 269,000 tons. Two of the eleven active refineries in the area were so badly damaged that they were not operated from that time on. Although repairs were pushed rapidly by the Germans, bringing production to 431,000 tons in one month, this should not obscure the real achievement of the low-level attack, which was to destroy almost all the excess refining facilities. From that point on, 400,000 tons a month was virtually a capacity performance.

Then for eight months Ploesti was not disturbed. The Italian campaign, the great air battles in the north to kill off the Luftwaffe, and the endless pre-invasion rail attacks combined during this period to occupy our air forces. However, in April and early May 1944, during blows at the Ploesti rail yards, severe damage was again dealt out to several of the refineries and capacity knocked down to 317,000 tons a month. Careful analysis of these attacks, which proved that oil targets could be hit and knocked out with a reasonable economy of force, was a strong contributing factor in the revision at this time of strategic priorities, placing oil first and putting into action the coordinated campaign against the entire German oil industry.

Now the names of the Ploesti refineries began to become monotonously familiar in 15th Air Force briefings. Four missions were flown against them in May, four in June, five in July and four during the first 19 days of August. By that time production was down 90 percent, and the Russians walked in to take over the remaining 10 percent. At that time only five of the eleven refineries were operating, and one of these, Astra Romana, was supplying over half the output.

Ploesti was never a soft touch. At first it was stubbornly defended by fighters, later by dense smoke and flak installations (see pages 50-53). In five months we lost 223 heavy bombers out of 5,479 effective sorties flown for an over-all combat loss ratio of 3.6 percent. Bombs dropped totaled 13,700 tons, or 2.5 tons per sortie. One hundred and eighty-eight enemy aircraft were destroyed in the area.

These operations, plus the 1943 low-level attack, resulted in a loss to the enemy of 1,334,000 tons of oil, which figures out to 97.5 tons of oil for every ton of bombs dropped. Analysis of the various types of mission flown over Ploesti reveals the following:

	Low-level 1 August 1943	P-38 10 June 1944	High-level 5 April- 19 August 1944
Tons of oil production lost	127,000	15,000	1,027,000
Bombers lost	54	24 (P-38s)	223 (also 28 fighters)
Tons of oil destroyed per bomber lost	2,300	625	4,600
Tons of bombs dropped	142	18	13,558
Tons of oil destroyed per ton of bombs dropped	895	830	75.5

From this the August 1943 low-level attack emerges as the most economical by far. It would have been even more so had all elements flown the mission as briefed. However, in behalf of the high-level missions, it should be brought out that these were in a position at the end of their campaign to enormously improve their statistical showing because only by then had they solved the smoke problem, greatest hindrance to the accuracy of their bombing. Finally, in behalf of the P-38 mission, it should be noted that losses were unduly magnified by enemy fighter attacks. If the mission had been conducted two months later, after fighter opposition had been effectively eliminated, and when smoke and flak remained as the hazards, results would have been a great deal better. But it must be remembered that when the mission was flown, the 15th AF was still trying to solve the smoke problem, and could not wait to eliminate fighters.

All production figures in this article, including monthly pre-attack capacities on the map opposite, are from official Rumanian refinery records.

Continued on page 38

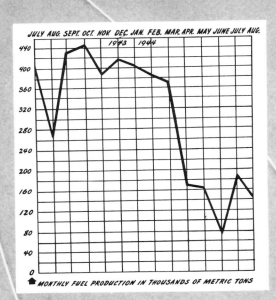

TO STEAUA
ROMANA 15 MI.
125,000

CONCORDIA VEGA
110,000

XENIA
22,000

ROMANA AMERICANA
92,000

DACIA ROMANA
15,000

PLOESTI

COLOMBIA AQUILA
45,000

STANDARD 36,000
(UNIREA SPERANTZA
33,000 ADD.)

ASTRA ROMANA
146,000
(PHOENIX 65,000 ADD)

+++++   R.R.

PRIMARY HIGHWAYS

REFINERY FIGURES SHOW MONTHLY
PRODUCTION IN METRIC TONS

0   ½   1 MI.

N

CREDITUL MINIER
45,000

JULY AUG. SEPT. OCT. NOV. DEC. JAN. FEB. MAR. APR. MAY JUNE JULY AUG.
1943   1944

440
400
360
320
280
240
200
160
120
80
40
0

MONTHLY FUEL PRODUCTION IN THOUSANDS OF METRIC TONS

ASTRA ROMANA

Owned by British and Dutch interests, this is the largest and one of the most modern refineries in Rumania. It is equipped with cracking facilities and special wax, polymer and other plants which together handle a fifth of Rumania's total refinery output. It almost completely surrounds a smaller refinery, Phoenix Orion, also British-owned and regarded as a particularly vulnerable target because of the great concentration of its equipment. This includes a lubricating oil plant, one of the few in Rumania. Total capacity of Astra and Phoenix before attacks was 211,000 tons a month. Actual combined production from July 1943 is shown at right. The low-level attack of 1 August 1943 did heavy damage to both, but because of the existence of excess standby facilities, they were soon producing more than before to compensate for reduced capacity at other refineries in the area. The main rail yards at Ploesti lie next to the Astra plant, and when they were attacked in April 1944, the refineries were again damaged. Phoenix was utterly destroyed on 5 May. Production at Astra fell to zero and was expected to remain so for 60 days. Actually recovery was much swifter. This is the only case in the Ploesti campaign where A-2 estimates of production varied more than slightly from the official refinery figures.

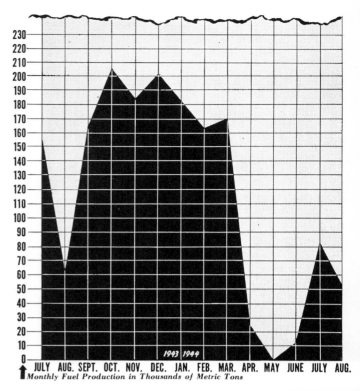

Monthly Fuel Production in Thousands of Metric Tons

Low oblique of Astra shows little apparent damage except for smashed tanks. Actually, capacity was down two thirds and due to go lower because of emergency nature of many repairs. Area included in this photo is indicated by dotted line at A in vertical at right, annotations correspond to those on vertical. Large wooden structure at lower left is a cooling tower. New construction (5) is believed to be a catalytic cracking unit, like those in newest U. S. refineries.

Old fashioned pipe still in Trumble Unit (7 in photo below) has been rendered useless by internal blast.

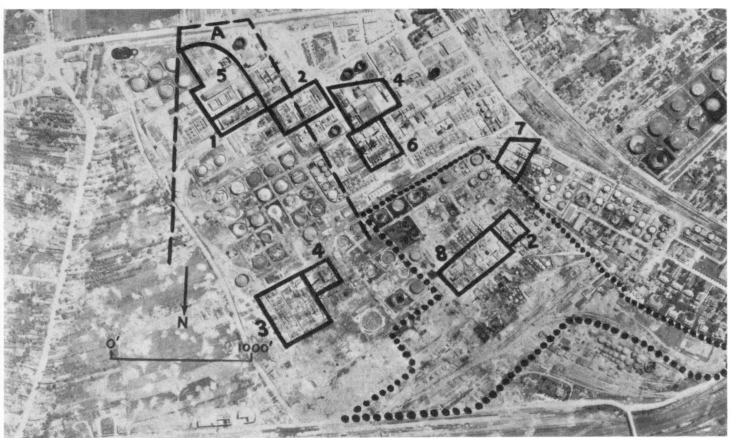

Vertical of Astra Romana and Phoenix Orion (bounded by dotted line) shows effects of numerous attacks. Annotated are stabilization plant (1), doctor plants (2), Dubbs units (3), boiler houses (4), probable catalytic unit (5), McKee unit (6), Trumble unit (7), and pipe stills (8). Most vulnerable part is the boiler house as the steam it produces is used to operate almost all units, is also needed to flush out refinery for speedy shutdown during attacks.

Continued on next page

CREDITUL MINIER

Although this is one of the smaller Ploesti refineries, its equipment is the most up-to-date. It has a sizable Dubbs cracking unit and has the only iso-octane (aviation gasoline) plant in Rumania. Its pre-attack capacity was 45,000 tons a month. Located a few miles south of Ploesti next to a large rail yard, from the air it is one of the most conspicuous refineries in the entire group. The low-level attack of 1 August 1943 did such damage to all its important facilities that production was completely halted and the plant never put back into working order. The Dubbs unit, the power plant and the pipe stills were all wrecked, also a pumping station. The latter is one of several which pump light fuels through pipe lines to the Danube terminal at Giurgiu. The bulk of Ploesti fuels has always been moved by rail.

Vertical of Creditul Minier shows the following: Pumping station (1), power plant (2), pipe stills (3), Dubbs unit (4), laboratory (5), machine shop (6), treating unit (7). A good deal of this refinery's tankage is still undamaged.

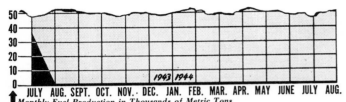

Monthly Fuel Production in Thousands of Metric Tons

Low oblique of Creditul Minier is annotated to correspond with vertical above. Destruction here and at Colombia Aquila and Steaua Romana testify to soundness of 1943 low-level planning which depended on each plane's hitting the specific building assigned to it. Where formations approached target on proper heading attacks were astonishingly effective. Where they did not, some refineries were missed all together some slightly, some seriously damaged.

STANDARD & UNIREA

Two refineries are contained in the area shown below, Standard Petrol and Unirea Sperantza, with a combined monthly capacity of 69,000 tons. The former had no crude production of its own, and up to the time of the low-level attack was inactive. Undamaged then, it operated at virtual capacity until April 1944, when successive missions seriously damaged it. Unirea was a standby plant for Phoenix Orion. It was put back into production after Phoenix was damaged, then shut down again. Later efforts to get it into production were halted by attacks in the summer of 1944.

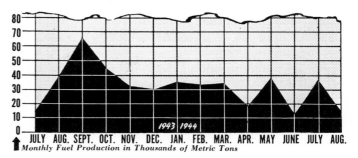

Monthly Fuel Production in Thousands of Metric Tons

Ground photo of Standard plant shows damage to stills in distillation unit. Chimney of boiler house (A in photo below) may be seen in top left. Water tank around chimney does away with need for building separate water tower.

Standard (left) is separated from Unirea (right) as shown by dotted line and by rail yard running through foreground of picture. All Ploesti refineries have extensive rail facilities, relying more on these than on pipe lines for shipment of products. Another line runs along the back of Standard, separating it from the bombed out Concordia munitions works in background of picture (5). Annotated are: Lubricating oil plant (1), distillation plants (2), boiler houses (3).

Continued on next page

ROMANA AMERICANA

Fourth largest in Rumania, this plant escaped damage in August 1943. Thereafter, whenever Ploesti was attacked, citizens fled here for safety in the belief that its ownership by American interests would spare it. Their hopes were shattered in May and June 1944, when Romana fell heir to a series of furious blasts which cut production from 109,000 tons in August 1943 to 12,000 tons in August 1944. Romana was hard to finish off because its vulnerable parts covered a large area, also because it was more heavily protected by blast walls than neighboring refineries. When it was viewed by the entering Russians, its wreckage evoked wondering admiration that the Americans should have dealt so harshly with what was theirs.

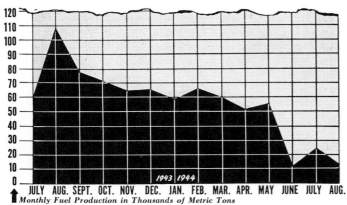

JULY AUG. SEPT. OCT. NOV. DEC. JAN. FEB. MAR. APR. MAY JUNE JULY AUG.
Monthly Fuel Production in Thousands of Metric Tons

First oblique takes in area shown at (A) in vertical at lower left. Tall columns in foreground are cracking towers. They are exceedingly complex in structure. If they can be

Vertical of Romana Americana shows distillation unit (1), boiler houses (2), distillation and cracking (3), machine shop and stores (4). Dotted lines show angles of obliques.

Second oblique takes in area shown at (B) in vertical at left. It shows clearly that the nearest of two boiler houses at (2) has been leveled. The machine shop and storehouses

destroyed the usefulness of the refinery is enormously reduced. However, they are ruggedly built, and experience proved that only direct hits could knock them out.

(4) are virtually destroyed. Distillation unit (1) has suffered heavily. Widespread damage to Romana's extensive tankage is plainly visible in this and the photograph above.

Distillation tower for gasoline was knocked over, righted again in an effort to keep refinery running. Note guy wires holding it in place. Small tanks are heat exchangers.

Continued on next page

CONCORDIA VEGA

This plant is the third largest in Rumania. It covers 46 acres, with the vital parts confined to 16 acres. Its equipment is modern and includes extensive cracking and distilling facilities. The latter are separated into three independent units, which makes them correspondingly less vulnerable to attack. Concordia's pre-attack capacity was 110,000 tons a month, average production about half of that. Hard hit during the low-level attack, it recovered rapidly, was not hit again until 5 May 1944. It was virtually knocked out on 31 May, but managed to maintain a small output until 10 August when it was finally flattened. Its storage tanks suffered more than any other refinery in Ploesti.

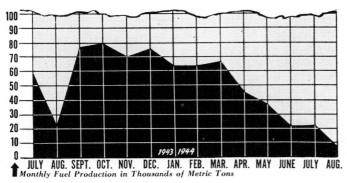

JULY AUG. SEPT. OCT. NOV. DEC. JAN. FEB. MAR. APR. MAY JUNE JULY AUG.
Monthly Fuel Production in Thousands of Metric Tons

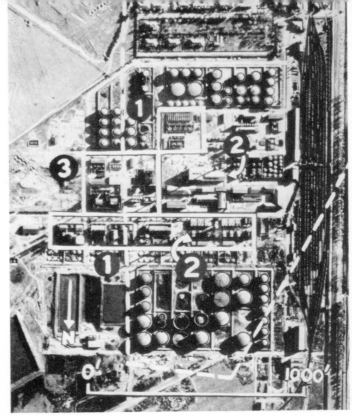

Vertical of Concordia shows distillation plants (1), boiler houses (2), cracking plant (3) before attacks of 1944.

Value of blasting tanks like this is that even if distillation facilities are undamaged, production must stop if there is no place to store the gas. Separate distillation units (1) are clearly visible. Closeup opposite was taken at (A).

Closeup of distillation unit shows debris surrounding four damaged fractionating towers, with truncated brick chimney visible just back of them. Dotted lines at (A) in picture on opposite page show the angle at which this photo was taken.

Continued on next page

COLOMBIA AQUILA

About the same size as Creditul Minier, this refinery had a pre-attack capacity of 45,000 tons a month. Its equipment, including a sizable Winkler-Koch cracking plant, was modern. It was virtually erased on 1 August 1943, operations being entirely suspended for 11 months. A trickle of production began to run through it in July and August 1944, as the critical condition of the other refineries in the area began more and more to throw the spotlight on Colombia as the best prospect for repair. Its production record, together with those of Creditul Minier and Steaua Romana, show significant similarities. These three plants were the ones most successfully attacked during the low-level mission and, as was to be expected, were knocked out for a longer period. However, considering the ultimate havoc caused in other refineries, and comparing this with their production records, it appears that Colombia, Creditul and Steaua were out longer in proportion to the damage done than the others. Whether or not this proves anything cannot be stated here now. It may well be that after Romana and Romana Americana were groggy, and in spite of continuing small production, ready to fold up after one more attack or (lacking new equipment) through the mere passage of time.

Vertical of Colombia Aquila is annotated to indicate location of stabilization plant (1), distillation plant (2), boiler house (3). Colombia's vital parts are concentrated in a smaller area than in most of the other Ploesti refineries.

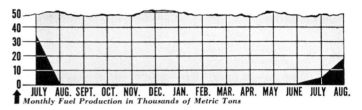

50	
40	
30	
20	
10	
0	JULY AUG. SEPT. OCT. NOV. DEC. JAN. FEB. MAR. APR. MAY JUNE JULY AUG.

Monthly Fuel Production in Thousands of Metric Tons

Oblique of Colombia Aquila shows many of its tanks intact. Next door is main Girgiu pumping station (4).

STANDARD

ASTRA ROMANA

XENIA

This is the next to the smallest of the important Ploesti refineries. It covers an area of 39 acres, with the important objectives confined to a little over one acre. Before being attacked, its capacity was 22,000 tons a month. However, it is old-fashioned and poorly equipped compared to the others, and in July 1943 it was not in operation. Ignored during the August 1943 low-level attack, it sprang into production at that time, and was soon operating at capacity in order to handle the continuing flow of crude from the neighboring oil wells, which could not be put through Astra, Phoenix, Concordia, Colombia, Creditul and Steaua because of the damage done to them at that time. Much of Xenia's equipment is obsolete. It has no cracking facilities and its only important installation is a distilling unit. Accordingly, as repairs were pushed at the more efficient refineries, production at Xenia was allowed to fall, reaching zero in March 1944. When attacks were resumed in April and May, Xenia was put into production for the second time. From then on the Germans ran Xenia as hard as they could. It was hit in July, but not seriously damaged. When the Russians arrived it was in operation.

Continued on next page

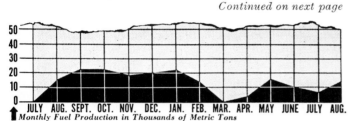

Monthly Fuel Production in Thousands of Metric Tons

Vertical and oblique of Xenia show how this small refinery escaped relatively unscathed. Only important installation is distillation plant and boiler house (1). Some tankage was destroyed. Tank below may be found at (A).

Closeup of tank (A above) that suffered direct hit. Blast wall is typical of those at all Ploesti refineries.

STEAUA ROMANA

Next to Astra, this is the largest refinery in Rumania, with a monthly output of 125,000 tons. It is located 15 miles northwest of Ploesti in the heart of the oil fields. It is well equipped, has extensive cracking facilities and two modern distillation plants, a McKee unit and a Stratford unit. It was here that one of the most heroic actions of the August 1943 low-level attack took place. The formation assigned to it arrived a few minutes after the defenses had been thoroughly alerted by another formation which had swung north after leaving Ploesti. In spite of this, all elements went in exactly as briefed, almost every plane hitting the individual pinpoint assigned to it. This put Steaua flat on its back for four months. It slowly recovered but was hit hard again on 6 May after an attack the night before by the RAF. Output sagged and, according to Rumanian production figures, continued to go down despite a temporary respite from bombing, reaching zero in June. Any further attempts to revive it were canceled out by a final heavy attack on 10 August, the same day that Romana Americana received its coup de grâce.

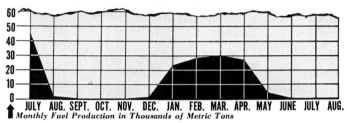

Monthly Fuel Production in Thousands of Metric Tons

Treating plant (above) at Steaua is wrecked. Area in this ground photo is shown at (A) in the vertical at lower left.

Steaua vertical shows process tanks (1), distillation (2, 3), boiler and power houses (4), Dubbs cracking plant (5).

DACIA ROMANA

Last and least of the active Ploesti refineries, Dacia has received less damage than any of them. It is included in this study because it did produce steadily during the period under review and because this puny production became more and more important as the over-all output of the area declined. At the start of the campaign its capacity was only 1.3 per cent of Ploesti's total. By the end of August 1944 this was up to over six percent. Not included in this article are four equally small or smaller refineries, Lumina, Noris, Cometa and Redeventza. These were either so tiny as to be unattractive targets or else were dismantled or hopelessly obsolete. It is believed that some of them were stripped of whatever equipment could be utilized to repair damage in the larger refineries.

Dacia covers an area of 25 acres, with the important objectives confined to three acres. It has a capacity of 15,000 tons a month. Most of its equipment is old and inefficient. It has no cracking facilities, but does contain a distillation unit and a small benzine plant. Almost dormant in July 1943, it was pushed to capacity after the low-level attack, along with Xenia and the other undamaged plants.

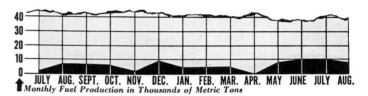

JULY AUG. SEPT. OCT. NOV. DEC. JAN. FEB. MAR. APR. MAY JUNE JULY AUG.
Monthly Fuel Production in Thousands of Metric Tons

Second ground shot (below) at Steaua shows heavy damage to a new installation, possibly a catalytic cracking unit.

Dacia oblique shows boiler house (1), distillation plant (2), benzine plant (3). Five of 2,000 smoke pots are visible.

Continued on next page

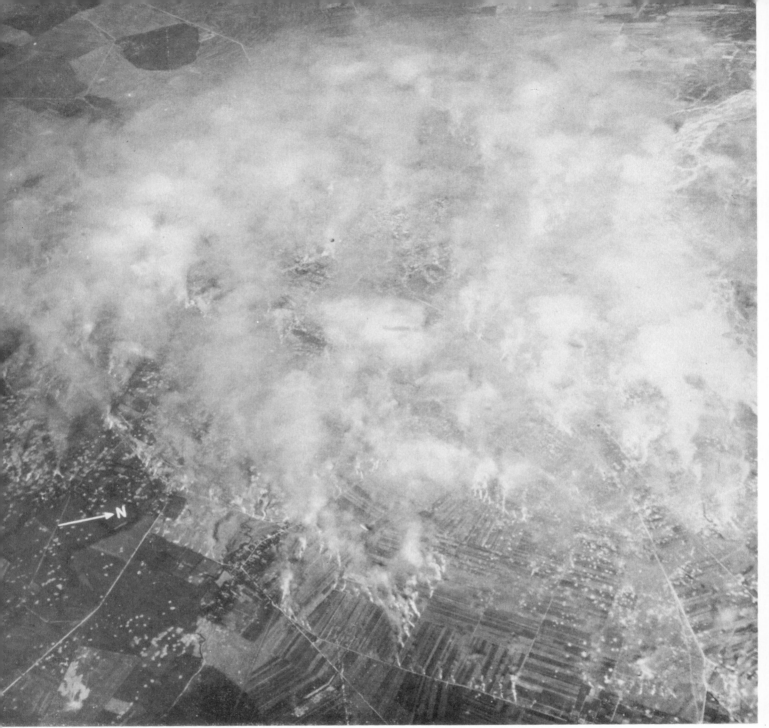

Screen is shown developing on 17 August. Romana Americana is at center right. White dots are bomb craters.

SMOKE DEFENSES

The map on the opposite page shows the layout of the smoke defenses of Ploesti as they existed in August 1944. It will be seen that they surrounded the town and all the refineries for a depth of at least a mile. They were stated to be most effective in high humidity, and ineffective in winds exceeding 50 miles an hour. In April the screen was much less elaborate than this, but was enlarged steadily until there were upwards of 2,000 separate installations, the densest concentration in Axis Europe. April and May at-

tacks were not much hampered by smoke, but by June it had become a serious problem. In July five large missions were flown, on only one of which was visual sighting possible, the others being conduced by PFF methods.

Various measures were adopted to deal with this passive but highly effective defense which could completely "black out" the entire area in 20 minutes or less depending on the strength of the wind. The first was a low-level attack on 10 June by 46 bomb-laden P-38s, designed to take the smoke system by surprise. Unfortunately the formation was jumped by defending fighters on the way in, and the element of surprise was lost. However, visibility at the low level was

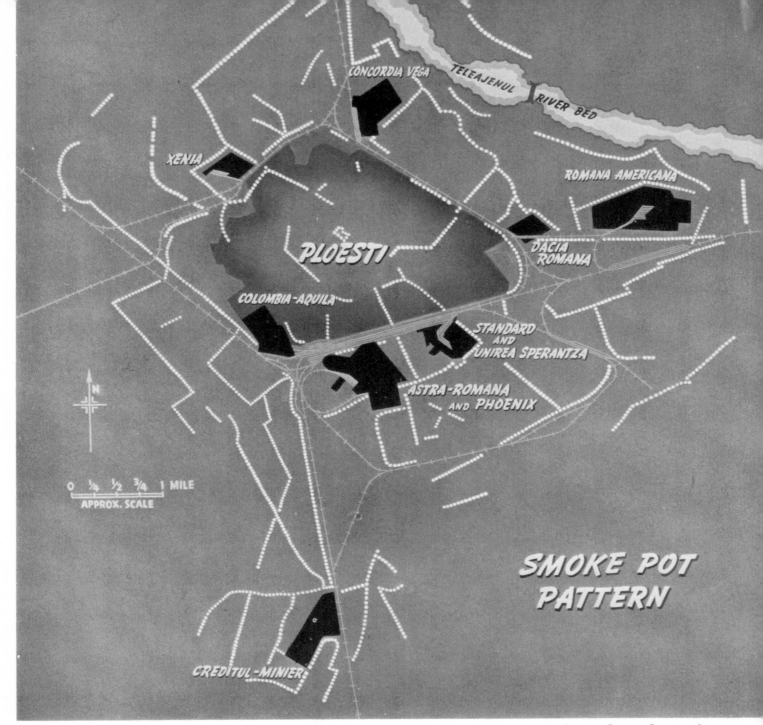

PLOESTI

CONCORDIA VEGA

TELEAJENUL RIVER BED

XENIA

ROMANA AMERICANA

DACIA ROMANA

COLOMBIA-AQUILA

STANDARD AND UNIREA SPERANTZA

ASTRA-ROMANA AND PHOENIX

0 ¼ ½ ¾ 1 MILE
APPROX. SCALE

SMOKE POT PATTERN

CREDITUL-MINIER

Each dot above is a separate smoke generator consisting (below) of pressure tank, smoke tank, nozzle.

sufficient to permit accurate bombardment. A second experiment involved attempts to circumvent the smoke by "blind bombing." This was done in two ways, by H2X and by offset methods. Both are described in IMPACT, Vol. II, No. 9. A third was tried when it became apparent that surface winds occasionally cleared parts of the target. A P-38 was positioned over Ploesti during the last three attacks in August to broadcast to the approaching bombers which targets were in the clear. Also, during this period an attempt was made to wear out the smoke by attacking over a period of hours. The chief of the Rumanian Passive Defense Command, confirmed the effectiveness of this strategy.

Continued on next page

Giant Wurzburg (left) and Freya (right) were used for early warning and for ground control of enemy fighters.

128 mm railway guns were largest in Ploesti. There were 24 of these, each of which could fire 1 shell every 5 seconds.

Gun laying was handled by small Wurzburgs.

Depth and strength of gun positions is shown here.

FLAK DEFENSES

The flak defenses of Ploesti were among the densest ever flown against by Allied airmen. They protected an area of about 13 miles square with 250 heavy and 400 light guns, not counting numerous Rumanian, Vickers-Armstrong and captured Russian weapons whose effectiveness was questionable. Like the smoke defenses, the Ploesti flak became heavier with the passage of time. Consisting originally of a fairly even scattering of 88 mm batteries throughout the area, they were strengthened with more 88s, with 105s and

with 128 mm railway guns. Our losses to flak rose accordingly, more than doubling in five months.

German radar in Rumania habitually picked up our bombers over Italy and tracked them in to Ploesti with ease, giving an average of 40 minutes in which to close down the refineries, get the civilians under cover and prepare the defenses. This early warning was supplied by giant Freyas. Gun laying was done by small Wurzburgs, one, sometimes two, to a battery. Allied jamming and use of chaff combined to render these useless, forcing the batteries to depend on optical range finding or remote station data. The smoke screen made optical methods useless (in addition to making

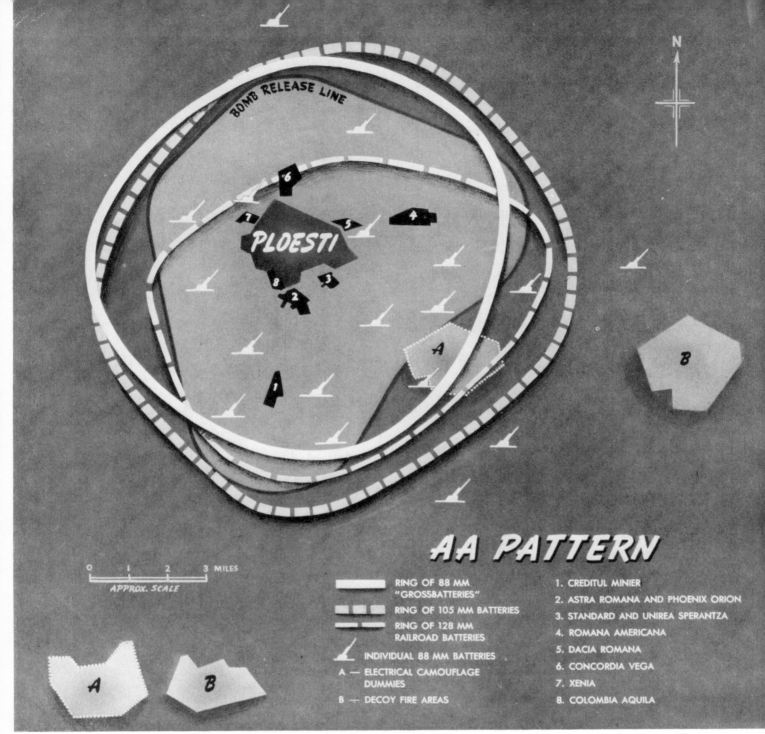

AA PATTERN

Scale:
0 1 2 3 MILES
APPROX. SCALE

Legend:

▬▬▬	RING OF 88 MM "GROSSBATTERIES"
▭ ▭ ▭	RING OF 105 MM BATTERIES
▬ ▬	RING OF 128 MM RAILROAD BATTERIES
⊿	INDIVIDUAL 88 MM BATTERIES
A —	ELECTRICAL CAMOUFLAGE DUMMIES
B —	DECOY FIRE AREAS

1. CREDITUL MINIER
2. ASTRA ROMANA AND PHOENIX ORION
3. STANDARD AND UNIREA SPERANTZA
4. ROMANA AMERICANA
5. DACIA ROMANA
6. CONCORDIA VEGA
7. XENIA
8. COLOMBIA AQUILA

Simplification of AA map shows the relationship of main Ploesti defenses to approximate bomb release line.

the gunners seasick, according to one report) and the Germans eventually resorted to the ringed defense shown on the map above, corresponding roughly to the bomb release line of our bombers. Here they were less bothered by smoke and could concentrate on the "incomers." Most of the 88 mm batteries finally were combined into "grossbatteries," consisting of from 12 to 18 guns each. Predicted fire was almost universally used. Gun positions were well protected by light weapons of 20 and 30 mm (see cut at right). One was occasionally knocked out by a direct bomb hit. Elaborate but ineffective electric camouflage areas and dummy fire installations (see map) also existed at Ploesti.

By radio a P-47 gives lowdown on enemy ground situation to tank columns in Northern France.

THE AIR-TANK TEAM

Tank Leader: "I am receiving fire from enemy tanks in the vicinity of crossroad R-13. Can you get him?"

Pilot: "I'll make a try." *(After flying over the position, he calls back)* "The enemy tank is too close to your position to bomb safely. Back up a short distance. and I'll go after him."

The enemy tank is soon knocked out.

This typical dialogue between a P-47 pilot and a tank leader was overheard on a recent advance in France, such as is illustrated above. It betokens a new kind of air-to-ground cooperation which consists, in brief, of assigning air units—usually P-47s—to cover armored columns.

Here is how it works. High frequency radios are mounted in tanks which move near the head of each column, and are operated by air-ground liaison personnel familiar with their characteristics. Thus, continual radio contact can be maintained between tanks and planes. All communication is by voice, and, to insure recognition, friendly vehicles are marked with red panels.

At a daily conference with the Tactical Air Commands, the G-3 for air requests a certain amount of air cover throughout the day. After the planes are in the air, the armored column control may request the fighters to reconnoiter the roads ahead of the column, or attack specific targets such as enemy tanks or gun positions. One flight generally goes down and works with the column, while another provides high cover. When the lower flight has expended its bombs, it changes position with the high flight. When both are out of ammunition, they may return to base, while a fresh squadron takes their place, thus providing continuous cover for the tanks.

These air-tank teams have met with great success. At first, tanks feared being hit by their own planes, but successful cooperation dispelled this fear. Knowing that "guardian angels" are overhead increases the confidence of tank personnel. and they move boldly ahead.